Love Affair with a Circus Girl

A story about love, survival, and tragedy

Alexander Druar

ISBN-13: 978-0-578-33299-4

Cover designed using KDP Cover Creator by Alexander Druar

Printed in the United States of America

DEDICATION

I want to dedicate this book with love to all the exploited children in the world, most especially to Lisa Yvonne French, whose beauty, talent, and charismatic personality brought light into my life from her world of darkness. She was truly God's greatest gift to me, and to those whose lives she touched.

CONTENTS

ACKNOWLEDGMENTS

I want to thank my friends and family members who have inspired me, during this long and emotionally difficult journey. I also want to thank my counselor Dr. Bridges, who without her encouragement and support, I might not have been able to make it this far. I also want to thank my wife and closest companion Petch, for being patient and understanding, and for helping me to publish this book.

1. Mystery Unsolved[12]

Lisa's life was cursed from the day she was born, despite coming into the world as a gift from God. At such an early age, she had become a child circus star. "Lavonne, Lavonne," the audience chanted, as she dropped out of the sky like a bird on her Cloud Swing, as if from Heaven - catching herself only a few feet from the ground by her wrists. Ironically, Lisa was afraid of heights, but she loved the cheers of an adoring crowd, accompanied by the symphonic roar of the lions and trumpeting elephants.

The little air dancer had been living a dream and a nightmare, simultaneously. At bedtime, Lisa would trade the spotlight for darkness, and the embrace of a loving audience for the arms of the devil. She sacrificed her innocence, in exchange for evil, and gave up her exuberant joy for unending terror. Despite being born beautiful, intelligent, and talented, Lisa's life was over, before it really had a chance to begin.

It's a warm and misty Sunday evening, August 4th, 1985. On the side of a secluded road in Davenport, Florida, an old white Chevy pick-up truck lay at rest with the hood raised. A thick fog penetrates the dense woods, creating a veiled cloak around the scene. Pam, a 16-

---

[1] "Darkness," directed by Robin Aubert and Petro Duszara, *Real Detective* series, Season 1 Episode 6, aired February 11, 2016.

[2] "French now admits killing her stepfather," by Beth Foushee, *Tampa Tribune*, September 15, 1991.

year-old Asian girl with dark brown eyes, stands beside the driver's side of the truck. Her short jet-black hair matches her T-shirt. She's wearing blue jeans and red high-top sneakers. She also has on a red high school football jacket, with a black letter H on the front.

Headlights appear faintly in the distance, piercing the darkness as they approach. The driver is a woman, who works at the local sheriff's office. She spots the young girl leaning against her vehicle, so she slows to a halt. The woman rolls down the car window to ask the girl if there's a problem.

"Are you okay?" says the woman.

"Yeah, I'm fine," says Pam. "I got car trouble, but I have someone coming for me."

"Alright then," the woman replies.

She rolls up her window and slowly drives away. Lisa, Pam's lover, has been crouching down on the floor of the truck, unseen by the woman from the sheriff's office. She is two years older than Pam and has shoulder length frizzy fire red hair. Her deep blue sapphire eyes can appear to change color with her mood. With a penetrating and powerful gaze, Lisa can capture anyone's undivided attention, like Medusa petrifying her prey.

Lisa's body looks like a ballerina, with small breasts and tiny feet. In contrast, she has the arm strength of a gymnast, due to all the years she has worked as an aerialist in the circus. Lisa has a pale complexion and an endearing smile, with freckles sprinkled around her nose. Her look is innocent, but her mind is sharp and focused. She's dressed in cut-off jean shorts, a sleeveless white T-shirt, jean jacket and pink sneakers. Lisa is a bit of a tomboy, but there is no mistaking her feminine demeanor and effervescent charm.

Lisa grew up in the wilderness, inside of a mobile home during her childhood, with minimal supervision. Her parents didn't do much to educate her properly. She never went to school except for the third grade, due to her circus life on the road. Lisa had to teach herself virtually everything that came out of a book, despite being challenged by dyslexia. She trained for circus life at the tender age of six, when most kids her age were starting first grade. Lisa was taught to perform an act on a 'Cloud Swing,' involving a 14-foot free-fall, catching herself only by her wrists. This is an extremely dangerous trick, especially for such a young child. No net was used during shows, so if Lisa made a mistake, she could have been severely injured or killed.

Lisa and Pam had just come from a local bar, where they had been drinking for several hours, and neither of them should have been behind the wheel of an automobile. The girls' truck isn't really having mechanical trouble, and they aren't out for a leisurely drive. Pretending to break down is merely a ploy, to lure Lisa's stepfather Alvin into a trap. The two lovers have something very heated and sinister in mind, but Lisa is already beginning to have cold feet.

Lisa claimed her stepfather raped her, since the age of just four-years-old, for a period of fourteen years. This day, after attempting to fend off another assault, she decided that he had forced himself on her for the last time, and she is determined to do something about it. Alvin had also threatened to kill Lisa and her mother Carmen on numerous occasions, and she took his threats seriously. This caused Lisa to live in constant fear for her and her mother's lives. So, after much persuasion by her mother and Pam, she decided it was time to put an end to the abuse and the threats, and fulfill her mother's wishes, by putting an end to her stepfather's menacing behavior.

Alvin had recently taught Lisa to fire a gun, and gave her a .357 Magnum revolver, so she could defend herself from a mentally deranged stalker named Charlie, who became obsessed with her. Lisa first met him at a flea market, close to where she worked in Auburndale, Florida while selling jewelry. This same gun was recently loaded and is tucked away in the glove compartment of their Chevy truck. Pam and Lisa are now prepared to confront Alvin, the minute he arrives to help them.

Out of the darkness and through the fog, the girls can see another pair of headlights growing brighter, as it approaches. It's a black Ford van, belonging to Lisa's stepfather. He pulls up in front of where the girls are standing and steps out of his vehicle. Alvin is in his early fifties and weighs about 180 pounds. He is unshaven with salt and pepper hair, has a scar on the side of his left cheek, and tattoos on both of his arms. A cigarette hanging from his mouth drops to the ground, which he extinguishes with his boot.

"What seems ta be the problem girls," Alvin asks. "Truck won't start? Did ya check ta see if ya run outta gas?"

"There's enough gas," Lisa replies.

Alvin looks under the hood and makes some adjustments.

"Now try'er," Alvin says.

Pam slides behind the wheel and turns the ignition key. It starts up right away. Then Alvin puts the hood back down, so that Pam can see out of the front window.

"I thought I told ya not ta go out tonight." Alvin complains.

"Well, if you hadn't been fighting with mom again, I wouldn't have felt the need to get away," Lisa replies. "You're always fighting with her and me; I'm sick of it!"

"Now ya listen here young lady," Alvin says. "Ya watch yer mouth or ye're gonna get it slapped; ya hear me!" Alvin shouts.

"Why don't you just try it and see what happens!" Lisa yells.

Alvin loses his temper and approaches Lisa with his right hand raised. As he takes a swing at her, Lisa grabs his wrist and bites him on the arm. Alvin screams in agony.

"I'm gonna get ya fer that," Alvin howls.

Pam retrieves the revolver from its hiding place, and shuffles it to Lisa, out of the window of the truck.

"Ye're dead ya little bitch," Alvin yells.

Pam quickly jumps out of the truck, retrieves a tire iron from the bed, and positions herself behind Lisa's stepfather. Alvin spins around to face her, taking his attention away from Lisa for the moment. He is out of his mind with rage.

"I'm gonna kill ya both, ya little tramps," Alvin shouts.

A metal clicking sound can be heard, as Lisa pulls back the hammer on the revolver. Alvin turns his head to see Lisa pointing his own gun at him. Her legs are spread apart, and both her hands are clenched around the pistol. Her piercing eyes, now turning grey, are transfixed on her intended target. Lisa's heart is pounding like a kettledrum, and her adrenalin is racing like electricity through a telephone wire. Sweat and tears stream down Lisa's face, while her blood boils and rushes to her pores. The fear and horror she suffered through for so many years at Alvin's hands turns to rage in a moment. Flashbacks of Alvin's sexual and physical abuse race through her mind, which only adds fuel to her fire.

"You're going to leave me and mom alone from now on!" Lisa demands.

Lisa and Pam agreed to kill Alvin when they hatched this plan, but Lisa was no killer. She was just a scared little girl inside her mind, who was terrified of this monster her mother had married. Lisa had dreamed about his demise repeatedly in her sleep. In her thoughts, it was so easy to imagine pulling the trigger. Now, in the heat of the moment, she's having second thoughts, when faced with the reality of destroying another human being. For a moment, time stood still, as Lisa tried to work out her internal conflict. Staring Alvin down in the moonlight and the mist, she felt her rage building, like a werewolf on steroids. However, her fear and conscience were winning the battle in her brain. She thought maybe she could frighten him, instead of killing him - just enough to make him finally leave her and her mother in peace. However, that thought quickly leaves Lisa's mind, as Alvin remains defiant and continues to provoke her.

"You, yer ma and yer little girlfriend are all gonna to die!" Alvin shouts. "Ye're both nothing but two-bit tramps, and yer ma is nothing but a dirty whore!"

"Go to Hell!" Lisa yells back.

"Ya haven't got the guts to pull that trigger," Alvin shouts. "When I catch ya, I'm gonna kill ya and yer bitch friend. Then, I'm gonna kill that good fer nothing ma of yers too, before I'm done."

While Alvin's gaze is directed toward Lisa, Pam swings the tire iron with force at Alvin's head. He whirls around and grabs the instrument from her hands just in time, and kicks Pam in the chest. She shrieks, as she tumbles to the ground, reeling in pain. Alvin now turns his attention back to Lisa again, and trudges toward her.

"Shoot him! Shoot him now!" Pam shouts.

Lisa senses that both of their lives are in jeopardy. The situation is spinning out of control. Suddenly, Alvin lunges at Lisa, wielding the tire iron above his head. Instinctively, Lisa squeezes the trigger. A shot rings out, followed by a high-pitched scream, as Lisa steps back from the force of the recoil, and Alvin is knocked backwards.

Alvin clutches his right shoulder, as blood trickles down the sleeve of his jacket. A moment later, he reaches for Lisa with his left hand.

Reflexively, Lisa fires a second shot, which penetrates his chest, followed by a third round. Alvin collapses to the ground moaning, and bleeding profusely from three places, as Lisa stands immobilized in shock, crying, and screaming. Pam looks on with delight and amazement. The gunshots apparently don't deliver an immediate deathblow, but Alvin is mortally wounded. Frightened by what has just transpired, the girls race to their truck, to flee the scene.

"We need to get out of here," Lisa says.

"I'll drive," Pam replies.

Pam grabs the wheel, and as she starts to pull away, she catches a glimpse of Alvin still struggling in the grass.

"He's not dead!" Pam shouts.

Pam jams her foot down hard to the floor, and deliberately runs over Alvin's limp disheveled body, until he lies motionless on the ground. Pam slams the truck into reverse and runs over his corpse a second time - just to be sure he's dead. Then, she spins the tires once more, steering the pick-up onto the road, as the smell of burning rubber fills the air. Lisa buries her face in her hands, crying uncontrollably in the passenger seat, leaving Alvin behind to die alone in the empty field. It's a death Alvin most certainly deserves, but one which Lisa will live to regret. She may have put a lid on her tormentor's maltreatment, but she hasn't put an end to her suffering. By killing Alvin, Lisa has unwittingly sealed her own fate.

"What did we just do?" Lisa demands.

"We snuffed that child-rapist!" Pam replies. "He'll never hurt you or your mother again! Now, he can go to Hell where he belongs!"

"I'm scared," Lisa says, as Pam continues to head toward Lisa's mobile home.

Just after midnight, a policeman spots Alvin's van parked by the side of the road, so he stops to check it out. When he steps out of his car, he notices a tire iron lying on the ground. He scans the landscape with his flashlight and sees a human body, face down in the field. He rushes over to see if there is any sign of life. At first, the man in blue assumes it's a hit and run accident, because he notices tire marks on the back of Alvin's jacket. The officer radios headquarters, and Detective Ray answers the call. Twenty minutes later, Ray arrives at the scene. As the detective inspects the body closely, he notices the bullet holes in Alvin's body - something the officer overlooked.

"This is no hit and run accident," Ray exclaims "This man's been shot three times! This is a homicide."

In the distance, Detective Ray notices a man in the woods, who has been watching them for the past several minutes.

"Look, over there," Ray says. "Come on let's go."

The two men give chase and discover the man is living in a makeshift camp nearby. The vagabond is dressed in rags and has a long black bedraggled beard. He smells like he hasn't washed in weeks. The tramp is thin as a rail and appears malnourished. His face and hands are riddled with grime.

As the detective and the officer look around, there doesn't appear to be anything incriminating at first glance. Ray initially assumes that this man must somehow be linked to the victim. The two men continue to search the area, hoping to find the murder weapon, or any other evidence, which ties this man to the crime. When Ray searches the drifter's pockets, he finds a roll of cash, which the suspect admits he had stolen from Alvin's jacket pocket.

"Did you kill that man across the way for this money?" Ray asks.

"I didn't kill nobody!" the tramp protests. "He was already dead when I found him."

Detective Ray is not inclined to believe the man's story, but he can find no additional evidence at the campsite, pointing to this man's guilt. The detective doesn't find any guns, and there are no blood stains on the man's shabby clothes or his hands. There was nothing else they can find to suggest this man is anything other than a thief. The evidence just isn't sufficient to charge him with murder, currently. However, Ray still decides to bring the suspect to the precinct for further questioning, and charges him with theft and suspicion of murder.

The next day, after identifying the victim, Ray must break the news to the dead man's next of kin. That turns out to be Alvin's wife Carmen and her daughter Lisa. Ray finds them both living in an old trailer, not very far from the scene of the crime. Carmen is in her forties, medium build with strawberry blonde hair, and hazel green eyes. In her prime, as a high wire performer, she was strikingly beautiful. However, with years of hard work in the sun, her looks have faded significantly.

Carmen is not clever like her only daughter Lisa. In fact, she is quite simple-minded and dependent. Her daughter Lisa is now more attractive and more talented, and receives most of the attention from men, including her mother's lovers. Carmen loves her daughter, but she is jealous and resentful of being upstaged. Conversely, Lisa is completely devoted to her mother, in a naïve and misguided way. When Detective Ray arrives at their home, both Lisa and Carmen act shocked by the news that Alvin has been murdered.

"Ma'am, I'm sorry to have to tell you this, but we believe we found your husband's dead body in a field not far from here," Ray explains. "He was shot three times, and then run over."

"Oh my God, no!" Carmen cries, as she begins to conjure up crocodile tears.

"I've been worried because he didn't come home last night," Carmen exclaims.

"Was there anyone who might have wanted to harm your husband?" Ray asks.

"I can't think of anyone," Carmen replies.

"There is this old guy by the name of Charlie, who has been following me around everywhere," Lisa explains. "He's out of his mind crazy and gives me the creeps. Perhaps my dad confronted him because he wouldn't leave me alone."

"Do you know where I can find this man?" Ray asks.

"Yeah, he works at a flea market in town," Lisa replies.

"Okay, well, thank you for your time," Ray says, as he is leaving. "I'm sorry for your loss. I will contact y'all later, so you can identify the body."

"Goodbye; thank you detective," Carmen says.

"Let us know when you find out who did this," Lisa says, as Ray closes the door.

Lisa and Carmen had kept their cool the entire time the detective interviewed them at their home. They are used to dealing with the police, and know exactly how to talk to them, calmly and innocently. Lisa and Carmen had just put on one of their best performances, while surreptitiously guarding their knowledge of the crime.

The detective later discovered that Charlie had apparently landed in prison, prior to the time of the murder. Ray knew he couldn't have committed the crime, despite his confession that he had killed Alvin. He told Detective Ray that he had ordered the hit from prison, but this old man is no crime boss; he's just crazy. Charlie had no visitors except for his sister, during the time in question. However, his sister did seem to fit the description of the young lady, who was seen by the side of the road, the night of the murder. It would be a strange coincidence, if the girl seen at the scene of the crime turned out to be Charlie's sister. Unfortunately, the woman who spotted the young girl near the crime scene didn't get a good look at her face because it was dark, and she was standing several yards away, so it was difficult to make a positive identification.

Detective Ray decides to pursue the sister as a possible suspect anyway, because he has no other leads to follow currently. After interviewing Charlie's daughter, the detective concludes that she is not the girl they're looking for after all. Even if Ray does discover the mystery girl's identity, it still won't prove that she is connected to Alvin's murder. However, she might have witnessed the crime, and may be able to give Ray a description of the killer. Locating the teen, without knowing her name, isn't going to be easy. Her life might even be in danger.

Not long afterwards, there is a second murder of another circus performer, who had also been shot dead. When Ray arrives to investigate, he hopes there may be clues, providing insight to the first crime as well.

"This can't be a coincidence; these murders must be linked somehow," Ray thinks.

The detective decides to go and check out a local bar, where some circus performers are hanging out, to see if anyone knows anything about either of the two murders. It's a motley crew of potential suspects. There is a bearded lady standing near the bar, a dwarf who is sitting on one of the bar stools having a cold beer, and a strong man with a moustache, standing in the corner of the room smoking a pipe. Several other performers from the circus are in attendance as well. Detective Ray questions everyone there, but no one is interested in talking to him or providing any information.

The circus world is made up of a tight-knit group of misfits, who are not about to rat-out any of their comrades, even if they're guilty of wrongdoing. Circus people and gypsies often don't trust the police. These performers may know something about one or both murders, but they are never going to tell the cops anything. Detective Ray finds himself up against a brick wall, and he is becoming frustrated.

"Sorry copper," the strong man says, "but we don't know nothing."

"Perhaps, if I'm able to connect these two crimes with the forensic evidence, it might lead somewhere," Ray thinks.

The next order of business is to try to find a ballistics match from the bullets found in the two different victims, to see if they were fired from the same gun. The bullets taken from Alvin's body were from a .357 Magnum - a very powerful firearm, normally used by a man. When the bullets are analyzed, it is determined that they were not fired from the same weapon. It is a fact that confounds Detective Ray. He was certain the report would show that the bullets came from the same gun, showing the two murders to be connected, but it now appears that they are not. Is it just an intriguing coincidence that two men from the circus were shot and killed, within a short period of time in close proximity? It didn't seem likely. Even though the guns used to commit these crimes were different, doesn't necessarily mean the killer isn't common to both murders.

"This is a mystery, which is becoming more convoluted by the day," Ray thinks. "What am I missing? Perhaps the killer is just being clever by not using the same gun?"

Ray doesn't believe in coincidences, like most detectives. It's a puzzle, leading him down another rabbit hole. There seems to be several clues in the two cases, but they aren't adding up and helping the detective to come any closer to solving these mysteries. At this point, the detective is becoming increasingly vexed. He not only can't find a link between the two murders, but there isn't adequate evidence to charge anyone with anything, other than theft, at the moment.

As time passes, the trail leading to Alvin's killer seems to be going nowhere. There is still at least one murderer on the loose in Polk County. If there is a third murder, perhaps it might help Ray find the evidence he needs to bring the perpetrator to justice. However, he's not hoping for this outcome. Ray believes he will eventually solve the two cases, without having to deal with a third victim. He has never had an investigation before that had so many twists and turns, without breeding results. For the next five years, there will be no further developments revealing Alvin's killer. The trail has gone cold.

It appears for the time being, that Lisa and Pam have gotten away with murder. Unfortunately for Detective Ray, it is another unsolved mystery for the file. It's highly unlikely that two teenage girls could have so easily manipulated and fooled an experienced detective, but that is exactly what has occurred. Ray is blind and can't see what has been staring him in the face from the beginning, because he's been tricked by a provocative 18-year-old siren, who has him completely bamboozled and under her spell. At this time, the detective never suspects that Lisa is involved in her stepfather's murder and continues to feel sorry for her and her mother. Lisa appears to Ray to be a vulnerable and fragile young girl, and not capable of committing murder with a powerful handgun.

Lisa is a master of manipulation, and she knows exactly what to say and do, to achieve the reaction she wants. She seduces Ray with her seductive eyes whenever they speak and controls his thoughts concerning Alvin's murder. Lisa has this kind of power over men and women, and Detective Ray is not immune to her alluring charm. This young circus girl is an illustrious provocatrix - there is no one she can't exploit with her sexual magnetism. Lisa is artful in her craft.

Deceit is a tool she has learned to use with precision, to fulfill her deepest desires, and protect herself from people who might try to harm her.

Anyone, who doesn't know how Lisa's mind works, can easily be manipulated by her. She can be conniving and cunning, not because she's evil, but because she has an inbred instinct for survival. Her actions are a manifestation of having been forced into confronting deplorable predators, who have infiltrated her domain. Her ingenuity and charisma have been her best defense for leveling the playing field against men, who have hunted her for sport.

Lisa didn't grow up with a father or mother who protected her. On the contrary, they have been her enemies, except that she isn't aware that her mother is also a threat to her. Lisa has had to rely on her wits and sex appeal, as a sword and shield against her enemies. She is a woman of the wilderness, no different than any wild animal. The circus tent is her home, the countryside, her backyard, and lions, tigers and elephants are her closest allies. Lisa was born and bred to survive in the jungle and trained to perform like a monkey on a swing. To her parents, Lisa is a commodity, groomed to be sold to the highest bidder.

Now that Alvin is gone, Lisa and her mom must figure out how to carry on by themselves. Their days traveling in the circus appear to be over for now. On one hand, Lisa is finally rid of the ogre she called daddy, but she also has a heavy burden to bear, and a terrible secret to keep. Despite her stepfather's vile brutality, Lisa must live with the memory and the guilt of killing her guardian. She may be tough for a teenage girl, but the memory of killing a parent is not something the human psyche is especially well designed to deal with.

As a result of being tormented by this terrible nightmare, Lisa begins abusing drugs and alcohol, to drown out the voices in her head. She even slits her wrists to kill herself, but fortunately she is unsuccessful and survives. By killing Alvin, Lisa has only replaced one demon for many others. Flashbacks of the rapes she endured and the murder she committed, torture her every waking hour, and haunt her in her sleep. For Lisa, there is no relief from the emotional pain and suffering her parents have caused her, and there's no escape from a destiny that will only end in disaster.

2. Air Dancing

1989 was the year the Berlin Wall fell, and just over three years after the fatal shooting of Lisa's stepfather. I had recently joined an ice show called 'Classical Ice' at Cypress Gardens in Winter Haven, Florida. At that time, the park was independently owned, and the Gardens still had its natural beauty and southern charm. Despite its name, the ice show featured laser lights and a space number. The Ice Palace was relatively small, but it could still seat over 1000 people. In between shows, I would sit out on the deck behind the theatre or in the dressing room reading a book, to avoid gossip and drama.

Occasionally, I would walk around the park and make friends. The beauty of Cypress Gardens was accentuated by several attractive young women who worked in the park and roamed the grounds every day. Many of them performed in the ski and ice shows, some portrayed southern belles of the Civil War era, and there were even several good-looking women among the general staff. For a young man in his mid-twenties, to be among so many desirable women while performing, was a dream come true.

We even had beautiful weather most of the time, except for the humidity. Then the management decided to add a new show called 'Air Dancing.' It was a circus style show, which featured a trapeze act. It was very exciting, and an excellent complement to Cypress Gardens' famous water-ski show, as well as our new ice extravaganza.

There weren't many thrill rides in the park, but the shows were exceptional, and the beauty of Cypress Gardens could not be matched anywhere in the world.

One afternoon, while I was in the dressing room, an unfamiliar face walked backstage. Apparently, she was looking for her mother, who worked as a stagehand in our show. Her hair was scarlet, frizzy and shoulder length. Her eyes were sea blue, deep and mysterious, and she wore rose-colored lip-gloss. This young woman was in her early twenties, slender, athletic, and about the same height as me. She was wearing white cut-off shorts, a hot pink t-shirt, and sandals on her feet. A black ribbon with a small gold medallion was fastened around her neck. At first, she didn't say a word to me. Instead, she gave me a piercing glance, as she locked her eyes on mine, and spoke to me.

"Have you seen my mom?" she asked.

"It depends," I replied. "Who's your mom?"

"Carmen," she said.

"Then yes, but I don't know where she is this minute," I replied.

"Okay," she said, smiling at me. "Can you tell her that her daughter is looking for her?"

"You're Carmen's daughter?" I asked with surprise.

"The one and only," she replied.

"Will do," I said. "I'm Alex by the way, in case you were wondering."

"It's very nice to meet you Alex," she said. "My name is Lisa - Lisa French."

"Enchante," I replied.

"What does that mean?" Lisa asked.

"It means, I think you're hot," I replied.

Lisa laughed.

"Thanks," Lisa said. "I have to go now."

"Wait!" I shouted.

Lisa stopped by the door for a moment, and then turned her head to look back at me.

"Will I see you again?" I asked.

"What do you think?" Lisa replied flirtatiously.

Lisa smiled devilishly, and as mysteriously as she had appeared, she vanished out of the backstage door. Now I knew that her mother worked with me, so all I had to do was ask Carmen, if I wanted to see her daughter again. I absolutely wanted to see this red-headed firecracker again. Ever since that afternoon, I couldn't get that girl out of my head. There was something about her that was very unusual compared to anyone I had ever met. I couldn't quite put my finger on it, but the look Lisa gave me before she left was powerfully enduring.

It was only a few days later when I noticed Lisa again; she was walking toward me in the park. It looked like she was coming from the direction of the Air Dancing show and headed in the direction of the Ice Palace. I thought, perhaps she was coming to talk to her mother again. Lisa walked right up to me and stopped to say hello, greeting me with her seductive smile and penetrating deep sapphire eyes.

"Hi Alex, remember me?" Lisa asked.

"Lisa French, right? How could I forget," I replied.

"Are you looking for your mother again?" I asked.

"Yes, but I hoped I would run into you again too," Lisa replied.

"Really - you did?" I asked.

"Yeah," Lisa replied with a smile.

"You're in the ice show, right?" Lisa asked.

"Yes, I'm a soloist," I replied.

"You're a performer too, aren't you?" I asked.

"Yes," Lisa replied. "I'm an aerialist in the Air Dancing show."

"How did you know?" Lisa asked.

"Your mom told me," I replied.

"You asked her about me?" Lisa inquired.

"Absolutely I did; I was curious about you," I replied.

"Hmm, me too," Lisa said.

"You asked about me too?" I asked.

"Maybe," Lisa replied, with a devious smile.

Lisa never took her eyes off mine the entire time we spoke. A strange feeling came over me, while standing next to her. I couldn't relax or turn my head. I felt paralyzed and mesmerized at the same time, as if I was staring into the eyes of a cobra. I started to sense my adrenaline surging and my heart beating faster. My palms were sweating, my mouth was dry, and I could hardly breathe. If I wasn't so intrigued with her, I would almost say I felt frightened. No woman had quite this effect on me in the past. Even though I dated plenty of attractive girls before, this young siren had a distinctive allure about her. It was more than simply charisma or star-power, however.

Standing in Lisa's presence, I felt a magnetic and debilitating force around me, which she controlled with her eyes. Whatever it was exactly, the experience was enchanting, exhilarating, and profoundly stimulating all at the same time.

"You're very cute," Lisa said to me.

Without warning, Lisa expeditiously moved in close to me, wrapped her right arm around my neck, and kissed my lips with force. Her embrace felt passionate and sensuous, and seemed to last for several minutes. I was completely caught off-guard and overwhelmed by her bold romantic assault. The encounter was intense, and completely unexpected. I had only just met this girl a few days ago. The way she kissed me was so intimate; it almost seemed like we had been lovers in a past life and had just been reunited. This was one of those moments that I knew I would never forget for the rest of my life. At some point, I remembered that we were still in public in the middle of the park, surrounded by hundreds of people, who for the moment ceased to exist. It felt almost like I had been knocked unconscious, and I struggled to regain awareness of my surroundings.

"Where did that come from?" I asked.

"No idea," Lisa replied. "I just felt like it.

"Did you like it?" Lisa asked, already knowing the answer.

"Are you kidding?" I replied. "I loved it - you're amazing!"

Lisa smiled with great satisfaction, as she stepped back from our kiss. Then she gave me that same devilish look again, while I attempted to regain my balance. By today's standards, Lisa's actions would probably be considered sexual harassment, but her public display of affection toward me was far from unwanted. I was able to glance away for the first time, but just for a moment. I caught a glimpse of one of my cast members staring in our direction, with her eyes wide open. Even though Lisa and I were among lots of people in the park, my colleague Renee seemed to have a private view of our passionate embrace. Then, my attention turned back to Lisa.

"You seem to have taken up all of my time again," Lisa said. "I need to get back to work now. Tell my mom I said hi, and I'll try to come see her again after my next show. If you keep showing up however, I may never get a chance to talk to her."

"Okay," I replied smiling, "but since I work with your mom it's not going to be easy for you to avoid seeing me."

Lisa smiled cheerfully. I was still a bit in shock from our impromptu encounter. As Lisa turned her back to leave, she looked like a dancer with her tiny little figure, except for her wild hair, which was never pulled back tightly against her head. She walked with one foot turned out to the side, as she glided across the pavement. Then she glanced over her right shoulder to look back at me, projecting her signature grin, as she disappeared into the crowd of people. I thought to myself again that this girl was so mysterious and exciting, and I wondered when our next rendez-vous might happen. After I returned to the Ice Palace, Renee stopped me to ask about Lisa.

"Who was that girl you were in a lip-lock with earlier today?" Renee asked.

"That was Carmen's daughter Lisa," I replied.

Renee was a typical showgirl - tall, blonde, slim, and curvy, with beautiful green eyes. However, unlike many ice performers, she was always very sweet and friendly, but kept her distance from me the entire time I worked with her. I'm sure from Renee's vantage point, Lisa was just another one of my many female distractions, but that couldn't have been further from the truth. Everything changed for me after meeting Lisa. I was completely captivated by her, and I had no interest in anyone else any longer. My romantic interlude with Lisa seemed like a fantasy, but it was very real. I understood I didn't know much about her, but that's what made the experience even more thrilling. I couldn't stop thinking about her, and it was driving me mad, wondering who this girl reminded me of exactly - no one really, which made her so special.

It wouldn't be until 1991, when I would find out the truth about Lisa's past, and what she had done in 1985. This precocious young shooting star in 1989 was destined to become one of the most notorious women in central Florida, and I was falling madly in love with her. Lisa would soon become famous; someone who people were going to read about in newspapers, watch on television, and see in magazines across the country. For the moment however, Lisa Yvonne French was only an anonymous circus girl, who was about to become my greatest lover.

In 1985, I was performing in my first ice show in Williamsburg, Virginia, about the same time Lisa was up to something completely different in Florida. That horrific event, which occurred one night in Polk County, would not only change the course of Lisa's fate, but it would also haunt her for the rest of her life. My love affair with Lisa would also eventually create a strong bond between us, which kept us connected well into the future for better or for worse. It would alter the course of both of our destinies, in a way we could never have anticipated, but not at all in the way we might have expected or hoped. This young woman was cursed from the day she was born. Lisa's aura tainted anyone who ventured to come close to her and might have been branded with the same black spot. I didn't realize it at the time, but I was never going to be able to walk away from her life, without a dark shadow from Lisa's spirit stalking me, wherever I walked.

Lisa and I started seeing each other more frequently, after we first met. It wasn't easy to spend time together because our shows were at different times, and we both had second jobs. In addition to performing in the ice show, I worked in the public relations department at the Gardens, and danced in a local theatre production of "A Chorus Line." Christine, a colleague, and friend of mine from the Ice Palace, also performed with me in this musical production. We only had small parts at the beginning of the show, so we were able to make it back to the Gardens in time to do our paid jobs.

Between the musical, the ice show and the public relations office, there was very little time to spend with Lisa, except very late at night. She was also working two jobs, and weekends were still workdays for both of us. Our days off were not well coordinated either. As a result, Lisa and I couldn't spend as much time together as we would have liked. Having so few romantic opportunities was a challenge for a new couple in love, but we tried hard to make it work.

After the Air Dancing show finished for the day, Lisa occupied her time in the evenings serving cocktails at a local watering hole. This was a bar in Winter Haven, where several of the men and some women were desperate to attract Lisa's attention, because she was so sexy. However, my baby only had eyes for me, and she didn't give anyone the attention they desired. All their advances fell short of making any impact, other than to cause them to spend more money on drinks.

Sometimes, the only way I could see Lisa more on weekends was to visit her at the bar. On Friday and Saturday nights, the pub was always packed with lots of people. One night, I sat next to this guy and struck up a conversation with him. He was good looking with long dark hair and broad shoulders. He introduced himself and offered to buy me a drink. He was checking out all the hot girls, while filling his glass with whisky and ice. Then he spotted Lisa moving toward us.

"Wow, she's phenomenal!" Billy said half drunk, referring to Lisa.

"I agree; she's my girlfriend," I said.

"No way!" Billy replied in disbelief.

"Yes way," I said.

"Get the Hell out of here!" Billy exclaimed.

"I'm not kidding; I can prove it," I said.

"Prove it then," Billy replied.

"Watch," I said, as I put my hand up in the air.

"Hey Lisa!" I called to her.

Lisa turned her head in our direction. She was wearing a red tank top, a jean skirt, red high heels, and the same black choker around her neck. Lisa still had on her makeup from the show and looked spectacular. She made her way over to the bar where we were sitting, while balancing a tray full of drinks.

"Hey baby," Lisa said to me.

"Hi Vonnie," I replied. "It's good to see you."

Then Lisa leaned over and kissed me on the lips, while my new friend stared with a blank expression on his face.

"I have to get back to work now baby, okay," Lisa said.

"Okay honey," I replied.

"Have fun, but not too much," I said smiling.

"Don't worry baby; I'm yours always," Lisa replied.

"Will I see you later?" I asked.

"What do you think?" Lisa replied, grinning.

That mischievous response was becoming one of her trademarks. As Lisa walked into the crowd, she turned her head to look back at me, as if to say - "I can't wait for later."

"You are so lucky," Billy said. "She's phenomenal!"

"She certainly is," I replied.

Lisa and I were both so busy that we never really had much time to go out on dates together. We didn't go to restaurants, the movies or on any trips together. We didn't have a chance to go shopping or dancing or do much of anything besides make love and sleep together. We never even went to Disney World together, even though we lived about 45 minutes away. We didn't do any of the things couples normally do because we worked constantly. We were lucky to have time to eat together. That's how crazy things were in those days.

Lisa would often come to the house where I was living, just to hang out with me late at night. I lived in a small in-law suite attached to Don and Carrie's house in Winter Haven, not more than a few minutes from the park. They were an adagio team, as well as a couple off the ice. In addition to performing, Don was also the operations manager for the park, so he was busy too. It was also difficult for Lisa and me to make any plans together. Whenever we saw each other, it was usually a spontaneous event. We would do our best to try to squeeze in a moment or two to see each other in between our shows, and after work, but it never seemed to be enough time. Lisa would always find me whenever she wanted to see me, and then leave just as suddenly. I could never keep track of the time nor of her. Sometimes, it felt like I was dating a shadow that I could never hold onto. She always seemed to make an appearance whenever the sun shined the most brightly.

When Lisa and I found some time to be together, it was primarily for lovemaking. Lisa was a spectacular kind of lover, who often thought about sex and her own sexuality. She never made love to me like any other woman I had known. For Lisa, making love was more of a ritualistic spectacle and an art-form. She craved the spotlight, and lovemaking was no exception. On the stage and in the bedroom, she always put on an unforgettable performance, choreographed for a standing ovation.

Lisa's opening act was designed to tease and create intense desire. She would turn on romantic music, light candles and then dress in something sexy. Occasionally, she would wear an old-fashioned red and white lace outfit, complete with long white gloves and high red boots. It must have been something she had worn in the circus because it looked more like a cabaret costume than a negligee. Lisa painted her face using plenty of rouge, dark brown eyeshadow, and rich crimson lipstick. She looked spectacular in the dim light; she was the featured act for the evening.

When Lisa saw that I was comfortable with a glass of Beaujolais in my hand, she would begin to move slowly and provocatively, as if dancing on a stage for an eager audience. She was exceptionally alluring to watch, and I was transfixed on her every movement. Her eyes never left mine, as she ran through what seemed to be a pre-choreographed routine. No one watching Lisa dance could resist her powers of seduction, while she was center stage. She was everyone's fantasy, male and female, commanding attention whenever she performed. By the time Lisa would allow me to touch her, she had driven me mad with desire. Before she let me kiss her, I had to finish sipping my wine.

During lovemaking, Lisa took me to another world. It was an intoxicating and addictive experience, beyond the temporary effects of any drug or drink. Her embrace was intense and sensual; her passion felt hedonistic and unforgettable. Time stood still whenever she kissed me. I could still feel the potent effects of her piercing desire throughout my quivering body, long after we fell asleep. I didn't want to dream about her afterwards, because the actual sensation of her expression of love and desire was so profoundly satisfying. It would have been a shame to spoil my reality with a carbon-copy in my dreams. The nights of endless passion with Lisa became irreplaceable memories, which have never left me, many years into the future.

I felt confident Lisa was my ideal partner. I truly adored her for the woman I knew her to be from my own experience. She was sweet, affectionate, and highly intelligent, although she never stepped foot inside of a classroom, for more than one year of her life. Lisa was confident, talented, and very determined, for such a young lady in her early twenties. Most importantly, Lisa and I felt comfortable around each other, as if we were next door neighbors growing up. Even though my childhood experiences were in the northeast, ice skating and going to Catholic school, and Lisa's early years were spent traveling with the circus, she and I were still very much alike, in almost every respect. If you believe in soulmates, Lisa and I shared one mind, one spirit, and one heart. We loved and admired each other tremendously. It seemed to be a perfect union.

Lisa's presence in my life was profoundly inspiring. The hours we were apart, I spent thinking about her feeling happy and fulfilled. I kept the secrets we shared, and I felt excited while anticipating the next time we would see each other again. Perhaps part of the reason our love seemed so intense was because our opportunities together were so brief and rare, but it kept the fire in our hearts burning with enthusiasm. Our relationship was never boring - never casual or superficial. We genuinely loved one another deeply. Our love always felt exhilarating and fresh, and we relished the moments we had together.

At this time, I knew nothing about Lisa's sordid past. I was completely oblivious to Lisa's dark history. I couldn't have envisioned myself sleeping with a killer; it would have been inconceivable to me. Lisa couldn't take the chance to tell me that she murdered her stepfather, for fear of losing me and being caught by the police. If I had known, it might have made dating her even more thrilling, but more likely, it would have caused me to panic and run away - and she instinctively knew that. I can't say for certain how I would have reacted at that time if I had known the truth. In 1989, Lisa was like a fairy full of fiery spirit and joy. If someone had told me Lisa was a dangerous fugitive on the run, I would have said they were crazy.

All I knew about Lisa's past was that she was a trapeze artist and handled exotic animals, while growing up in the circus. I didn't care that she was poor and lived in a trailer with her mom, while we were dating. It didn't matter to me that she didn't have a father or siblings. I never even thought to ask about them. I knew that Lisa didn't go to a fancy private school, her religion was irrelevant, and her wardrobe - immaterial. I adored Lisa for who she was, and for her personality and charm - nothing more. This exceptional and extraordinary girl who I fell in love with was simply irreplaceable. There was nothing anyone could have said to me that would have tarnished my image of her or spoiled my feelings for her.

It may have seemed to my friends that Lisa and I were just having fun, based on the nature of our relationship, but our connection was much deeper than people could have imagined. It was much more than just a summer romance or sexual liaison. Lisa and I had a spiritual connection and were so devoted to one another. I was beginning to become quite serious about her in a short period of time. I started to picture us having a life together beyond Cypress Gardens. However, with a girl like Lisa, it was challenging to imagine what our future might look like. She was not really the type of girl you settle down with to raise a family. Lisa was more like a muse, who appeared in my life to inspire me.

At the time, it seemed like Lisa and I were born for each other, because of how effortlessly we fit into each other's lives and one another's hearts - being together felt so natural. It didn't matter to me what kind of a life we had together, as long as we were never apart for too long. We had only been dating for just a few short months, but it seemed like we had been together for over a decade. I knew I would never find another woman quite like Lisa. She was so special, and so full of life. I really couldn't imagine my life anymore, without her being a primary part of it.

One afternoon in between shows, I met Lisa for a tryst among the beautiful flower gardens and colorful trees in the park. The place where we met was a very secluded pathway, except for the occasional guest walking by. We stopped at an especially tranquil place along the trail, and I turned to face Lisa. I looked into her eyes, while holding her hands, and proposed, placing a Cartier engagement ring in her hand. Lisa smiled enthusiastically, while not saying anything at first. She looked up at me and slipped the ring on her finger. Then she wrapped her arms around my neck and kissed me. After several minutes, she stretched her hand out to look at it.

"I love it!" Lisa said enthusiastically. "Yes honey, I will marry you!"

Lisa and I were officially engaged. Only a few months ago, I never could have imagined meeting someone like Lisa, much less believe I would be engaged to her. We were both feeling jovial, and we walked back toward the Ice Palace together arm in arm. It seemed like everything in my life was falling into place and could not have been better.

During this moment, Lisa had completely forgotten about the .357 Magnum revolver she had stashed in the ground, only yards away from where we were just standing. Lisa's luck seemed to be finally changing, and she also couldn't have been happier. She had traded a revolver for a ring and hate for love, creating a paradox in her mind, which only she was aware of and could comprehend.

Lisa's star was finally beginning to shine again, and she felt thrilled to be moving away from her dark past, to create a new life for herself with me. She was hoping she could finally be happy for once in her miserable life. Lisa's nightmares now seemed like they were in the rear-view mirror, and she was beginning to believe that she had nothing more to fear. However, Lisa still held her secret deep in her soul. It must have been tearing her up inside, not to tell me what she had done before we met. For now, the only tears she shed were tears of joy.

3. The Rumor

Despite Lisa and my engagement, our future together was still uncertain because of what was happening with the park. Cypress Gardens had just been bought by the Busch Corporation because they wanted to own Sea World. Their plans included selling off Cypress Gardens in a separate deal after the initial sale, so no one knew what would happen to the Gardens. Since Busch Gardens in Tampa also produced an ice show, Classical Ice was on the chopping block, and I would have to find a new job. This development would cause challenges with my relationship with Lisa if I had to move. My best options to find work were in Tampa or Orlando, which were only 45 minutes away.

I was offered a paid position in the public relations department at Cypress Gardens, but I wouldn't be making as much money as I had been performing. The money they offered me was ridiculously low, but in hindsight, I probably should have accepted it. The work I had been doing was initially on a volunteer basis, but now I had an opportunity to be compensated financially for my efforts. It just wasn't an attractive offer, and so I turned it down. I would have been better off performing in Tampa at their show if there was a position open. One of my colleagues, Victor, ended up taking a job there in the chorus.

Lisa and I were both entertainers, so job uncertainty is always part of the landscape in our industry. If I couldn't find a job in the communications field, I could always teach skating. I just hoped this change wasn't going to cause a strain on my relationship with Lisa. Although Lisa was not well educated, she was highly intelligent and versatile. I believed she could do anything she set her sights on, so I wasn't concerned about her finding another job, if we moved away together. However, I don't remember talking to her about moving away with me. I'm not sure how she would have reacted to that possibility, but I hoped she would stay with me, no matter where I decided to go.

What I didn't realize at the time was just how attached Lisa was to her mother. It was unlikely she would have wanted to live too far from her. Even though the ice show was closing, Carmen would have easily found another job within the entertainment department at Cypress Gardens. Both of Lisa's jobs seemed secure. Winter Haven didn't have much to offer me though, once the ice show closed, unless I stayed working in the public relations office.

I thought about trying to get a job in the other ice show in Tampa, but it didn't seem like they needed another soloist, and they appeared to be working their performers to the bone with low pay, so I never applied. Once again, I think I should have talked to the producers, but a guy named Kevin, who was doing adagio pairs and the solo, discouraged me from auditioning. It probably would have been a relief to him if I had taken over the solo part. I still had plenty of time to think about what I was going to do before my show ended. Whatever options were available, I wanted to stay close to Lisa. If I taught skating in Tampa or Orlando, it would take some time to build up a student base, and I wasn't sure I could keep my head above water until then. As long as Lisa and I weren't too far apart, nothing else mattered. However, something unforeseen was about to happen that would completely change my plans, as well as to disrupt the trajectory of both of our lives.

Unknown to me at the time, apparently one of the water skiers who knew Lisa, told her I was cheating on her with some blonde, but no names were mentioned. I did have two close blonde female friends, Suzette and Christine, both of whom I had previously dated. However, when I started seeing Lisa, I was completely faithful to her. I was so in love with her; no one else existed in a romantic way.

Unfortunately, Lisa decided to believe the rumor and reacted badly, instead of asking me if it was true. She would later refer to this mystery woman as my 'kissy friend.' I did not have an affair with any other woman while I was dating Lisa. I didn't even have the time to see anyone else. I barely found the time to see Lisa. It was simply a vicious rumor started by someone, who was obviously jealous and wanted to cause discord in our relationship. Instead of confronting me about it, Lisa decided to have a 'girls' night out' at the bar where she worked. I begged her not to go, and to spend time with me instead, but she wouldn't listen.

Lisa and I never seemed to have enough time to spend together in the first place, and I couldn't understand why she insisted on going out without me. It seemed like there was nothing I could do to change her mind. Lisa was upset about the rumor, and she wanted to make me jealous. Her plan included having my friends bring me to the bar later in the evening, so I would catch her with someone else. It was a juvenile idea, but Lisa's mind worked this way. Deep down, as beautiful as she was, Lisa was also very insecure and feared that the people she loved the most would leave her, like her biological father had done.

I never realized how possessive and insecure Lisa felt, despite being so desirable and talented. She could have had any man or woman she wanted. I couldn't imagine her feeling insecure about herself or with our relationship. She should have known that I was obviously in love with her, and if she felt there was a problem, she should have come to me to talk about it, instead of staging a dramatic scene, which could only end badly. Lisa apparently had what is known as 'Borderline Personality Disorder' (BPD). One of the symptoms is having an intense fear of abandonment. Our relationship was still very new, and I had dated several women in the park in a short period of time, so perhaps it shouldn't have been too surprising that she might have felt a little insecure. I think if I had known more about Lisa's past, I would have understood her feelings better.

There were many beautiful women in the park, but to me, no one could compare with Lisa's best qualities, and I felt no one was better suited for me. I just wish she had understood that. We still had a lot to learn about each other, and my reputation in the park didn't help to calm her fears. Lisa felt very hurt by the rumor, and she decided to make a statement to me in grand dramatic form, which defined her character. When Lisa did something for attention, it was usually on a large scale, and she made sure everyone was watching when she made a spectacle. Growing up a child star put Lisa at center stage and in the spotlight, and she wasn't about to be upstaged by some blonde with designs on her fiancée.

Since Lisa decided to go out with friends for the night, that left me to hang-out with my colleagues Rob and Melvin, who worked as character actors at Cypress Gardens. We went to play pool and drink beer, so I could try to take my mind off what Lisa was doing without me. As the night rolled on, I started to get depressed. I was feeling anxious because I wanted to be with Lisa instead. I wasn't feeling jealous especially, even though I knew she was at a bar being hit on constantly. When Lisa was waitressing, that sort of thing happened all the time, and I learned to ignore it. It may have felt different to me this time because Lisa was socializing and not working. I trusted Lisa, but I really missed her, and I couldn't understand why she didn't want to be with me that evening.

I decided to go to the bar where I knew she would be, after my friends encouraged me to put down my pool cue and go find her. When the three of us arrived, a very large young man and an attractive young woman were walking outside with their arms around Lisa, who appeared to be intoxicated. The three of them gave me the impression by their body language that they were planning to go home together to have sex. Even though I don't think of myself as the jealous type, Lisa was in front of me with her arms around two attractive people. I knew Lisa to be bi-sexual, so it wasn't a stretch for me to imagine her intensions weren't pure.

I walked up to Lisa and demanded that she give the engagement ring back to me. She handed it over without hesitation or resistance. Then the three of them walked away and disappeared into the night, without a fight. Lisa didn't try to plead with me or offer any explanation. She just left without expressing any kind of emotion. I didn't realize it, but that would be the last time I would ever see her again for the next 28 years. It was a night that I would regret for the rest of my life. Lisa didn't do anything wrong that night, as far as I knew, but I wouldn't be sure of it until many years later.

Appearances can be deceiving, and in this instance, the thoughts in my head didn't line up with reality. Apparently, the man and the woman with Lisa were just friends of hers bringing her home, because she was drunk. However, Lisa had told my friends to bring me to the bar that night, so that she could serve up a little revenge for what she perceived as my infidelity. At the time however, I believed that Lisa was the one being unfaithful, and I had run into her by chance. Lisa was deliberately trying to make me jealous, but I over reacted. What Lisa and I believed to be the truth was one great big lie, and we both paid a heavy price for the deception. We paid the price with our lives. It seemed our relationship, which I thought was so strong, was extremely fragile in the end, and hanging by a string which had just broken.

There are pivotal life changing events that we need to be conscious of when they're happening. When these moments occur, the decisions we make at the time will inevitably have a profound impact on the direction of our lives. We need to be thoughtful about our choices, which will inevitably alter the path to our futures. This was one of those moments, which I didn't recognize or appreciate. This seemingly small incident set Lisa on a collision course that neither of us could have possibly predicted at the time. We didn't pause to think about how our actions that night might change our destinies. In hindsight, I can clearly see that we made poor choices, because ending our relationship unintentionally sealed Lisa's fate, and caused me unending suffering.

Afterwards, I didn't allow myself to feel sad about losing Lisa. Instead, I felt angry and betrayed. The regrettable aspect was that we broke-up over false pretenses. It was all a monumental misunderstanding. We were both still in love with one another, but too stupid and too proud to talk to each other about our feelings the next day.

A few days later, I learned that Lisa had deliberately written bad checks, and she appeared to be using cocaine, which I discovered by accident. Drugs were always something that turned me off about people, and it disturbed me to become aware that Lisa had been using them. Illegal drug use is a form of self-abuse, and I have never approved of anyone who used them. I also didn't like it when any of my girlfriends smoked cigarettes - it's a disgusting habit, and it usually caused me to break up with them, if they didn't quit.

I still regret not going to talk to Lisa the next day, but I was still angry and didn't want to talk to Lisa again, especially after I found out about her secrets. I shouldn't be surprised that she didn't want to tell me about the murder, because she probably knew how I would react. I was so intolerant of even the slightest bad behavior. I never knew it at the time, but Lisa did all those things behind my back. She was able to hide everything from me easily because we weren't together long enough for me to catch her. Lisa never drank much in front of me, and I never saw her smoke or do any type of drugs. I never had any reason to suspect that she had several vices, but I probably should have guessed. I probably would have ended our relationship sooner if she had told me about the murder. Perhaps, I might have had compassion for her, knowing the child abuse she suffered at her stepfather's hands. That may have made a difference in the way I might have reacted. It's hard to say. I was a different person when I was 25 years old.

After what I discovered, I decided that I didn't want to have anything to do with Lisa anymore. If she was not really the woman who I fell in love with, then I didn't want to try to reconcile. I just assumed at this point that Lisa was no good, and that I was lucky to have found out before I married her. I felt so betrayed, and I couldn't think straight. I lost the pure feeling that I had for her, and I just couldn't get it back. I thought I had been deceived, and it made me angry. However, I was just fooling myself into believing that I didn't love her anymore.

Sometimes it helps, just to take a deep breath, and step away from ourselves for a moment. We tend to only look inward and concentrate on how we are feeling at the time, to the point where we lose our ability to empathize with others. Lisa was in pain because of her childhood, my perceived infidelity, and our break-up, but she didn't communicate how she was feeling to me, nor did I try to understand her. She may have thought I didn't love her anymore, but that wasn't true. I couldn't see the forest for the trees because I was too focused on feeling sorry for myself. I realize now that what I was experiencing was pure ego and stupidity. Pride is one of the worst things to have in excess, and Lisa and I were both guilty of wallowing in it.

Not long after Lisa and I broke-up, I found out from Carmen that Lisa had been fired from her job at Air Dancing. I was shocked by the news, but I was still angry with her. Instead of feeling sorry for her, I acted like I didn't care. I knew from what Carmen told me that

Lisa was very upset. Apparently, Lisa chose not to show up when it was time to shoot a commercial for her show. She was one of the featured performers, and not making an appearance during filming caused a lot of grief on the set. Lisa was still unsettled about what had happened between us, and she wasn't in the mood to smile for the cameras. Lisa knew there would likely be consequences, but she didn't think it was enough to get her fired. The entertainment director disagreed and terminated her as soon as he found out what happened.

I know I should have gone to talk to her to find out what happened and try to console her, but once again, my pride got in the way. This was my chance to make things right, but instead I didn't give her a chance to explain because I was behaving selfishly. Lisa needed me and I wasn't there for her. Perhaps, I didn't love her as much as I thought I did at the time. Communication is key in a crisis, and I should have tried harder to empathize with how Lisa was feeling. She not only didn't have me anymore, but now she didn't have her job she loved either. All of this sent Lisa into a deep depression and caused her to retreat from the world and indulge in more destructive behavior.

What seemed like only days after our break-up, Rob came to me and asked if it was okay with me to ask Lisa out. He knew we had been engaged, and that it might cause bad blood between us, if I saw them together. Rob and I weren't exactly friends, but we did have to work in close proximity, since he and I were both part of the entertainment department. I told him that since Lisa and I broke-up, I didn't really have much to say about the matter, so I didn't object. Instead, what I should have done was to tell him to go to Hell, and then go talk to Lisa about getting back together. I must have lost all sense of reason. I certainly was not in touch with my true feelings, because my sentiments were obstructed by my ego. Humility is a gift, which should be nurtured, and pride is the devil's curse. If I had been honest with myself, I would have admitted that I was still in love with Lisa, and that I wanted her back.

What I didn't realize was that I would never be able to completely purge Lisa from my mind or my heart for the rest of my life. I was ill-fated to be in love with her forever. I let my pride get in the way, and it's something I will always regret. Sometimes in life, you just need a friend to shake you and say - "Don't be stupid, go and get her back if you love her." In my case, no one said that to me - not even Lisa's mother. I wish someone had talked some sense into me back then. Once you've lost a meaningful relationship, it's hard to feel the same way about someone else ever again. It's not better to have loved and lost, rather than to never have loved in the first place. Losing someone you love hurts badly, and you never forget it for the rest of your life.

'Classical Ice' had its final curtain call, but instead of sticking around town, I decided to get as far away from Lisa and Florida as possible. Things didn't turn out the way I wished, and I was feeling terrible about everything that had happened. I just wanted a fresh start and to try to forget about Lisa. So, I decided to move across the country to Los Angeles. What I didn't realize was that Lisa's spirit would follow me wherever I decided to go, and I would never be able to purge myself of her presence in my mind and heart.

4. News from Abroad

I had a friend named Tom from high school, who was living in Los Angeles, and he suggested that I come out to live in California. I asked if I could stay with him for a couple of months, while I searched for a job. He agreed, so I got in my car and drove across the country with everything I could fit into my little Mazda to Northridge, California. I eventually landed a marketing job at American Communications & Engineering, a telecommunications company in Simi Valley. On the side, I taught ice-skating in North Hollywood at an Ice Capades Chalet, which was in one of the malls. I lived there in 1990 for about a year until the company I worked for was bought by Sprint-Gateway, and I was forced to look for another job again.

Unknown to me during the same timeframe, Lisa flew to Hollywood to do a photo-shoot for Gallery magazine. Apparently, her mother and boyfriend Stephen came up with another one of their money-making schemes, which involved exploiting Lisa's physical attributes. Stephen took provocative photos of her on the beach and sent them to the publisher of Gallery. It wasn't a surprise that the magazine was interested in her because Lisa was extremely sexy and photogenic. Representatives from Penthouse magazine also solicited Lisa later to do an expose with them as well.

It seemed that no matter how far I went to get away from Lisa, forces in the universe brought us closer together again. However, I never knew she was there at the time, so our paths never crossed directly. I was connected to the entertainment industry because my new girlfriend Anita worked for Paramount Studios. She should have been an actress because she was also extremely beautiful and had a propensity for drama. Instead, she was a secretary because she could type 100 words a minute.

After losing my job at AC&E, I spent a couple of months trying to find other work, but nothing turned up. I probably should have focused my attention on teaching ice skating, but I was trying to concentrate on pursuing a different career path. At the Ice Capades Chalet, where I was currently teaching classes, they wanted to take 60 percent of my earnings from my private lessons. I didn't think that was fair, so that was the reason I didn't want to develop a skating business at that rink. I just wanted to teach group classes, so I could get free ice-time.

There were plenty of other clubs I could have taught at in the region, but I just didn't want to pursue teaching, while I was still very young. Instead, I decided to investigate doing another ice show. I had spoken with a performance director from Disney on Ice, but they didn't have a role that interested me. I had an older friend from the ice rink in North Hollywood, who was a professional costume designer and actor on Star Trek. He was also a former professional ice show skater, and he helped me to choreograph a routine to "That's Entertainment" for auditions. He gave me a phone number for a show producer named Rosemarie, who was producing a new show in France, so I decided to give her a call.

My girlfriend and I were having relationship problems, but I wasn't sure I felt ready to leave her and go away to Europe for six months. A little while later I happened to be playing golf with my brother Joe and his agent Michael in California. I asked Michael if he thought I should go to France to do another ice show or stay in Los Angeles. This is what he told me:

"Listen Alex, you'll never regret the things you choose to do in life, as much as the things you choose not to do," Michael said.

He was telling me to go to France.

By good fortune, I was chosen by Rosemarie to be the lead soloist for a show called 'Fantasia sur Glace' at Walliby-Stromph theme park in a little provincial town in France called Hagondange. It is about three hours east of Paris by train, in the Alsace Lorraine region. It seemed like it would be a great adventure, so I decided to go. I didn't know anyone in the cast, but I didn't care. I was supposed to share an apartment with a guy named John from England, who used to be married to a friend of mine from Buffalo, New York. However, he decided to live with a female friend of his instead, so I ended up with my own place, which suited me perfectly.

We were living in a very small town, so very few people spoke English. I had studied French for about five years in school, so I had at least a working knowledge of the language. However, reading and writing a language is a lot different than speaking it. It was easier for me to read and write French versus trying to talk to someone, who spoke the language fluently. Fortunately, it wouldn't be long before I felt comfortable speaking, since I made many new friends at the park and in the town. I also dated several French women, who helped me to improve my language skills, among other things. French women have a reputation for being great lovers, and I can say unequivocally that it's no myth. At this point, Cypress Gardens and Lisa French were not on my mind anymore. However, something would happen later, which would unleash a specter from my past. Lisa's name would resurface into my present life from across the ocean, as if her spirit was permanently attached to my soul.

One day, a letter arrived for me in France from a girl who used to work at a Kiosk next to the Ice Palace. She and I had developed a friendship, while I was performing. I kept in touch with her when I moved to California, and I must have given her my address in France.

When I opened the envelope, I was surprised to discover there was an article inside written about Lisa, by a reporter from the Tampa Tribune. Lisa's photo and name were splashed all over the page. However, it was the content of the story, which shocked me to my core.

The article said that Lisa Yvonne French had been arrested at a boyfriend's house in Arcadia, Florida in December of 1990 on first-degree murder charges, for a crime that she and a girl named Pam had committed in 1985. Lisa had avoided being implicated for over five years, until Carmen's boyfriend Stephen was arrested on illegal weapons charges, and sold her out to the police. If it hadn't been for Stephen's cowardly confession, Lisa would have likely never been caught. Even though Detective Ray would like to take the credit for solving the crime, he played no part in figuring it out. The only thing he really did was to initiate the arrests of Lisa and Pam. Imagine my profound confusion and consternation when I read the article.

"How was this possible?" I asked myself. "How did I not know that I was engaged to a killer?"

I had fallen asleep next to Lisa dozens of times in the past. I was really stunned and vexed by this revelation, and I tried to make sense of it all in my mind. The girl I knew was sweet, gentle, and delightful.

"How could this be the same girl, who three years prior to our introduction, shot and killed her stepfather?" I wondered. "This couldn't possibly be true! Lisa couldn't be a murderer!"

It was hard to process this in my head; this was incredible news. I had a completely new life - having lots of fun and adventures with new people and traveling around exploring Europe. I was trying to forget the heartache I left behind in Winter Haven. Now, here was Lisa, back in my life again in a foreign country, haunting me from thousands of miles away.

The murder wasn't the only news either. The article went on to say that Lisa had been seven months pregnant when she was arrested, and gave birth to a baby girl, while she was incarcerated. Lisa named the baby Joy, even though she was forced to give up her child for adoption. It was typical of Lisa to see beauty and find happiness among the chaos and drama in her life. This is one of the things that made Lisa so special, and something I loved about her.

When it was time for Lisa to give birth, she was marched out of prison in ankle bracelets, which were never taken off during her labor. Apparently, the police thought she was going to run away, while having her baby. It's unconscionable that any woman had to be subjected to this type of inhumane treatment. One of the female nurses allowed Lisa to hold her child for a while, before her baby was taken away from her permanently. Lisa begged her mother to take care of her baby while she was in prison, but Carmen refused even though she knew that it would break Lisa's heart.

Whatever guy Lisa was living with before she was arrested didn't seem to be interested in taking care of her baby either, even though he might have been the father. Lisa told me that she thought Joy might have been Carmen's boyfriend Stephen's child, because she said he raped her around the time she became pregnant. Joy could also have been Rob's, her boyfriend after me, or she could possibly have been mine. Lisa never really knew for sure. When I first read the article, I dismissed any thought of Lisa's baby being mine, because I calculated when Lisa and I had last slept together. It had been at least 10 months prior to Joy being born. I assumed, after reading the article, that the baby must have been Rob's, since he dated Lisa right after me. Apparently, it didn't cross Lisa's mind that her baby might have been ours. Who the true father of Joy is - remains a mystery. Hopefully in the future, I can discover whether I am Joy's biological father. If I am, I wish that I will be able to find her and tell her about her mother and me. Unfortunately, the adoption agency was unwilling to help put me in touch with Joy's adoptive parents.

In many respects, Carmen was a self-centered, cold-hearted woman, who subjected Lisa to many years of sexual and emotional abuse. Lisa's exploitation by the men in Carmen's life seemed to be a pattern of despicable behavior condoned by her mother. Lisa didn't feel comfortable going to the police, after being assaulted repeatedly, because she said they rarely believed rape victims at that time in Polk County. Circus performers and gypsies usually don't have good relations with police. According to Lisa, when Carmen's boyfriend Stephen raped her in 1990, she stayed silent, because she said Stephen was a dangerous man and might try to harm her. She also didn't want to make him angry by filing a complaint, because she feared that he might reveal her secret - and she was right.

This was one of Lisa's biggest dilemmas in her life. Her mom kept choosing men, who she feared and constantly had to defend herself against. Carmen was gifted at choosing bad men and inserting them into Lisa's life. Stephen betrayed Lisa to the police, to get a reduced sentence after he was arrested on illegal weapons charges. He told police that she had confessed to him about the shooting. Talking to anyone about the confrontation with Alvin was one of Lisa's biggest mistakes. Unfortunately, no matter what the men in Carmen's life did to Lisa, her mom always turned a blind eye, and allowed Lisa to be victimized and traumatized by them. It's hard to imagine why Lisa never learned that her mother was at the center of almost all her suffering. She should have realized this very early in her life and run as far away from her as she could go.

Despite Carmen's exploitation of her daughter, Lisa loved her mother intensely. She and her mom had an unusually close relationship, even though it was mostly one sided. After being around both Carmen and Lisa extensively, it wasn't hard for me to imagine that Lisa would have done anything for her mother, including killing someone for her. Carmen obviously lied to Detective Ray, when she told him she didn't know anything about her husband's death. The prosecution should have charged her with obstruction of justice, at the very least. Why they never called Carmen to the witness stand during Lisa's trial is another mystery. And, why her mother never showed up for her daughter's trial was something Lisa could never understand.

Before the murder trial began, prosecutors struck a deal with Lisa's girlfriend Pam. She was promised a lesser sentence if she testified against Lisa in court. Without Pam's testimony or the murder weapon, the girls would have likely both been acquitted. Perhaps Lisa would have never even faced a trial, due to lack of evidence. The prosecution's lawyers must have persuaded Pam into believing that she would face first degree murder charges if she didn't cooperate. Lisa shouldn't have told the police where they could find the revolver that was used to kill Alvin - another unforced error. Now that the police and the prosecution had the murder weapon, along with Pam's testimony - that was all the evidence they needed to convict Lisa of murder. Fortunately, the charges were reduced from first to second degree, allowing Lisa to narrowly escape the death penalty.

Lisa testified at her trial, that her stepfather Alvin raped her for 14 years, since the tender age of four-years-old. This revelation shed a different light on Lisa's character at the trial, compared to the one the prosecution attempted to portray in court, and what the media tried to paint in public. Instead of Lisa being demonized as a cold-blooded killer, the trial became more about a child who had been the victim of sexual abuse. If Carmen had been there at the trial to corroborate her daughter's story, it's possible the murder charge might have been reduced to manslaughter or even dropped completely.

Unfortunately, Carmen couldn't be bothered to show up to defend her only daughter, and she was apparently never subpoenaed by Lisa's defense attorney. Perhaps Carmen was afraid that her testimony would have shown her own guilt and culpability. Lisa's mother not showing up for her trial was one of her biggest disappointments and heart breaks. Most mothers would have been there to support their child every single day, but not Lisa's mom. This was the kind of say nothing, do nothing mother, Lisa was unfortunately stuck with.

Lisa's testimony alone was not enough to gain empathy from the jury, especially without a witness to substantiate her claims. The fact that the confrontation between the girls and Alvin was planned, was a key factor in the jury's decision to hold Lisa accountable for premeditated murder. Jurors wondered why Lisa didn't go to the police, instead of taking the law into her own hands. Lisa's defense was that she didn't think the police would believe her, especially at that time, and in that backwoods county. Thirty years ago, women were often saddled with the burden of proof in cases of rape and incest. It's still true to some extent today. Even Lisa's own mother was unwilling to admit her knowledge of what had been going on with her husband and daughter; so, what were the police going to think?

Lisa testified that her stepfather had threatened to kill both her and her mother, and that they were both in constant fear for their lives. She also claimed that she only intended to confront her stepfather, to get him to stop the attacks and threats. Lisa tried to explain that she changed her mind about killing her stepfather on the night in question. However, during the confrontation, events escalated to the point where Alvin had left her no choice, and she was forced to defend herself. Since Carmen wasn't there to testify to the sexual abuse, Lisa was ultimately sentenced to 12 years in prison. However, she only served four years, before another attorney was able to orchestrate a reprieve. She was released on probation, which she later violated and wound-up spending three more long years behind bars.

My reaction to the news about Lisa's capture and conviction probably should have been one of sympathy, compassion, and concern. However, I was in shock after hearing the news, and I really didn't know what to think or how to feel. When Lisa realized she might be facing the death penalty, she must have felt extremely frightened, alone, and desperate for help. She was only 24 years old at the time, and just beginning her adult life. I can't imagine what she must have gone through; it must have been terrifying. I was still very young too at this time, and unable to experience the level of empathy for Lisa that I should have felt. I didn't know what to think about Lisa anymore, nor did I realize my true feelings for her. I was in a total state of confusion and denial - full of mixed emotions.

The person I read about in the article was not the person I knew and loved, only a short time ago. I wasn't even sure what to think about her story about being raped. It was just so horrible to imagine. It seemed more likely to me, that she made up the story to escape the death penalty. If I was thinking that way, I could only imagine what a jury, who had no relationship with her, thought about her story. I contemplated going to visit Lisa in prison, but I was afraid to see her, because I was worried that she might still be angry with me. My mind was rejecting everything I had just learned about what happened to Lisa, after I left Florida. It seemed that all Hell had broken loose, the world had turned upside down, and dark forces had penetrated my soul. I felt lost and overwhelmed.

I tried putting the revelations about Lisa out of my mind, while spending my last few weeks in France, but it was quite impossible to achieve. It affected my ability to concentrate during performances. The tranquility that I had experienced, since I became acclimated to my new environment in France, suddenly became in a state of upheaval. Before leaving Europe, I spent my last day in Paris, where I met a woman named Laurie in a Cabaret, the night before I flew back to California. She distracted my attention from Lisa, while spending a memorable night together at her apartment, after she finished work. Our one night of passion was an attempt to escape from the torment that plagued my mind.

When I arrived back in Los Angeles, my friend Tom reminded me about Lisa all over again. I was beginning to feel like Lisa's spirit was following me everywhere. I just could not escape her presence in my life. Tom had recorded an episode of 'Hard Copy,' which was a real-life detective show, which featured Lisa's story about the murder, and her life as a circus performer. During the episode, it showed a photograph Lisa had taken of herself in a leopard skin bikini, which she had given me a copy of when we were together.

Tom knew about Lisa, because he was supposed to have been my best man at our wedding, if it had occurred. While I was in France, Tom moved out of our apartment and in with his girlfriend Helen. When I returned to America, I was fortunate to be invited to stay with them for a few days, before moving back to New York. Helen and her brother Louie were both at the house when I arrived. Neither one of them knew anything about Lisa.

Tom was anxious for me to see the Hard Copy episode about Lisa he recorded, so he put it in the video player for all of us to watch. The story illustrated what I had read in the newspaper article. The documentary was even more sensationalized than the article in the Tribune. It made Lisa out to be a diabolical killer and evil genius. Often, the media doesn't care about the truth - they only want to create drama for ratings. After watching the video, Louie wasn't convinced that I knew Lisa, much less that we had been lovers. I didn't blame him for being skeptical because the story is unbelievable. Tom had a habit of playing practical jokes on people too, and I think Louie and Helen both assumed this was another one of his childish pranks. Louie and Helen tried to act like they had caught onto our little prank.

Lisa was incredibly gorgeous, reminiscent of a movie star, but the segment on Hard Copy portrayed her as a dangerous criminal. Neither Helen nor her brother could bring themselves to believe that a friend of Tom's had such an intimate relationship with someone, who was so notorious and deadly. I didn't blame them for having doubts, because I was having a hard time believing it myself. I think my connection to Lisa might have made them a little nervous too, because I was staying at their house. Perhaps it made them look at me with an increased level of apprehension and suspicion.

"There's no way that you know her dude," Louie said to me.

"Yes way," I replied. "I can prove it."

This was the second time I had to prove my relationship with Lisa. So, I opened my briefcase and showed everyone the same photograph of Lisa in a leopard skin bikini, which appeared in the Hard Copy episode. Helen and her brother were amazed when they saw the same picture they had just seen on the video.

"Dude, that's crazy," Louie said. "You weren't lying."

"I told you," I said.

"So, you were engaged to this chick?" Helen asked.

"Yes, I was," I replied.

"However, I knew nothing about this whole murder affair when we were together," I said. "This is all new to me too. I only found out this happened a couple of months ago. I would have never known about any of this, if not for my friend from Cypress Gardens sending me a news article, or if Tom hadn't shown us this Hard Copy episode."

"Wow, that's crazy man," Louie said.

"I still can't believe it," Helen said.

Despite everything I had learned about Lisa recently, she was still a beautiful young woman, who I still loved and adored. In the past, I instinctively had respect for Lisa's abilities, after she told me that she learned martial arts from her mom's boyfriend. She probably could have snapped my neck in two seconds if she had wanted to. Lisa never made a move to hurt me, and I never felt afraid of her the entire time we were together. In fact, she never showed me or anyone else any type of aggression in my presence. However, Lisa did have a look that occasionally made me nervous. It was a stern and focused stare, and when she used it, I knew not to upset her further. Fortunately, I only saw that look of hers once or twice. When she and I were in bed together, I was always able to close my eyes and fall asleep next to her, having complete confidence that I would be safe in her arms.

Lisa was not the woman she appeared to be on the exterior, but she was also not the woman who was being portrayed by the media either. She was not a cold-blooded killer. On the contrary, Lisa was a fearful and vulnerable young woman, who had been victimized repeatedly by the people closest to her. If she ever acted violent toward anyone, it was only because they had threatened her or showed aggression toward her first. If no one displayed any type of hostility against Lisa, I believe she would have never hurt anyone. Any type of dog will bite when it's been mistreated, hurt, or threatened. You can't blame the dog when it tries to defend itself. Lisa was not an aggressive person naturally, but everyone has survival instincts. People will defend themselves or those they love, if necessary. If Lisa killed her stepfather, then he must have abused her and pushed her into a corner with no way out.

When I was with Lisa in 1989, she was always delightful and pleasant. We never fought about anything, so she never had any reason to feel threatened. I may have been the only person close to her, who treated her well. Lisa always acted sweet and affectionate with me, and she never once gave me any reason to fear her. She was everything I ever wanted from a romantic partner. She was always joyful, and fun to be around. She was never argumentative, belligerent, aggressive, nor emotionally volatile. She was never depressed, never cried nor became angry in front of me. I didn't recognize the person they were talking about on Hard Copy. That wasn't the young woman I knew at all. After discovering her secret, Lisa had become someone I never knew existed. Reading the article from the Tampa Tribune and watching the video had really thrown me for a loop. I started to question everything that I thought I knew about her, but I didn't find any answers.

By 1992, I ended up in Ft. Lauderdale, Florida to teach ice-skating, after a brief stent in Birmingham, Alabama. One of my many regrets was not to find out where Lisa had been incarcerated, so I could have tried to go visit her. I found out many years later that she was confined near the panhandle, not far from Tallahassee. After everything that happened, I was afraid to get involved with Lisa again, but I know I should have gone to see her anyway. I might have been able to bring her encouragement, and perhaps some small amount of comfort. I regret that I didn't go.

I was afraid Lisa was still angry with me, so it was hard to predict how she would have received me from behind bars. I was very anxious about what her reaction might have been. Seeing her dressed in an orange jumpsuit surrounded by armed guards was just too much for me to absorb. In any case, going to visit Lisa would have been the compassionate thing to do. Regrettably, I didn't make the effort. I was not emotionally prepared to subject myself to what likely would have been an extremely painful experience. I just couldn't bring myself to do it. However, I should have concerned myself more with Lisa's suffering, and not with how seeing her would affect me. I am ashamed that I didn't have the courage to go when I had the chance.

Probably the best opportunity I had to go talk to her was when I lived in Ft. Lauderdale. If I had gone to see her in 1992 or 1993, perhaps I would have been able to change her outlook for her future and given her hope. I might have had the opportunity to correct the mistake I made in 1989, and still have a chance to redirect the course of both of our lives. This was another pivotal moment in my life when I failed again to do the right thing. I didn't act when presented with the chance to reach out to someone I loved, who needed my support and encouragement.

When Lisa was released from prison, after serving only four years of her sentence, her mother was not there waiting for her to welcome her home. If she had been wiser after regaining her freedom, she should have chosen not to see her mother ever again. Lisa served time in prison because of what her stepfather had done to her, and because of what Carmen wanted her to do to her husband. Lisa told me that her mother had encouraged her to get rid of Alvin by any means necessary, because she was afraid of him and didn't want him around anymore. Lisa knew exactly what she meant and decided to sacrifice her life for her mother. Even though it was Lisa's defense that she shot her stepfather, due to all the years he raped her, the real reason Lisa told me she killed her stepfather was because her mother asked her to do it. Yet, despite this great sacrifice, Lisa's mother only went twice to see her in prison and never attended her trial. Lisa's biggest mistake she made during her life was trusting and loving the wrong people, present company excluded.

After Lisa was freed from prison in 1995, she struggled to find work. No one wanted to hire a convicted felon, who was sent to prison for murder. Despite this major obstacle, Lisa managed to work for several companies over the next 25 years. She first earned her license to be a hairstylist, but unfortunately, she was allergic to the chemicals and had to stop cutting hair. Later, she earned her commercial driver's license, after someone told her she could never handle a big rig. She worked toward achieving her commercial driver's license mainly to prove she could do it.

Lisa loved driving a truck for two main reasons: First, the money and benefits were very lucrative. Second and most importantly, driving gave her a sense of independence, peace, and serenity because no one was there to torment her. Many people in Lisa's life caused her constant turmoil, so being on the road alone allowed her to escape the constant barrage of harassment and negative energy encompassing her life and draining her spirit. Unfortunately, Lisa's career as a truck driver came to a crashing end one snowy dark night in Kansas.

While on a trip across the country, Lisa hit a patch of black ice and lost control of her semi-truck. She disregarded the advice not to drive in bad weather and decided to take the risk anyway. Lisa's attitude was often defiant and overconfident, and almost proved to be fatal in this case. After hitting the ice, the truck fishtailed, and Lisa was unable to regain control of the vehicle. It went off the highway and slid down an 80-foot embankment in the dark. When the truck finally came to a stop, she found herself unconscious, bleeding from all parts of her body, and dangling in the air upside down - her frail body still strapped to her seatbelt. The crash knocked her front teeth out and caused trauma to her head, neck and back. It was a miracle that she was still breathing. If Lisa hadn't been found in a timely manner, she would surely have died of her injuries. Fortunately, she was rescued and brought to a nearby hospital, where it took weeks for her to recover. Lisa survived the crash against all odds, cheating death one more time.

Lisa always seemed to find a way to survive traumatic events in her life. No matter how bad things became for her, she shook off her negative experiences, and tried to stay positive. She kept moving forward, without looking back. Lisa had a child's spirit, something that was quite special and remarkable about her. Her optimistic outlook was often what kept her alive and motivated. At this point in time, Lisa had suffered more devastation to her mind and body than most people could endure during their lifetimes. However, she still suffered emotionally in silence. No one ever suspected the pain she felt by the smile on her lips and the glow in her eyes. Lisa French was simply a survivor.

5. The Early Years

Lisa French didn't grow up like other children. She was born into circus life, where there were no laws or rules - only survival. As a young girl, Lisa was ardent and full of wonder, living in a world of adventure. She learned to train bears and dance in the air on a high wire. She became a child star before her teenage years and thrived on the clamor of applause and the cheers of an avid crowd.

Lisa loved all animals like most children, except for the kookaburra bird, because one attacked her one day. She was comfortable being around extremely dangerous wild animals at a very young age, like Mowgli in 'The Jungle Book.' That doesn't mean that Lisa's life was never in danger - far from it. She was often unsupervised, while interacting with the lions and tigers. Her favorite animals were the elephants, which she loved to ride during shows.

Lisa's life wasn't defined by freedom and fun, however. She had to practice her routines alone for hours every morning or face severe consequences from her stepfather. Lisa traveled with her parents across the country in a mobile home, moving from town to town. It was difficult for her to make new friends for more than a few days, outside of her extended gypsy family. Later, Lisa's parents managed their own circus, using their family name. Her life wasn't only about rehearsing and performing. She also had to feed and train some of the animals, clean their cages, and take care of them when they were sick or injured. It was a very hard and lonely existence. Lisa longed to have more contact with people her age and have time to enjoy her childhood.

Like any other child, Lisa had a natural curiosity for learning. However, she never had the opportunity to attend school formally for more than one year, nor did she have a tutor. The circus tent was her classroom; the beasts and performers were her teachers. Whatever Lisa learned was mainly through experience. Things like reading, science, and math, she had to teach herself, despite being dyslexic. Her parents were also not well educated and didn't teach her to read or write. Lisa never attended church services, so she didn't learn much about religion or morality. However, she still claimed to be spiritual, and believed there is a much better place to exist, outside of life on earth.

Lisa's life was often filled with torment and terror. Death was not something she was afraid to face. Occasionally, she thought it was a preferable option to her reality. Her parents did very little to ensure her safety. In fact, Carman and Alvin put her life in danger daily. By the age of six, Lisa was taught to perform a life-threatening act on a Cloud Swing. It involved a 14-foot freefall, often from 40 feet in the air with no net, while catching herself only by her wrists. The act helped bring in more money for the family, which took priority over Lisa's safety.

Ironically, even though Lisa performed very dangerous tricks from high above the ground, she was afraid of heights. She learned to be brave and get over her fear to please her parents and to keep herself alive while performing. If Lisa missed even once, she could have been severely injured or died. In those days, circus performers often worked without a net, which didn't seem to bother Lisa's parents. Despite the danger, she loved performing. Lisa felt thrilled listening to the cheers from the crowds chanting her name - 'Lavonne,' prior to her dives through the air. Lavonne was a nickname, which came from her full name, Lisa Yvonne. I called her 'Vonnie.' Having that much positive attention as a child felt intoxicating, especially when most of the attention she received at home was negative and hurtful.

Unfortunately, Lisa had to go through Hell, before she could experience her audience's adulation. While most kids Lisa's age went to school, were making friends, skipping rope, and having fun, Lisa was risking her life every day on a high wire and Cloud Swing, with no one to catch her if she fell. This wasn't a hobby for her, it was her job. Apparently, child labor laws didn't seem to apply to the circus back in the seventies. It was a very lonely and stressful existence, especially since Lisa didn't have any brothers or sisters. There were some other children traveling along with their parents in their caravans, but Lisa didn't have many opportunities to play with them.

A traveling circus is no place for a young child to grow-up, especially not for a young girl. For some children, who have never experienced the reality of circus life, performing, and traveling the country with exotic animals might seem like a dream come true. For Lisa, it was both Heaven and Hell. Her biological father left her family when she was only four years old, leaving her and Carmen destitute and vulnerable. Lisa's biological father leaving the family was the beginning of all her troubles.

Soon afterwards, Lisa's mother married Alvin, who wasted no time sexually abusing her. Lisa's parents obviously had no morals, so they didn't give Lisa any guidance about what is right and wrong. Lisa was merely a source of income to them, and an object of exploitation. Alvin and Carmen were both drug addicts, alcoholics, liars, and thieves. It's not surprising that Lisa acquired some of their bad habits. Her stepfather Alvin was a despicable child molester, and her mother was an accomplice and an enabler. Both were unfit to be parents.

When the shows were over and the crowds were gone, Lisa would go back to her filthy, cluttered trailer, and realize that her life was merely an illusion to others. Her reality was something much different from the spectacle the public witnessed under the big-top. Lisa especially dreaded bedtime because of her stepfather's forced rape rituals. This daily assault was much worse than her nightmares could ever have been. Lisa cried every evening after supper because she knew what was coming next. Her mother Carmen would pretend not to hear or see anything, every time Alvin left her bed to go to Lisa's room. Their family lived in a trailer, so there wasn't much distance between anyone at any given time. It was not possible for Carmen not to have known what her husband was doing with her daughter late at night, while she pretended to be asleep.

Lisa French grew up in an isolated world, surrounded by good animals and evil men. Her childhood innocence had been stripped away from her by the shocking age of four. It was stolen by the same people Lisa should have been able to trust the most - her parents. The person tucking her in bed was the Boogeyman, and Lisa's mother was his accomplice. Lisa's cries at night always fell on deaf ears, veiled by the cover of darkness. No one listened to her screams, dried her tears, or kept her safe from the devil. Lisa's dreams were her only sanctuary from her terrifying incestuous horror story, end even those were often filled with terror.

When Lisa awakened in the morning, the cycle of unending betrayal and suffering would begin all over again. Hovering 40 feet above the ground during the day, allowed her a temporary escape from the clutches of this monster. When Lisa was high above the earth on her Cloud Swing, no one could touch her. If she were to fall to her death, at least she would never have to fear the darkness again. As much as Lisa was afraid of heights, she was more afraid of her bedroom. When other little girls her age were dreaming of sugar plum fairies, Lisa was suffering through an assault worse than being attacked by a mythical dragon. She wondered what she had done to deserve such pain and punishment. Certainly, God no longer existed, or she must be in Hell with Lucifer.

Lisa never allowed anyone to see the ugly side of her world, nor did she ever allow it to break her spirit. For a very long time, she kept this secret to herself. Lisa never told anyone for a long time, about the unspeakable violence she had suffered throughout her childhood. If she allowed someone to get close enough to look deeply into her eyes, they could see the frown behind her painted smile, and sense the abyss of her lost soul. To hide her pain, Lisa wore a happy face like the clowns in the circus, because it was the only way she had any hope of experiencing genuine affection from true admirers.

Most children, suffering from the same circumstances, would likely shy away from people, believing everyone to be another Freddy Krueger. However, the anguish and isolation Lisa experienced during her childhood, only inspired her to express herself positively in front of an audience, who she imagined loved and adored her. Above all else, Lisa was desperate to receive genuine love, especially from her mother. She used everything at her disposal to feel the kind of pure love she longed to experience. Unfortunately, the way she went about it, using her body and sexuality, only guaranteed that she would continue to be mistreated by everyone around her. Lisa would never feel truly loved and appreciated in the way she so desperately desired - unconditionally.

Like the ring-the-bell game at a carnival, Lisa's star rose during the day and fell at night. This was her fate - to explode in a blaze of glory. Regardless of the heights she would achieve in her life, Lisa's destiny was written in the stars to come crashing down to earth in a fiery ball of flames.

6. Reconnecting

I have always been fascinated and intrigued by Lisa French's life and character. Throughout my own life, I have never forgotten her or completely lost the feeling I used to have for Lisa. I had been curious to find answers to so many questions that remained unfulfilled for nearly 28 years. I often thought about trying to find her, but I wasn't sure where to start looking, or what the consequences might be. I thought that if I had a chance to talk to Lisa again, I might find some answers to some of my questions, and it might give me some sense of peace. It could also accomplish quite the opposite as well. I combed the internet for several years with no success.

I finally did a Google search for her and found out she had changed her last name and moved to the Chicago area. However, I didn't know if she was still living there. I noticed during my internet search that she had been arrested again in 2015 in Florida. Her mugshot showed that she was overweight, and she looked like she had been taking hard drugs. I was so shocked by what I saw; I almost didn't recognize her. It was heartbreaking to see her in such a neglected state. I tried looking for her again on Facebook using the name Taylor, and I finally found her.

In one sense, I was surprised to learn that Lisa was using social media. She had four profiles listed for some odd reason. In any case, I was very excited to finally track her down. Since her pages on Facebook were public, I started reading some of the things she had written, and how desperate she said she had been feeling. She wrote about how depressed and unhappy she had been for a long time and had little hope for her future. Much of what she wrote was very dark and full of sadness and despair. It was especially painful for me to read some of her posts. Here was a woman, who was larger than life to me at one time, and now in 2018, Lisa had sunk to a very low point in her life. She was jobless, penniless, existing on welfare, and stuck living with her parents at the age of 51. It seemed like she had given up on life all together. Lisa was just barely surviving and wallowing in self-pity. Again, this was not the Lisa I fell in love with in 1989.

When I first saw that she was married, and living a new life in Illinois, I felt encouraged and happy for her. I thought that Lisa had finally made a decent life for herself. However, after reading her social media pages, I discovered whatever life she had known in Chicago was short-lived. I really became overwhelmed with sadness thinking about Lisa's state of despair. Lisa was suffering, lonely and depressed, and I felt terrible for her. My reflex reaction was to try to contact her right away and to see if I could help, but then I hesitated. I had to ask myself, if I really wanted to dig up the past and risk getting involved with Lisa again. After all, she was a convicted felon, who spent several years in prison. Surely, that experience must have changed her tremendously.

"What if she was still angry with me?" I thought. "What if she couldn't forgive me for leaving her?"

Perhaps Lisa no longer had feelings for me, after everything she had endured. Lisa proved herself to be dangerous and becoming involved with her again might cause me harm. I really didn't know what to expect and I wasn't sure what to do. I wrestled with the idea for several days, until I finally found the courage to send Lisa a message. It took Lisa almost a week to respond to me, but her initial reaction was positive. She told me she was happy to hear from me. We sent messages back and forth for a few days, until she finally allowed me to have her phone number. I felt anxious about calling her and hearing her voice for the first time in a long time, since we broke up on bad terms in the past. I had broken off our engagement, due to what I perceived as her infidelity. She also thought I had some part in her losing her job, because of something I said to her mother. Despite my anxiety, I finally called her. As I listened to the rings, my heart and mind were racing with nervous energy, while memories from our past streamed through my head like a music video.

"Hello," Lisa said in a raspy voice.

"Hi Lisa, how are you?" I asked.

"Terrible!" Lisa replied. "My back is killing me and I'm on strong medication. I'm really in a lot of pain, and I'm suffering from severe depression. Why are you calling me? I just want to be left alone!"

"Well Lisa, I wanted to see how you were doing, and to ask if I could help you in some way," I replied.

"You can't help me, so go to Hell!" Lisa shouted.

Then, she hung up the phone.

"That didn't go well," I thought to myself.

However, I was determined not to let her behavior deter me. I waited 28 years to have this chance, and I wasn't about to give up now; so, I called her back. The second time around, I managed to persuade her to talk to me. She was still angry with me after all this time, not only for breaking-up with her, but also because she thought I caused her to be fired from her job at Air Dancing. I tried to explain that I had nothing to do with her being fired, but I wasn't sure if she believed me. I knew it would take a long time to rebuild trust between us, after everything that had happened. Lisa wasn't inclined to trust men in general, especially ones she perceived to have hurt her.

Unspeakable things had happened to her over the past three decades. Perhaps I was just too late. I should have never ended our relationship the way I did. I loved her so much, and yet I threw it all away so easily. I can never forgive myself for doing that. I don't know why I expected Lisa to pardon me. By the end of the call, I assured her that I was going to try my best to help her, as much as possible. Lisa told me that she appreciated my offer before saying goodbye. I really felt ashamed that I had waited so long to reach out to her. I didn't want to admit to myself that I still loved her, but I did.

One of my first objectives in helping Lisa was to get her in touch with some health care professional friends of mine, who I thought could give her good advice and moral support. I wasn't confident that Lisa was currently receiving the best medical care, because I knew she didn't have much money, and still suffered from back pain. I also hoped Lisa would transition away from her current group of friends, who likely did nothing but create more trouble for her. Lisa was associated with drug addicts, alcoholics, and criminals. I wanted her to break free from their influence and her dependence on them. Unfortunately for people like Lisa, once they become involved with a group like that, they tend to stay in those circles for most of their lives. It makes it very difficult for someone on the outside, to help them to cut those ties permanently. However, I knew if Lisa couldn't make better friends and break her old contacts, I was going to have a Mount Everest size challenge trying to help her form better habits.

Lisa told me that in her teenage years, she felt like a loser, and that's why she hung out with bad people. It surprised me to hear her say that, because I always saw Lisa as someone who was extraordinary - a rare jewel. She was blessed with talents far beyond the average person, but apparently, Lisa had learned from the people she hung-out with, that she wasn't special. It's often the case that when people are jealous of someone, they do their best to bring them down to their level. When Lisa was with me, she said she felt special.

That's how I wanted her to feel because Lisa was an extraordinarily exceptional woman.

I have never been someone who took drugs or drank to excess, unlike many of Lisa's friends. Unfortunately, most of the people in Lisa's life reinforced or encouraged her bad habits, and negative mindset. I was trying to change that; however, I was only one of many voices in Lisa's life. She spent three decades developing bad habits and believing in a negative image of herself. It was going to be an uphill battle to help Lisa to change almost everything she had learned. All I really wanted was for Lisa to be happy and healthy, and value herself and her life.

Lisa and I started communicating every day after our initial contact. The more we talked, the better she seemed to feel and act. It became difficult for me to tell that there was anything wrong with her anymore. She seemed like the Lisa I used to know and love again. She was happy, energetic, flirtatious, and seemingly not in pain as much anymore. It was almost as if her emotional happiness had a positive effect on her mind and body. It was quite remarkable for me to witness her transformation, within such a short period of time. As a result, our relationship started to feel like old times. It was very encouraging and intoxicating to interact with her in such a positive way again.

After a while, I became aware that I was falling in love with her all over again. At the same time, it concerned me about being emotionally involved with Lisa, while I was trying to help her. It might ultimately have a negative impact on both of us. If we started to have problems in our relationship, there could be severe consequences to Lisa's emotional and physical well-being. Her mind was very fragile and volatile, and I didn't want to upset her. Our renewed relationship could easily become like a double-edged sword. Accepting her or rejecting her romantically could have an equally harmful effect on her. There was also the issue that no one else seemed to be willing or able to offer Lisa much emotional or financial support. Her parents were useless, so it was either me or nobody. I felt uncomfortable being the only one responsible for her, but I had no choice, except to deal with the situation alone, in the best way possible.

I tried to discourage developing a romantic relationship with her, but Lisa craved attention and had a desperate need to be loved. I also found it challenging to resist her advances, because I was still in love with her. She had no intention of making it easy to keep the lines in our relationship from being blurred. I tried to focus on my objective to help Lisa, and not risk what I was trying to do, by giving into my desire for her. However, Lisa seemed to be a lot less interested in my help, and a lot more interested in reviving our past love affair. I wasn't certain if that was how I truly felt as well.

Most of all, Lisa needed someone she could trust. I knew she needed me to be her best friend more than her lover. In spite of my efforts to manage our relationship, Lisa was always in control. She knew what she needed, and she took what she wanted. She knew exactly what she was doing. When Lisa was feeling happy, she and I got along very well. We were always good friends in the past, and naturally compatible. Ever since our first kiss, Lisa was still the one steering the course of our relationship. Deep down, I knew that it was unlikely we were going to be able to be only friends, but perhaps I wanted more in the end anyway.

Having a relationship with Lisa is like a poker game; you are either all-in or you fold. There was never any middle ground, especially between us. I didn't want to admit it, but I was finally recognizing that I had been in love with Lisa my entire life, and how I felt about her wasn't about to change. It was impossible to resist or control my feelings for her. However, I couldn't be sure if I was just clinging to our past or developing new feelings for her. I knew my involvement with Lisa could be dangerous for both of us, because this woman was not the same person who I fell in love with 28 years ago. I also knew that she could kill if she felt threatened or hurt. I needed to be extremely careful.

I realized that I may have never really known Lisa, as well as I thought I did in the past. Her mental state bounced around like a pinball. It was probably never stable in the past, but I never noticed because she kept it hidden. I couldn't fix Lisa's emotional or physical problems, so the best I could do was to try to persuade Lisa to seek professional help. I offered to pay for her psychiatric care, and I did end up paying for her visits with her primary care physician. I knew that Lisa had gone through Hell during her life, which was why I wanted to help her now, and possibly make up for abandoning her.

I couldn't imagine what prison life was like for her, but somehow Lisa made the best of it. She managed to find happiness and peace, even while she was incarcerated. Lisa showed me a review about herself during her time spent in prison. It stated that she was cooperative and helpful, and demonstrated good behavior with a friendly attitude. That didn't surprise me, because Lisa had such a charismatic personality, and could transform herself like a chameleon. She made friends easily, not only among the other inmates, but she apparently became a favorite among the staff as well.

If Lisa had been well educated, and grew up in a decent family, she might have become a politician because everyone loved her. She certainly could lie as well as any of them. People simply liked Lisa the minute they met her. She adapted to everyone, whether they were rich, poor, tall, short, black, or white. She had a gift, when it came to winning people over with her charm and complimentary style. I noticed Lisa often changed her accent and tone of voice to match whatever person she spoke to. She had a remarkable gift for gab, and I admired her for it.

Despite Lisa's positive attributes, her mind had been damaged from all the years of mental and drug abuse. I'm certain she must have also experienced brain trauma from her truck accident. She had also become paranoid and seemed to suffer from hallucinations. Occasionally, Lisa would see imaginary people in my room during video calls. It was bizarre, and it caused Lisa to become very agitated and distrustful of me. When I posted things for work on Facebook, or if I was chatting with friends, she would accuse me of pursuing other women. Eventually, I was forced to unfriend her, so that it would no longer become a source of controversy.

Lisa's emotional volatility was like a rollercoaster and a great source of stress for me. I didn't know how much longer I could tolerate it. Some days she felt happy and acted normally, and other days she was belligerent and verbally abusive. It was difficult to deal with her antics because I had strong feelings for her. Lisa's behavior reminded me of my sister, whose conduct before she died was equally bad. It's likely both had similar mental disorders. Lisa had never acted jealous in the past, but now she expressed it openly. I continued to try to discourage a romantic relationship between Lisa and myself, because of her erratic behavior - but that also had negative consequences. The more I pushed Lisa away, the more hostile she became. She began drinking again too much and pursuing other harmful relationships. Lisa was obviously very insecure and suffering from mental illness, so I continued to encourage her to see a psychiatrist, but she didn't take my suggestion seriously enough.

Lisa's mother and stepfather did nothing to take care of her, other than allow her to live with them. Ironically, it was Lisa's land that everyone was living on in Florida - property that Lisa's parents had swindled from her. The 10 acres of land that the house is sitting on in Fort Meade, bordering Lake Wales, is real estate which Lisa had been given the option to buy from her ex-husband, during their divorce. While she was in prison, her parents manipulated her into giving them power of attorney, allowing them to exercise the option to buy the land on her behalf. However, after they bought it, they built a house on it, and gave Lisa nothing, which I believe was Dave's plan from the beginning.

It was clear that my relationship with Lisa was growing more complicated by the day, due to all her capricious behavior. Despite Lisa's conduct, I still loved her, and I wanted her to experience happiness in her future. I understood that Lisa had been treated badly most of her life, and suffered every day from physical pain, so I tried hard to overlook it when she acted intolerably. Regardless of our tumultuous relationship, we were both still very anxious to see each other again. Lisa needed more attention than I had been able to give her, due to living three states apart. I wanted to see her again for my own reasons, including coming to terms with our past. So, I made plans to have a reunion in mid-September down in Florida. The conditions at her house were so deplorable and stressful, so I agreed to have her stay with me, when I came down to see her. I knew that was going to be very risky, but with Lisa everything was a high-risk gamble.

I figured that staying at a nice quiet relaxing place, somewhere near the beach, would be the best choice. I planned to fly into Tampa, and have Lisa come to pick me up at the airport. I also booked a place in St. Petersburg at the Grand Plaza Resort Hotel because it offered everything we needed. There were plenty of places to eat at the hotel and around the area. I thought that between the pool and the bay, it would be a good place to relax in the sun - free from stress and her toxic parents. I also tried to plan a dinner reunion with former Cypress Gardens Ice skating friends of mine, who were still living in the area. I thought it might be fun for both Lisa and I to unwind, see some old familiar faces, and have some laughs together.

As the time drew near to see each other, we were both very nervous and filled with emotions and expectations. It had been almost 30 years since we last saw each other in the flesh. Not only had we both changed, but we also lost our youth and innocent spirits.

We weren't a young naive couple in love any longer. We both had been through so much since those days. It was hard to know for certain how we would feel, and what would happen when we were face to face again for the first time, after so many years. I was confident that our first meeting would go well. However, Lisa's emotions were so sensitive, that I couldn't predict how long it might be before her mood changed, triggered by something I did or said to her.

Lisa's state of mind didn't deter me from following through with our plan to see each other again. Even so, she and I were both still extremely nervous about our rendez-vous. I had always regretted acting impulsively in the past when I broke off our engagement. It tormented me for years that we didn't give ourselves the chance to make-up. If Lisa and I had worked things out and stayed together, our futures might have looked quite different. She might have even been able to avoid prison, and much of the pain she suffered through.

Perhaps staying together might have led Lisa in a better direction in her life. On the other hand, it may have ruined mine. I had an exciting life in Lisa's absence, but I'm not convinced I have been happier for it. There's always been something missing in my heart, but I could never put my finger on it. I was beginning to understand just how vital a role Lisa had played in my life. I didn't know how, but Lisa had filled a void, which couldn't be replaced by any other woman. Perhaps if we had stayed together, it might not have been too late for Lisa to change her bad habits, while she was still young. It was hard to say what would have happened or what might have been. I know things turned out very badly for Lisa, and I felt very sad and guilty about that. Since I couldn't change her past, I decided that maybe I could influence her life in the present and future - only time would tell.

I'm not sure how I would have reacted if Lisa had told me about the shooting in the past. I probably would have freaked out completely. Lisa didn't want to tell me for fear of being caught, and potentially losing me. I was so naive at 25 years of age. I didn't really have the capacity to understand the entire context of what had occurred between Lisa and her stepfather. I'm certain that I would not have turned her in, but I probably would have suggested to her to get the advice of a good lawyer, instead of continuing to hide the truth from the police. Maybe I would have just asked her to go away with me. I can't say for sure.

I would like to believe that I would have stood by Lisa, but my instincts probably would have told me to run away. If she had told me her story, perhaps I might have been able to process it calmly, but I doubt it. In any case, I will always regret not speaking to her again, after that night at the bar. Despite my lack of empathy in the past, I was now determined to try to make-up for it, by putting my full support behind her in the present.

7. The Jeep

During one of our conversations, Lisa told me that the only car her family had was about to be repossessed. She said if that happened, she would have a hard time going anywhere, because she and her parents lived miles away from everything. The house she lived in sits next to Lake Buffum in central Florida. A couple of Pontoon boats were docked in the backyard next to the lake, but her second stepfather Dave, stubbornly didn't want to sell either of them.

In any case, Lisa needed help buying another car because she had no job, no money and poor credit. If Lisa didn't have an automobile, she probably couldn't find a job, buy groceries, or go to the doctor. Lisa also needed to find work to make the car payments, because I didn't want to have to make them for her. Unfortunately, when it came to dealing with Lisa, I constantly found myself in an untenable position. I didn't realize at the time that she had a serious drinking problem. I probably should have asked her more probing questions before deciding to help her. When I knew Lisa in the past, she didn't drink much around me. I only saw her drunk that one night when she came out of the bar with her friends. So, I didn't understand that I needed to be concerned about Lisa driving drunk.

I had a friend named Gregg, a car salesman in the Tampa Bay area, who I asked to help Lisa pick something out for her to drive, and to try to help her find a job selling cars. She could sell anything with her magnetic personality, and she understood mechanics. If she did well, she could afford lease payments, move into her own apartment, and away from her toxic parents and their filthy home. I felt Lisa had a good chance to be offered a sales position, so I wasn't too worried about her making the payments. It was only a matter of days before someone would come to repossess their current vehicle, so I had to act fast. Lisa's stepfather Dave hadn't made payments on their car for months, so I didn't really have much time to consider my decision carefully.

Against my better judgement, I told Lisa that I would help her by co-signing a lease. I knew it wasn't a good idea, but I was committed to helping Lisa change her life. At least this way, the dealer would still own the car. She would be renting the vehicle for a maximum of three years, and the monthly payments would be relatively low. I thought it was something she could handle. Lisa was thrilled that I said I would help her to regain her freedom. She hated having to ask Dave to borrow his car, whenever she needed to go somewhere. His Kia was a filthy disgusting smelly mess inside - like everything else he touched.

On the day Lisa planned to go to the dealership to look for an SUV, she couldn't hold back her enthusiasm. She took her mom and her little dog Kricket with her, when she went to meet Gregg. In typical fashion, Lisa arrived a few hours late for her appointment. The dealership was about 45 minutes away in Tampa, but traffic wasn't the reason they were late. When Carmen and Lisa finally made an appearance, Gregg had rearranged his schedule to accommodate them.

First, they checked-out a small Buick, which I knew she wouldn't like. Lisa really wanted a Jeep because it was more her style. She was still a bit of a tomboy at her age, with a feminine twist. Lisa was a woman, who was used to being outdoors and getting her hands dirty. A Jeep fit her personality better. Gregg showed her a royal blue Jeep Compass next, but she hated the color. After looking further, they came across another one, which Lisa liked much better. This Jeep had metallic white paint with black trim along the sides and the roof. It was a basic model, but it did have Bluetooth for her phone and a radio, but not navigation or leather seats. Lisa wasn't a novice when it came to automobiles. She held a commercial driver's license (CDL) and had advanced knowledge of commercial truck engineering. She knew how to repair them if they ever broke down on the road. Between Lisa's and Gregg's knowledge of automobiles, they didn't really need me to be there at this point.

A new vehicle would be safe and reliable, and something Lisa and I would have our names on together, which made her happy. I knew that in Lisa's mind, she had started to envision us as a couple again and buying a car together would make that statement. Buying this Jeep together would bind us together, for better or for worse. I didn't realize at this time, that helping Lisa with this Jeep would become a source of tension and division between us, and it was something I should have anticipated happening.

Now that Lisa had chosen a ride, all I had to do was to come up with a deposit and have the paperwork signed. Gregg told Lisa that the car would be ready to pick up in about a week or two. Lisa was as thrilled as a teenager, knowing she was getting a new car. She could hardly breathe when she spoke to me about it. It pleased me to see how happy and respectful she was acting for a change. Everything about Lisa's attitude and spirit just seemed to be transformed. She felt like she had a new lease on life, and not just because of having a new car soon. It allowed her to have new hope for her future. She talked about nothing else each time we spoke. It seemed like a huge weight had been lifted from her body.

Lisa would finally be able to come and go as she pleased. She would no longer be stuck at home with her toxic parents, who did nothing but create stress for her. Carmen and Dave had been going through a long divorce proceeding with no end in sight, and Lisa was caught in the middle with nowhere else to go. Now, she would be able to get away from the house whenever things became ugly, which was a great relief to her. Ironically, Lisa had less freedom at age 51, compared to when she was a child. Lisa was used to traveling constantly when she was young, so being trapped at home with no way to leave was like living in a prison.

A few days before Lisa was supposed to pick up the Jeep, I started to worry about her going alone to the dealership. I assumed she would be nervous and excited the day she needed to pick-up her car. I suggested to Lisa that since the dealership was a fair distance away, it would be a good idea to take an Uber to get there, instead of driving her stepfather's crossover. Her plan included leaving it at the dealership since it was about to be repossessed. Despite my advice, Lisa insisted on going alone and driving the black Sorrento. Once Lisa had an idea in her head, no one could talk her out of it. She was going to do what she wanted, but I had a bad feeling that things were not going to go smoothly. I should have planned to fly down to help her, and I regret that I didn't.

When the day finally arrived for Lisa to pick up the Jeep, she was having a hard time getting ready. I texted her to see how things were going, but she responded by saying that she hadn't left yet. This went on for hours until the afternoon, which caused me to become increasingly nervous. I couldn't understand what was taking her so long to leave, but Lisa would not give me any clear answers to my questions. Her appointment was supposed to be around 11 am, and it was now 1:30 pm, and she was still at home - at least that's what she told me. Perhaps she left already, and something happened along the way. She had been so anxious to have her Jeep all week; I couldn't imagine what was holding her up.

It was now around 2:30 in the afternoon when I received a call from Lisa; she was crying. Apparently, she had been stopped by the police for rear ending someone along the route.

"This is going to be a real problem," I thought to myself.

Lisa wanted me to talk to one of the officers. I didn't see how I could help, but I wanted to find out from a credible source what had happened, so I agreed. Fortunately, it didn't seem like she was going to be charged with DUI. However, she was going to be receiving a ticket for reckless driving. The officer handed the phone back to Lisa, and I suggested to her that maybe she should forget about picking up the car today.

"Lisa honey; I know you're having a stressful day," I said. "Why don't you take an Uber home, and you can try again tomorrow, okay?"

"No Alex," Lisa replied. "I'm fine; I can make it there today. I will be alright; don't worry."

"Okay then," I said. "Call me when you arrive, okay?"

"Okay baby; I love you," Lisa replied.

Lisa started driving again, determined to make it to the dealership. A few days later, Lisa told me that she had not one, but two accidents on the way. If I had known, I would have tried harder to keep her from picking up the Jeep that day. Lisa claimed she had taken sleeping medication, instead of her anti-anxiety pills, and that was the reason she had the accidents. I suppose that was a plausible explanation, but when Lisa was in trouble, the truth always became elusive. I could never count on Lisa to be completely honest.

Just when I thought things were going to be better for the remainder of the day, I received a call from Gregg. He told me Lisa never showed up at the dealership. I wondered why she hadn't called me if she encountered more trouble. Apparently, Lisa was stranded on the side of the road somewhere, not far from the dealership. When I hung up the phone, I called Lisa and asked her what happened. She told me she couldn't drive the car any further, so I told her to wait there, until I could see what I could do to help her.

Then, I called Gregg back to see if he could arrange to pick her up. He told me he would go look for her and left the dealership in a hurry.

Gregg spotted Lisa standing next to the black Sorrento in a parking lot along the highway. It was still relatively new, however Gregg told me how filthy and disgusting it was on the inside. Lisa slid into Gregg's car, leaving Dave's car in the parking lot to be repossessed. After they arrived at the dealership, I spoke with Gregg again and told him to make certain that Lisa hadn't been drinking. I instructed him to not let her have the Jeep, until he felt she was completely competent to drive. He assured me that he would keep her there for at least an hour - long enough to be certain she was okay to drive before giving her the keys. Gregg told me he would make up some excuse, like needing to have the car washed, to keep her waiting.

Just when I thought nothing else could possibly go wrong, it did. Apparently, I wasn't going to be able to lease the Jeep, because I lived out of state. I didn't understand why I didn't know this information before this moment, but this news couldn't have come at a worse time. I wasn't sure what I was going to do. Lisa sat patiently at the dealership with no way to get home, if she couldn't have the new car. She would have nothing to drive, and now she was stuck in Tampa, far from home. This was a total disaster! I could already imagine what was going through Lisa's mind. She would be extremely disappointed and depressed. Her spirit would be crushed if I couldn't fix this problem. I wasn't going to let that happen.

This Jeep was one of the only things keeping Lisa's spirits up. Thoughts about how terrible Lisa's life had been all these years, rushed through my mind. This was the one thing that made her happy again, and I decided that I couldn't take it away from her now. I promised her this Jeep, and I felt obligated to follow through with it. After all the effort she made to get to the dealership, I couldn't let her down now. It would destroy her. Besides, I still felt guilty about walking away from her all those years ago, leaving her to suffer endlessly for most of her life. So, I told Gregg to let me talk to Lisa.

"Hi Lisa," I said.

She was crying uncontrollably, so she didn't say anything at first.

"Don't worry honey; we'll buy the Jeep instead, okay?"

"Really?" she replied, as she tried to hold back her tears.

"Yes," I said.

"Oh, thank you Alex," she replied.

"You're welcome Vonnie," I said.

When Gregg took hold of the receiver, I asked him to redo all the paperwork, so I could buy the Jeep. Now the dye was cast. I was all-in with Lisa now, and I was hoping the gamble would pay off in her favor. I was still thinking that Lisa was in no condition to drive home, after all she had been through that day. I tried to convince her to stay overnight in Tampa, but she wouldn't consider it. Lisa was determined to head home with her new car, despite everything that happened. I didn't understand the urgency, and I told her I would pay for a hotel room for her.

It was now close to 6 pm. Lisa had spent the entire day just doing something as simple as picking up a car and driving it home. She managed to make the simplest of tasks complicated, and full of drama. If she had just listened to me when I told her to take an Uber, none of this would have happened. Lisa finally made it home safely, and for the moment, she was truly happy. That was all that mattered to me.

This whole ordeal made me start worrying about my liability with the car, since the registration was also in my name. I knew I should have given this more thought previously, but when it came to Lisa, my mind stopped working, and my emotions took over. If Lisa hurt someone with the Jeep, it could become a big problem for me. All my chips were in the pot, and it was too late to turn back now. I was either going to win or lose big. Winning for me meant that Lisa would survive and find happiness again. I was prepared to stick by her, for as long as it took to accomplish that goal.

However, from that point on, that Jeep would become a constant thorn in my side because Lisa could not seem to follow through on securing a job. Therefore, I had to continue making payments or my credit would be damaged. In any case, she now had freedom and happiness. I felt I owed it to Lisa to give her a second chance at life, after leaving her in the past. I loved Lisa tremendously, but the main reason I think I helped her was out of guilt. I never knew how much she meant to me, until I spoke with her again for the first time in decades. Even if Lisa wasn't the same woman I used to know, and if she didn't love me the same way anymore, it didn't matter. I still loved her so much and longed to have her in my life again. I wanted our relationship to have a second chance, and I was willing to do almost anything to make that happen.

8. Beach Rendez-Vous

Lisa and I had been communicating almost every day for three months since June 2018. By this time, I knew what to expect from her behavior. I could tell that Lisa was traumatized, due to everything she had been through in the past three decades, so I tried to be as understanding as possible. All her suffering, along with the time that had gone by, had a noticeable effect on her attitude and behavior. I was aware that many of her outbursts were not really directed toward me, but a manifestation of her frustration and pain.

At this moment in Lisa's life, her emotions were mercurial. She wasn't the same woman I used to know and love anymore. I don't know why I expected her to be the same, but I did. So many things had happened to her since 1989, and it had taken a toll on Lisa's demeanor and state of mind. I was not the same person I used to be either, for that matter. Fortunately, Lisa enjoyed communicating with me, but she seemed emotionally distant at times. Occasionally, it almost felt like we had just met for the first time.

Lisa was not in a good frame of mind during this time. She acted paranoid, erratic, nervous and afraid most of the time. It was as if she had suffered a permanent mental breakdown. Lisa was broken and I wanted to fix her, but I just didn't have the tools or the expertise to make her well again. All I could manage was to offer her love and friendship and try to do my best to take care of her from a distance, making sure she had money for doctor visits. It concerned me that my efforts were not going to be enough to make a difference.

Dealing with Lisa was often like dealing with a young child. Sometimes, she would call me extremely upset because she had an argument with one of her parents, or because something bad happened to her. Other times, she made up some convoluted story to tell me that she thought I was naive enough to believe. Most of the time, I could see through her lies because I anticipated them, but occasionally some more subtle things would slip through the cracks. I knew that telling fantastic stories became Lisa's proclivity to get what she wanted, but I was wise to her tactics. It was necessary for me to be perspicacious, to stay one-step ahead of her.

Lisa also experienced hallucinations when she spoke to me on video calls. Occasionally, she would tell me she could see someone in my room while I was talking to her, though no one else was there. I thought this may have occurred because of her drug use, lack of sleep, brain damage or perhaps a combination of all three. These delusional episodes, along with her mood swings, were beginning to create arguments and division between us. I didn't know what to do about it, so I considered cancelling my trip to Florida. After further consideration, I decided that I needed to go, as much for myself as for her sake.

Lisa and I were both very excited to see one another again, despite the problems we were currently experiencing. Our assignation was set for mid-September. I also planned to get together with some former colleagues of mine from Cypress Gardens for a reunion dinner. The plan was for Lisa to pick me up from the Tampa airport, and afterwards spend a week together at St. Petersburg Beach in a nice resort hotel, overlooking the bay. I chose this location, not only for its relaxing atmosphere, but also because it had everything we needed to enjoy ourselves, without leaving the hotel. I wanted to make sure we had a peaceful environment for both of us to reconnect. I also wanted to see if I could make a significant impact on Lisa's life, by spending time motivating her to feel hopeful for her future.

In the back of my mind, I had romantic thoughts about what might happen between us, but I kept trying to convince myself that it was not the main reason for my visit. We both still had strong feelings for one another, but I didn't want that to interfere with my mission of offering Lisa something to look forward to in her life. I was painfully aware of how much Lisa had changed in 28 years. She was not the same sweet, friendly, and precocious girl that I used to know from our past. It was heartbreaking for me to see how cruel life had been to her over the past three decades. No one seemed to have taken good care of her or truly love her, and I couldn't understand why. I had the privileged opportunity to love Lisa in the past and care for her, but like many others; I also failed to give her the love and support she deserved.

The long-anticipated reunion day had finally arrived. Lisa and I were very nervous and excited to see each other again. After disembarking from the plane, I discovered that the Tampa Bay airport was a bit of an obstacle course. I struggled to find my way through to the right baggage claim, where Lisa was supposed to be waiting for me. I knew that if I didn't hurry and find where I needed to go, she would become anxious. I decided I'd better send her a text message to let her know that I would be there shortly. As I walked toward our rendez-vous point, I finally spotted someone from the back who looked like Lisa. The woman had dark brown, shoulder length hair; she was wearing ripped jeans, a pink tank top and aqua flip-flops. My hands started to become moist with sweat, my heart began pounding in my chest, and my mouth became so dry that I could barely swallow. My nerves were on full alert - I was exhilarated and panicked at the same time.

"Lisa!" I shouted. "She must not have heard me," I thought. "Lisa!" I shouted again.

This time the woman whirled around like a ballerina on point, and glanced in my direction, as I continued to walk toward her. She didn't seem to recognize me at first, but as I walked closer to her, an exuberant smile formed across her face. It was Lisa alright. A tidal wave of emotion swelled up inside me, almost knocking me off balance.

"Hey!" Lisa exclaimed with excitement, as she hurried toward me.

Lisa was beaming with joy and my heart was racing. This was a surreal moment seeing her in the flesh again for the first time in almost 30 years. It was like seeing a ghost from my past, which had been haunting me my entire life. I felt like I had gone back in time to recapture a memory, and a moment of sheer bliss. I can't even begin to describe the exhilaration we were both experiencing. Nobody in the world had quite the same effect on me as this extraordinary woman. This feeling inside me had never changed or faded away completely. Lisa walked straight up to me, in a moment of Deja-vu, locked her arm around my neck, and kissed me intensely. I hadn't been kissed like that for a very long time. When Lisa finally opened her eyes, they were laser focused on mine, and her deep gaze penetrated my soul. I was spellbound to be holding Lisa once again, after so many years of separation. It was thrilling to feel the warmth of her breath on my neck, the soft touch of her kiss on my lips, and the power of her embrace. The experience was paralyzing.

I had thought about Lisa for so many years, wondering where she was living and what she had been doing. Now at last, she was here with me in my arms, and I never wanted to let her go again. It only took seconds to realize that I was still in love with her. At that moment, it seemed like Lisa and I had always been meant to be together, but somehow, a cruel twist of fate had interfered with our destinies and drove us apart. As if by cosmic forces, we were drawn together again - this time for eternity, and that's all that mattered to me.

I had so many questions for her, which raced through my mind like the Indy 500. What role was I chosen to play in Lisa's life now?

Was I supposed to be her friend, her savior, her lover, or something else? What role was Lisa supposed to play in my life? Would she contribute to my happiness or cause my world to be destroyed? Perhaps it might be a little of both.

It was very difficult to imagine how events would unfold. In any case, I was determined to be a part of Lisa's life for the foreseeable future. I didn't want to make the same mistake with her twice, so I told myself that I would never abandon her again - no matter what happened. In that light, I decided to focus my attention on her emotional needs, as well as necessities concerning her health. I also had a strong desire to make our relationship last this time, regardless of the consequences. I was putting all my chips on the table.

After retrieving my suitcase from the baggage claim, Lisa and I strolled jubilantly out of the airport arm in arm. Lisa's dog Kricket had been waiting patiently for us in the backseat of the Jeep. I put my luggage away and then we headed toward the beach. We were both very happy to be together again. This excursion also gave Lisa an opportunity to get away from her parents, and that feculent drug infested house in Fort Meade. She never stopped smiling, as we pulled away from the parking garage, and drove off on our new adventure.

Along the way, we started to feel hungry, so we decided to stop at Subway for a bite to eat. Since it was a very hot day, we brought Kricket inside with us because we didn't want to leave her in a hot car. I put her emotional support leash on, but we left her vest in the car because it was packed in a suitcase. As we started to order, the person behind the counter asked if Lisa's dog qualified as a service animal. We replied 'yes,' and thought that would be the end of it, after receiving our food and sitting down.

Unfortunately, some old female busybody, who knew one of the Subway employees, took it upon herself to stick her nose in our business. She confronted us saying that Lisa had lied about her dog being a service animal, and that we should take the dog out of the store. Apparently, she preferred that the dog suffer in the heat. We tried to brush her off, but she kept pressing the issue. She would not leave us alone and took a very threatening posture with us. I finally had enough of her rants, so I rose from my chair and told her to back off. After successfully defending our position, the woman finally conceded and left the store with her tail between her legs.

I was surprised that Lisa sat at the table quietly and let me handle it. It's likely that if Lisa had been alone, she might have reacted more forcefully. I could see from the expression on her face that the barrage of attacks had made her upset, and it made me angry. It's precisely because of ugly people like this woman that Lisa had an emotional support dog in the first place. Lisa told me that she was pleased that I stood up for her. It was better that I confronted the woman, instead of allowing her to do it. We finished our lunch with Kricket at our feet, without further incidents. Then we left the restaurant and headed to our beach destination, which wasn't far from where we stopped to eat.

The Grand Plaza Hotel was right on St. Petersburg beach. It had an outdoor pool, a few restaurants and bars, and a band for evening entertainment. Staying here would give Lisa and I a chance to become reacquainted in a comfortable setting, without any interference from outside influences.

There were no dogs allowed, but since Kricket counted as an emotional support dog, she was allowed to roam freely with us. She was an ugly little grey overweight Chinese Crested, which didn't have all its teeth. Still, Kricket had a certain endearing appeal. People at the hotel seemed to like her, and her mama was very proud of her baby. Lisa may have felt like Kricket was her only friend in the world, who loved her unconditionally. Having that little dog tag along with her everywhere seemed to keep Lisa content and grounded. At the time, I didn't appreciate how important that little dog was for Lisa's happiness and peace of mind, but I would soon learn the hard way.

Initially, the time we were spending together felt very pleasant. We ate breakfast on the veranda, overlooking the bay watching the seagulls. In the evenings, we had dinner outdoors and danced to live band music on the beach, under the stars in the moonlight. The sand felt cool beneath our feet, and there was a warm gentle breeze from the bay, caressing our faces and keeping us warm. It seemed more like a dream than reality. In my wildest imagination, I never thought I would be together with Lisa again. She was also demonstratively happy, possibly for the first time in years. Her smile touched my heart and filled me with joy. This night, I could not have been more at peace. This was one of those experiences, when I wished I could stop time and savor the moment forever.

It felt like the old days, except we were much older, and had more time to spend together. Perhaps that wasn't a good thing. I was still waiting for the other shoe to drop, waking me up from my dream. It all seemed too good to be true - the lines between reality and fantasy were bleeding together. I was worried that this encounter might ultimately have a pernicious effect on both of us. However, I didn't want to think about it at the moment. I only wanted to try to relive our past, which was something I should have known was impossible. I longed for this feeling to last because I hadn't been so satisfied in such a long time. We held each other closely, and then kissed under the stars, trying to make-up for every second we'd been apart.

When we went back to our room, Lisa reminded me that she rarely had a good night's sleep. She suffered from severe back pain and had to lie on a broken-down mattress at home. She also had insomnia, likely due to her past night-time abuse from her first stepfather. When Lisa finally did fall asleep, even her dreams denied her escape from her reality. For the first time since we were young, we were sleeping together again, by the sea. In bed, we listened to the sound of the waves brushing against the shoreline and absorbed the comfort and intensity of each other's passionate embrace. We made love to each other well past midnight, as if we were still in our twenties, without a care in the world.

That night, Lisa fell asleep quickly. She must have been exhausted after our passionate evening and the excitement of the day. Lisa felt safe and relaxed for the first time in a long time, so she was able to sleep through the night peacefully, without interruption. I was still wound up from being with her again, so it took me longer to relax enough to doze off. I was still a little nervous and didn't want to fall asleep. I was afraid Lisa might be gone when I woke up in the morning, like in the movie 'Groundhog Day.'

My mind started to wonder, and I began to worry. Maybe, this was all just a ploy by Lisa to seek revenge, luring me into a trap for all the years of agony she had suffered. Perhaps, I would be dead before daylight. I already knew that Lisa was capable of planning and executing the perfect murder. I don't know why, but I didn't seem to care. I felt like Lisa and I were inexplicably tied to one another, and it might be our destiny to live and die in each other's arms. I experienced a strange premonition, listening to the waves break and draw back again. It was like we were on the Titanic, alone in our bed, not realizing what ill-fate was in-store for us. Despite sensing tragedy, I felt calm and unafraid - ready for anything destiny threw at us.

It was hard for me to predict whether Lisa would have nightmares while she slept. I wondered if she happened to have one, perhaps she might think I was trying to hurt her and would unconsciously attack me in her sleep. It was a little troubling imagining that this might occur, while I was sleeping next to her. I wouldn't be prepared to defend myself if anything happened, but it was a risk I was willing to take. I don't know why, but despite these thoughts, I instinctively felt safe with her. I had always felt secure with Lisa in the past and nothing had changed in the present. I doubt most people would have been comfortable in my place, if they knew Lisa was emotionally unstable and had been convicted of murder.

Lisa didn't need a gun to kill someone. She was strong enough to choke any man to death or break his neck. It would be relatively easy for her to do if she caught someone off guard. She wasn't a fragile little girl anymore. Lisa had been trained in martial arts and spent over seven years in prison. I just needed to remember not to scare her, while she was sleeping. I was willing to risk my life to help Lisa, and I understood exactly what I was doing by being in bed next to her. I closed my eyes and allowed my conscious thoughts to slip away. I held her hand, with my head resting gently against her breast. I finally drifted off to sleep, lulled by the sounds of the shore and her respiration. We were both at peace and happy - nothing evil could touch us.

9. The Reunion Dinner

I had planned a little reunion dinner in Winter Haven, for whoever could make it from the 'Classical Ice' show in 1989. Lisa and I were getting along well, and I was hoping she was going to feel comfortable seeing some old familiar faces. We needed to go back to her house in Fort Meade to pick-up Lisa's mom, because she didn't have a car to drive herself to the restaurant. Since Carmen worked backstage with me in the ice show, she was welcome to come along. We had to stop by the house anyway, because Lisa decided to leave Kricket there for the remainder of our stay on the beach. I was worried that being separated from her support dog might be a mistake, but it was her choice. Lisa's well-being was dependent upon having Kricket around. When she wasn't close by, Lisa's emotional stability was at risk of falling apart.

Fortunately, when we arrived at the house, Dave wasn't there. It took Carmen forever to get ready, and I knew we were going to end up being late. It took longer to get to Winter Haven from Fort Meade than I anticipated, so when we finally arrived, Don and Renee were already waiting for us at the bar. It had only been a few years since I saw Don, but I hadn't seen Renee since the show at Cypress Gardens ended. She was going to be remarried in just three days, so it was a good opportunity to wish her good luck and offer up a toast to her future. I purposely didn't tell her who I was bringing to dinner, because I wanted it to be a surprise. While Renee was sitting at the bar, she turned her head just as we walked through the front door. She suspected that my mystery guest might be Lisa, but I think she was still surprised to see her in the flesh anyway. Renee might not have recognized her immediately, if not for Carmen's presence. Lisa's appearance had changed dramatically, due to her weight and age, but Renee looked very much the same. Renee was more familiar with Carmen since she worked with us every day, and only saw Lisa a limited number of times in the past.

I didn't realize it at the time, but Don's former skating partner Carrie had been living in her car for several days prior to our dinner party. Apparently, she lost her job at SeaWorld, where she had been working for 18 years, and now she couldn't find other work. I discovered that was the reason why I had trouble contacting her. It was really shocking to me to be faced with the fact that not just one, but two people I knew well at Cypress Gardens were in serious financial trouble and in poor health. I was disappointed that more of my colleagues from the show couldn't come, even though there were several skaters from the show still living in the area. After exchanging greetings, we all sat down at our table to enjoy Mexican food and Margaritas and talk about old times.

The cast of "Classical Ice" was small. There was Robyn, who left soon after the launch of the new show, Terry-Lynn, Jennifer, ('Buffy') Don and Carrie, Brian and Kathy, Frank and Anita, Victor, Debbie, Kelly, Forest, Renee K, Renee S, the Boltons, and me. Victor, Terry-Lynn and I, and the pair teams were the lead soloists. It was a fun show and a wonderful time in all our lives. Don used to say it was a 'Holiday on Ice,' because somedays, he and I only had to do two shows a day, because our counterparts performed in the other two shows. For me, it was especially satisfying because I was in love, performing, surrounded by beauty, and I never felt more alive.

After catching up on our present lives, I brought up a story from our show days, which was especially memorable to me. I was sitting on the outside deck of the Ice Palace one day, chatting with another girl named Lisa, who worked at a kiosk next to our theatre. Suddenly,

I heard the opening music of our show beginning. I sprang to my feet and dashed through the back door and tried to hurry to get ready for my cue. I wasn't in costume yet, nor did I have my skates on, even though we were supposed to be ready at least 10 minutes before show time. Fortunately, I was in the second half of the opening number, so I still had a few minutes to get ready, but it was going to be tight. I threw on my costume and laced up my skates - all in under two minutes. I was frantic, but somehow, I made it on time. I was the front end of a glow in the dark horse and Don was the back end. It sounds weird, but it looked cool from the audience's perspective.

Later during the performance, there was a short break in the show, so that all the skaters could change costumes. A conductor, played by Carrie, came on stage wearing a Mozart head and a tuxedo. Behind her was a water fountain that was turned on during her speech to the audience. When the spotlight went out, the fountains turned off, and Carrie was supposed to skate off-stage in the dark. Then, everyone in the audience heard a splash, and afterwards there was total silence.

A minute or so later, the spotlight came back up. For a moment, all the audience could see was a leg with a skate on it sticking out of the fountain. It was Carrie's leg! She had fallen into the fountain, while trying to find her way off stage. It was so dark in the theatre, and there was no glow tape on the floor to help her find her way to the exit. It was hilarious, but she could have been hurt or even drowned, if she became stuck. The audience roared with laughter because they thought it was part of the act. The turmoil completely took the focus off the next performance on stage. Fortunately, with some help from the stagehands, Carrie made it out of the fountain unhurt, and the show continued. Everyone at the table had a good laugh over that story.

I was surprised that Lisa was quiet most of the night, and that Renee and Don didn't have more questions for her about her life, or about what she had gone through, after spending time in prison. Perhaps it was my fault for dominating a lot of the conversation. During dinner, Lisa drank at least two large Margaritas. It may not have been a lot for a celebration, but Lisa was an alcoholic, and she shouldn't have been drinking at all. It almost seemed like consuming alcohol was more important to her than virtually anything else in her life. Trying to take a drink away from her was like trying to take candy from a baby, except that Lisa could scream louder and break your hand, if you touched her glass.

Lisa was controlled entirely by alcohol, even more than by drugs. I knew that she did it to mask the pain of her life, but it was destroying what was left of it. Lisa almost died of liver failure, and she even spent time in Hospice waiting to die. By some miracle, she recovered, but not without repercussions. She was overweight and in very bad shape, because of her excessive drinking and lack of exercise. Lisa's health was poor. She was on so much medication that I was scared she would die right in front of me. That was something Lisa just didn't understand, and why her habit made me so upset. Plus, I still had a bad memory from that night at the bar when we broke up. Otherwise, it was an enjoyable evening.

Lisa and I still had to take Carmen home before going back to the beach. We probably should have left her at the house, but Don said he wanted to see her, and Lisa wanted to take Kricket home. I didn't realize it at the time, but Don's warehouse happened to be very close to Carmen's place, and that was where he stayed while he was in town. He could have dropped Carmen off more easily than us since they both were only 10 minutes apart. However, I don't think Don wanted to spend any more time with Carmen, nor did he likely want to have to explain to Dave why he was taking his wife home alone.

If Lisa had wanted to contact me in the past, she could have easily found me, if she had known where Don's workshop was in Lake Wales. Don and I kept in touch over the years, and saw each other on occasion, so he could have given Lisa my number, if she had asked him for it. I didn't discover this fact until after I left St. Petersburg and went to talk to Don at his warehouse. It made me realize that no matter how far our paths took us in different directions, the experiences we had with people we've met in the past are indefinitely linked in our subconscious minds in the present. Who we have become as individuals is a product of our history.

It was late when we returned to the beach, so Lisa and I decided to go to bed as soon as we returned to our room. Lisa had to have her usual nighttime drink, even though she still had alcohol in her system from dinner. Unlike at her home in Fort Meade, when Lisa slept next to me, she fell asleep almost at once. Occasionally, she would wake up during the night, and pour herself another drink before going back to sleep. I was sensitive to the fact that as a child, Lisa had been touched inappropriately by her stepfather before going to sleep. I was careful about not making too much contact with her while she slept, for fear she might have a defensive reaction to being touched. However, I always kissed her goodnight, and held her hand before she closed her eyes.

When Lisa was happy, she was enthusiastic, affable, and entertaining. She had an infectious smile, and a certain way of talking to people, which made it seem like she was their best friend. She had a knack for making strangers feel special and knew precisely how to relate to ordinary people. Her charismatic flair could melt even the coldest of hearts. However, Lisa's mood could turn on a dime if something annoyed her. Occasionally, she would act frightened and panicked or defensive if she felt threatened. Anyone who didn't know her might feel intimidated or confused by her erratic behavior. I was starting to get used to it, and I understood what things triggered severe reactions from her. Lisa could experience a full range of emotions all in the same day, which is a sign of someone who has Borderline Personality. I was put off occasionally by Lisa's antics, but I convinced myself that Lisa would never deliberately hurt me.

For years, Lisa suffered through so much pain and anguish. She acknowledged that it was remarkable that she was still alive. She fought a constant battle with depression and self-hate. Lisa had no fear of death - in fact she welcomed it. Whatever happened to her didn't seem to matter to her. Somehow, no matter how many near death experiences Lisa faced, she always managed to survive. It gave her a false sense of invincibility.

From my point of view, Lisa was the toughest and bravest woman I've ever known, but now she was a broken woman, who was prepared to give up. Our renewed relationship didn't seem to be enough motivation to inspire her to change her mindset. Lisa desperately craved love and attention from her mother and son especially, but she never felt the warmth from them she longed to receive. Lisa needed help and to feel like her presence in people's lives mattered. I was the only one who cared enough to offer her the love she desperately desired. Unfortunately, my love alone wasn't enough to keep her satisfied or calm.

Lisa was a creature of habit, and it was going to take a lot to convince her to change her self-destructive proclivities. Most of the time, she ignored the advice I tried to give her. In 1985, Lisa made a Faustian pact with Lucifer, and as a result, she would never be free from his torment. After years of fighting back depression and feelings of hopelessness, Lisa was finally experiencing joy again periodically, since we rediscovered one another. I just didn't know how long it would last or how much time I had left to spend with her. The prospect of losing Lisa again after all these years was unbearable for me to contemplate.

I think Lisa's mom and stepfather were jealous of her. They resented Lisa and treated her badly like Cinderella, because of their embedded, envious feelings. Carmen claimed to love her daughter, but her actions told a different story. At the very least, Carmen and Dave could have kept their house clean, and had fresh food in the refrigerator, so that Lisa wasn't living in a filthy drug infested garbage dump. What Lisa really needed was to be able to leave her parents' house permanently, and not have to wait on two lazy and ungrateful degenerates, who refused to do any work for themselves. I wish I could have taken Lisa away from that hellhole she was living in, but unfortunately, I didn't have the resources to do it. I also had other people in my life and responsibilities to them as well.

Lisa seemed to be at peace with me for the moment, while we were together. She was being well cared for, but her drinking was still a wedge issue between us. What I really wanted to do was to help Lisa find a job, so she could afford to move to a place of her own, and then help her to find a good psychiatrist. The best I could do at the time was to help Lisa relax and have fun with her, so that she would be motivated to want a better life for herself. I thought that spending a week together with her should have been a good start toward that goal. However, it seemed like the pathway to Lisa's recovery was such a long rocky road ahead. I was committed to take that journey with her for as long as necessary, because she was worth saving.

Lisa's eyes were dilated frequently from drinking too much, and they appeared to have no color at all occasionally. They looked like two black circles, and all I could see was darkness and death. I felt that someday soon, I would become lost in Lisa's stare and drawn into one of her nightmares. During our rough-water journey, I couldn't see land through the thick fog of her psyche, and there was no wind to fill our sails. We were just drifting along in a treacherous ocean without a rudder, into oblivion. There seemed to be only stormy seas and dark clouds ahead on the horizon, and black vultures circling above our heads.

10. The Meltdown

Things started out well the next morning, but Kricket was noticeably absent. Lisa and I decided to go for an early breakfast at IHOP across the street from the hotel. As usual, Lisa made friends with the waitress and an older couple, across from where we were seated. She wasn't shy about eating either. She ordered lots of food, as if she hadn't eaten a decent meal in weeks. Lisa had to borrow my glasses to read the menu because she didn't have a decent pair of her own.

After we finished breakfast, we walked out of the restaurant, and headed toward the shops along the road. I noticed that Lisa had stolen one of the mugs she had been drinking from, so I voiced my disapproval. After a minute or two, she walked back into the restaurant to return the mug. She did it mainly to satisfy me, not because she felt any remorse. Lisa sought approval from people she loved, and gaining my respect slowly became important to her again. Lisa's mind was instinctively focused on pleasing people because she was so desperate to experience love and gratitude in return.

When children are denied real love by their parents, they never stop trying to seek it in other relationships. Lisa didn't feel badly about stealing the mug. However, it didn't sit well with her because I showed disapproval of her actions. It took courage on her part to embarrass herself by returning the mug, so that she could regain my respect. I was proud of her for doing the right thing. Shoplifting is usually a behavior of a teenager, and not expected of a 51-year-old adult. Lisa was highly intelligent, but she still had the emotional maturity of an adolescent.

"I just wanted a souvenir Alex," Lisa said.

"Do you want to get arrested again?" I asked her.

"No," Lisa replied.

"We're going to some souvenir shops now," I said. "I will buy you 10 mugs if you want - just don't steal."

"Okay Alex, I'm sorry," Lisa replied.

"Forgive me?" she asked.

"Yes Vonnie," I replied, kissing her.

Lisa put her arm around me and smiled, as we continued to walk together down the street. She had formed several unseemly habits in her life, and stealing was one of them. When a child grows up without proper supervision, guidance, and discipline, they form bad habits which are tough to break as adults. Despite her intelligence, Lisa was still very much like a child, who hadn't been brought up properly. Long before I ever met Lisa, she had the instincts of a wild animal trying to survive. She learned at an early age that her parents wouldn't protect her. Lisa had a powerful thirst to feed her own basic needs and desires, because they were often left unsatisfied. Her parents never taught her anything about morality. Their behavior was often even worse. Unfortunately, Lisa's greatest influence in her life was her mother Carmen, who was a drug addict, an alcoholic and a pathological liar, like her husband Dave.

When Lisa and I entered one of the shops up the street, she wanted to try on beachwear. She needed to look for a top that would cover up her protruding belly, which became that way from drinking excessively. Even though Lisa had gained weight, she still had a tiny little backside, like she did in her twenties. As a result, she had to pick out a separate bikini bottom from the rack and try to match it up with a different size top. After doing a thorough search, I found a small bikini bottom with a cute rope pattern on each side, which exposed the skin. Lisa tried them on, and they fit her perfectly. The lady who was helping us found a top to match that Lisa liked. I also picked out a straw cowboy hat for her, some sunglasses, and a short sleeve yellow shirt with a marlin on the back. I bought a couple of items for myself as souvenirs, including a white hooded shirt and a shot glass for my collection.

Lisa and I enjoyed shopping together, which was something else we never did in the past. Usually, Lisa shopped at thrift stores because she didn't have much money to spend on clothing. Her wardrobe was eclectic - nothing matched. Most of the things she bought for herself cost less than ten dollars, but she never complained about not having nice clothes to wear. She did have a few nice dresses and shoes, but for the most part, her wardrobe consisted of clothing from the Goodwill and the Salvation Army. It was a shame because Lisa in her prime was strikingly beautiful. Dressing Lisa with secondhand rags was like putting a brown paper bag over a bouquet of roses.

As bad luck would have it, there was a liquor store next to the gift shop. Lisa insisted on going in. I should have tried harder to talk her out of it, but I didn't think it would have done any good. She wasn't satisfied buying just one bottle either. Lisa had to purchase at least six bottles of various kinds of spirits. She used her debit card to buy the booze, which was given to her by welfare. She spent over 100 dollars, after ignoring all my objections. Lisa received about $750 dollars per month for food, medical care, and necessities. It was not enough to survive on if she had to pay rent or make a car payment. Now a significant chunk of that money was wasted on liquid poison. I should have told Lisa that I wouldn't allow her to bring more than one bottle to the room, but I didn't want to start a fight with her.

No one should be allowed to spend welfare money on liquor or illegal drugs. Giving an alcoholic and drug addict free money is simply a way of guaranteeing they will continue their bad habits. It just shows how messed up the welfare system is in this country. Sometimes it can do more harm than good. People need to earn their own living and would be much better off if they received help finding a job, rather than receiving other people's money for doing nothing. Lisa was well enough to do certain types of work, and so were her parents. However, why should anyone work if they're getting checks for free in the mail each month? Instead of America being the land of the free, it has become the land of free stuff.

Against my wishes, Lisa brought the box of liquor back to the room. I was annoyed, but I tried very hard to refrain from arguing with her, hoping we could still enjoy our evening together. We decided to have a nice dinner in the hotel that night, so that we could dress up a little and celebrate being together again. Eating out together was another thing we never did in the past. The hotel had a circular glass enclosed restaurant on the top floor, which had a panoramic view of the bay. I thought it would be very special to have dinner up there to celebrate being together again. Lisa dressed up and put on makeup and high heels. She looked extremely beautiful, and she seemed so happy. I didn't want to do anything to spoil her mood.

We must have taken the wrong elevator because it let us off at least one level below the restaurant floor, so we had to climb up a couple of flights of steep winding stairs. It was harder on Lisa because she had on a long dress and high heels. The restaurant was crowded, but the panoramic view of the water was magnificent. Lisa was very excited to be having a dress-up dinner, surrounded by such beautiful scenery. As expected, the first thing she ordered was a fruity alcoholic cocktail. I didn't mind her having the first one since we were celebrating, but then the waiter asked her if she wanted another one, and she said yes. I argued with her about it, which I probably shouldn't have done, because she became agitated. I tried to take the second drink away from her, but she defended it like a dog would with a bone. She made it seem like her drink was her only source of oxygen, and if I took it away, she wouldn't be able to breathe. Lisa was going to do what she wanted to do, and I couldn't stop her. Lisa was happy for once in her miserable life, and that's mainly what mattered to me now.

The seafood we ordered was extraordinarily delicious, and the atmosphere could not have been more exhilarating. I tried to enjoy these precious moments of happiness with Lisa, because they were unlikely to last for very long. Adjusting to her new character was challenging for me, because I didn't remember her being so capricious in our youth. I guess it was natural for us both to change in the past three decades, but Lisa's psychological development seemed to have stopped altogether since then.

I suppose in the past, Lisa was trying very hard to make me like her and didn't want me to know about her past. She certainly hid what she did in 1985 from me very well. Some of Lisa's bad habits wouldn't have made much difference to me then because I was so in love with her. I also didn't have the same sense of responsibility that I do now. I might have ignored many of her indiscretions, if I saw her doing them in the past, but it was difficult for me to ignore them in the present. It's much easier to overlook things when you're younger.

I had plenty of bad habits in the past too, but none of them had anything to do with substance abuse or stealing. However, I never went through anything like Lisa had to endure. I tried not to judge, because I thought it would be more prudent to offer her help. I wanted to try to be understanding about her drinking, but at the same time, I didn't want to watch her harm herself. I just couldn't understand why someone so close to death, due to alcohol abuse, would choose to keep drinking excessively, after so narrowly escaping death.

After dinner, Lisa and I went back to the room, she wasted no time opening another bottle of alcohol. We started arguing again because she was unrestrained drinking a superfluous amount of Saki. I couldn't stand by and watch her continue to destroy herself - it made me upset. The main reason why I was in this relationship with Lisa was to help her recover, not watch her kill herself. I became very frustrated and told Lisa that if she kept drinking this way, I didn't want to be with her anymore. She reacted with defiance. I was putting Lisa on the defensive, and she responded by acting hysterically. What I couldn't understand was why she felt the need to drink so much, when she was under no pressure at all now, and having a pleasant evening.

At that moment, I realized I had made a mistake by losing control of my own emotions. I was only making matters worse. After several minutes of arguing, I tried to change gears and attempted to be supportive, by speaking to her more gently. Lisa calmed down to a degree, but she was still on the defensive, so I encouraged her to go to sleep. I think she was tired anyway, probably from the alcohol she drank.

By this time, Lisa was very stressed-out, and I knew that the argument had been mostly my fault. I am not the best person to be around if you're an alcoholic. It really irritates me to watch someone drink herself into a coma, especially someone I love deeply. Lisa fell asleep soon afterwards, and I thought everything would be okay. I was very tired too, so I lied down next to her and fell asleep, hoping things would be better in the morning. Unfortunately, things became much worse. Lisa's liver may not have been in good shape, but I should have realized that her mind was even more fragile than her body.

I woke up suddenly in the middle of the night, and when I saw that Lisa was gone, I started to panic. It must have been around 2:00

or 3:00 am. On her pillow, I noticed that she had scribbled a note. This is what it said:

"Dear Alex, I love you very much, but I can't go on without you. I'm down by the shore."

I called her cell phone immediately to see if she would answer her phone. Fortunately, she picked up the call, but she didn't say anything at first. I only heard the crash of the waves, until she finally spoke.

"Alex," Lisa said crying. "I'm sorry; I don't know what to do anymore."

It was hard to understand her because she was crying while she spoke. I asked her to try to calm down, so I could comprehend what she was saying.

"I'm in the water," Lisa said.

"Hold on Lisa, I'll be right there!" I shouted in reply.

I was frantic with fear. I'm not sure if I hung up the phone or just left the line open. I was completely freaked out. I didn't think; I just acted. I quickly threw on a shirt and a pair of shorts, and flew out the door, sprinting in bare feet. I took the elevator down from the ninth floor to the lobby. When the elevator doors opened, I raced toward the beach.

Within just seconds, I closed in on the shoreline. I could see a tiny light that appeared to be emanating from Lisa's cell phone. She was lying down on the beach by the water's edge, playing with her phone. It looked like she might have been trying to text me. She was obviously still distraught because she believed we weren't going to be together any longer. We both had very high expectations for that week, and it had turned into a total disaster. I knew it had been my fault.

However, Lisa's despair went much deeper than our relationship. She was disheartened about her entire life, and tired of living in pain and fear. Her current feelings were rooted in her past, but it was affecting her sensibilities in the present. It really wasn't me who she was so upset with, as much as it was her parents. Her life had been one long inescapable firestorm, and she was on the verge of giving up. And now, Lisa felt she was losing my support too, which she desperately needed. I was her last hope, but she felt my support for her was drifting away.

Lisa didn't understand that I had no intention of letting her go again. I left her once in the past, and I swore to myself that I would never do it again, no matter what happened. Lisa had reached another critical turning point, and this crisis might prove to be deadly. I knew that Lisa needed psychiatric help, but now she needed an emergency response team. Instead, all she had was me, and if I messed this up, Lisa's blood would be on my hands.

The moment I reached her, I sat her up and tried to console her. Lisa was exasperated and in deep despair. I tried to coax her to come away from the beach, but then she suddenly became belligerent, and walked into the water, attempting to escape. It was very early in the morning, and thus still dark outside. Only the lights from the hotel and the moon's glow helped to keep Lisa in my sight. The bay appeared black, like a huge oil spill, and there would be no visibility underneath the surface. As Lisa began to submerge; her body slowly disappeared from my vision.

"Lisa, please come back in!" I shouted.

I called to her repeatedly to come out of the water, but she ignored me. Lisa only went further out into the bay, in a recalcitrant manner. I was alarmed, thinking that she might vanish completely, determined to drown herself. At this point, I started to panic again, due to the nature of this precarious dilemma. If Lisa dove underneath the water in the dark, it would be almost impossible for me to save her. I was not a good swimmer, and not very strong or skilled at water rescues. I had never been a lifeguard in the past, so my best chance was to cajole her into coming back to shore.

Unfortunately, there was no one else on the beach who could help me. For some reason, it never occurred to me to call 911, because I was engaged in negotiating with Lisa. By the time anyone arrived, she could have drowned herself anyway. In fact, if she heard me calling for help, it might have triggered her to go under the water sooner. So, I said anything I could think of to get her to come back to the beach. Finally, Lisa started to walk back toward me, to my great relief. She appeared to be calmer, and I thought everything was going to be fine.

In an instant, Lisa's demeanor changed capriciously, and she became obstreperous, as we walked off the beach together toward the pool area. She began shouting and carrying on about people who had mistreated treated her. Lisa's life had been hellish, and she didn't need anything more in her life to go wrong. She certainly didn't want any more pressure from me. I was upset with myself for allowing things to become so heated. I knew by this time, that Lisa's emotions and state of mind were extraordinarily brittle. I should have taken better care to be more patient with her. It was my mistake, but unfortunately, the situation had become intractable.

For a long while, Lisa didn't want to go up to the room to calm down and change her wet clothes. She was still extremely agitated, carrying a lifetime of pain, anger, and disappointment. She needed to vent, and I was the unfortunate recipient of her rage. I should have been more patient and allowed her to get it out of her system. However, behavior like that frightened me. We were sitting on lounge chairs behind the hotel, and I didn't want her to cause a scene, and wake up the other guests.

It seemed that the more Lisa became sober and off medication, the more she felt the emotional pain of her past, and the agony that it had caused during her life. All this pent-up energy and lack of sleep contributed to her irritability. After several minutes of ranting by the side of the pool, Lisa finally relented out of sheer fatigue. My hope for now was that Lisa would finally calm down, as I escorted her back inside the hotel. However, the drama was still not over. This was only just the beginning of scene two, in a three-act drama.

As we approached our room, Lisa threw another fit in the hallway. She began to make threats and started hitting herself in the face, so that she could tell someone that I did it, I think. Maybe it was her way of punishing herself; I didn't know for certain. This new tactic of hers to garner attention completely caught me off guard and caused me more trouble than I expected. Fortunately, there was a hotel worker nearby, so I asked him to call security. While I had my head turned, Lisa began hitting herself in the face again, which the staff employee witnessed this time. I had never seen anyone do that before, and it rattled me. Her behavior was so bizarre and disturbing to watch.

I was hoping that the hotel security guards would arrive soon, but the police came instead. I was just grateful that someone had come to help her, and that I didn't have to deal with her antics alone any longer. Not long after the police arrived, they separated Lisa and me to ask us each what had occurred. That was standard protocol, under the circumstances. At this point, I was sure Lisa's blood pressure must have been very high, because she had been extremely agitated for several hours. However, Lisa had learned to act calmly at an early age, whenever the police arrived.

After they spoke to us, an officer wanted to know if Lisa could go back inside the room, so they could go. I said no because I believed Lisa to be suicidal. I told them that she could change her clothes and gather her things, and then go home in a taxi. I didn't want to let her back in the room in case she tried to do something crazy again. Our room was on the ninth floor with a balcony. If I went to sleep, Lisa could potentially jump to her death. Then I would be in trouble with the law because they might assume that I had murdered her.

However, I was more concerned that I would be emotionally devastated if Lisa died dramatically. I didn't want anything bad to happen to her; and I especially wanted to prevent her from killing herself. Somehow, our romantic reunion had turned into my worst nightmare. Lisa had become more trouble than I could handle. As much as I hated our time together to end this way, I was forced to let her go, even though it hurt to watch her leave. It was terribly painful for me to have to go through this experience. This wasn't the way I imagined things would turnout, but I probably should have expected it.

What really annoyed me the most was the fact that, when I told the male police officer that I believed Lisa was suicidal, he spoke to me, as if I was crazy.

"Maybe she was just going for a late-night swim?" he said. "A lot of beach goers drink and go swimming at night."

"I don't think most people swim with their clothes on?" I said.

"Some do," he replied.

"What a moron this guy is," I thought to myself.

He was obviously an incompetent, lazy old fool and had no real concern for Lisa's safety or well-being. She was obviously right about certain redneck police officers, who had no real interest in helping people. The female officer seemed more understanding. It's too bad she wasn't the one in charge. She probably had a hard time dealing with her colleague's attitude problem. I felt sorry for her.

"If this guy is Saint Petersburg's finest example of a police officer, everyone in this town is in trouble," I thought to myself.

This officer couldn't pass an eye test, much less an IQ test. He was just so annoying and stupid - a complete disgrace to the police force. I should have taken his badge number and discussed the incident with his supervisor.

I was really heart-broken watching Lisa pack-up all her belongings. The female officer helped her change clothes and to put all her things on a dolly. As Lisa was escorted out of the room, she began shouting again out of frustration. I assumed that I would never see her again, which made me even more upset. It felt like another Deja-vu moment from 1989. A different time and place maybe, but the same outcome. Perhaps no one can change what's meant to be after all. No one can go back in time, to rewrite history, like in the movie 'Time Machine.' No matter how many times the leading man went back to save his fiancé from dying, she continued to die in different ways. Destiny has a way of infiltrating and interrupting even the best-laid plans.

It had been a wish of mine to see Lisa again and perhaps rekindle our romance, but now that dream had turned to dust. Never in a million years did I think that I would ever see her again, after I left Florida over 28 years ago. Now, after only a few short months being in contact with her, our relationship appeared to be over once again, in the blink of an eye. I was crushed and I didn't know what to do. My world began to crumble around me, while Lisa had to endure a long and lonely car ride back home. I could only imagine how she might be feeling. I knew she must have been sad and depressed, and I wished I could have done something to console her. She had lost her new Jeep and me all in one day. I had done what I said I wouldn't do - I abandoned her for the second time, and I didn't feel right about it.

I wondered if this would have happened, if little Kricket had still been with us. She was like a baby buffer and security blanket for Lisa. That ugly fat little grey pooch could always make her smile. Since Lisa lost both of her children, Kricket was the only living thing, which gave her unconditional love. Lisa's emotions seemed more stable when she had her baby girl with her. It was a silly looking little pet, with its head of hair a mess, and its tongue sticking out. Her little dog looked more like a cartoon than a canine. I think Lisa said she had rescued it from the side of the road somewhere. She told me Kricket was her miracle dog and made her laugh whenever she felt like crying. Lisa needed that little dog now more than ever. It was her decision to leave her dog home for the last few days of our stay, but it ended up being a very bad idea. I was never convinced in the past that emotional support animals were much more than an excuse for people to bring their favorite pets along with them. However, this experience taught me how valuable an animal can be to someone, whose sanity is hanging on by a thread.

After Lisa had gone, it became very lonely at the beach. Emotionally, I was in a very bad place, but I was sure it was much worse for Lisa. I was alone with my thoughts and had to spend the rest of the day and night by myself. I didn't want to call or text Lisa too soon after all the brew-ha-ha, but I was still very worried about her. Instead of making things better for Lisa, I probably had made things much worse. I was tormented by this recent break-up, even more than in the past. I had regretted all my life ending our relationship prematurely, and now history was repeating itself. This had been my second chance to make things right, and I made a mess of everything.

I had to remind myself that I was in Lisa's life to help her, and not to get back together with her. However, it was impossible for me not to feel strongly about her. I wasn't ready to leave Florida just yet. I also didn't want to take Lisa's Jeep away from her permanently. I couldn't do that to her. That wouldn't be fair or helpful. I also didn't want to make the long drive back home alone, while I was feeling so badly. Most of all, I had no desire to abandon Lisa once again, but perhaps that was exactly what I had done.

It was a very long and lonely day, and I didn't have much to do now by myself. I spent most of the day in my room, alone in bed with the balcony door open. The sounds of seagulls and the waves breaking against the shore, felt calming and peaceful. I kept replaying the events of the week in my mind, trying to figure out what had gone wrong. I blamed myself for Lisa's breakdown. Lisa was not the same woman that I used to know at all. Mentally and emotionally, she was broken inside. It was a fallacy and a fool's quest, thinking I could somehow relive our past and find love with Lisa once again.

I felt guilty for not being in Lisa's life when she needed me the most, while she faced a murder trial and prison. She also had to give up her child for adoption, because her mother refused to take care of her baby, while she was incarcerated. I completely failed in my objective, after having a unique opportunity to help Lisa assemble her life again. I should have realized that it was impossible to have a normal relationship with a woman whose mind had been shattered, over decades of abuse and neglect.

I was out of my depth, and I knew it. Lisa needed professional help, which I was willing to find for her. If I didn't contact her again, I knew she would probably never receive the care she so desperately needed. Lisa was likely distraught and feeling helpless, and I had contributed to her sadness. I could not leave Florida, without trying to fix my mistake, unlike in the past. This time I was determined to act differently. Lisa's parents were not going to give Lisa what she needed to recover and to have a better life, so it was still up to me to do something for her. I wasn't sure Lisa would trust me ever again after what happened, but I was adamant about giving her and our relationship another chance.

As dawn turned to dusk, I found myself in solitude. I began to feel hungry because I hadn't eaten all day. I decided to go to dinner outside, next to the hotel, so I would have some company. It was windy that evening on the beach. Saint Petersburg was having a red sea and sky at the same time. Instead of feeling comforted by the other guests around me; I felt cold and completely alone. They appeared to form a wall around me, further isolating my spirit, as I sat by myself in the moonlight.

The wind began to blow more briskly, and the noise it made drowned out the conversations of the dozen other people having dinner beside me. The warm breeze carried with it the taste of salt from the sea, as well as the aroma of dead fish, which had washed upon the shore. The smell of death was in the air. It was almost as if the events of the morning had poisoned the atmosphere and foreshadowed the future. I felt like I was about to have my last supper, as a waitress brought flatbread and a glass of blood red wine to my table. I was overcome by a feeling of betrayal and regret, as grey clouds formed over the bay. I sensed a storm was coming, as tiny pools of silver dollars began to form on the boardwalk, and I was about to be caught in the rain.

11. Repairing the Damage

The next day, I checked out of the hotel and started driving toward the east coast. I wasn't sure where I was going yet. A part of me wanted to go home and forget about Lisa, but another part couldn't let her go. The reason I became involved with Lisa from the start was primarily to help her, and I wasn't finished with that job. Instead of getting on I-95 to drive back to North Carolina, I checked into another hotel, not far from Lisa's house. I wanted to stay close by to see what would happen next. I just couldn't bring myself to leave her alone and depressed with no means of transportation.

My friend Don was still in town working on his next ice rink project for another ice show overseas. I thought after I was settled, I would pay him a visit and talk about what had happened at the beach. I drove over to his warehouse the same day, after he gave me directions. Ironically, his warehouse was only about 10 minutes from Lisa's house, which no one had ever realized. I drove by the place a couple of times trying to find it, because the warehouse was set back from the road, and it was not well marked.

When I knocked on the door, I was surprised to be greeted by Don's ex-pair partner and ex-girlfriend Carrie. She was equally shocked to see me too. Unfortunately, I couldn't get in touch with her in time to have her come to the reunion dinner. Until recently, she had been sleeping in her car, and I didn't have her cell number. Carrie looked frail and unhealthy. The last time I saw her was when we performed together in 1993, at Busch Gardens in Williamsburg, just two years after Lisa was arrested. She invited me to come inside the trailer and asked me what I was doing there. Inside the trailer, it was dark and musty, with a distinct aroma from the cats which roamed around the place. It wasn't much, but at least it was clean, compared to where Lisa was living. It was still a trailer at a warehouse, and not a proper place to live.

Carrie explained that she had been let go from her job at SeaWorld. She previously held a position there as a pyro-technician for 18 years. Since she couldn't find another job right away and didn't have much savings, she was now homeless. Carrie told me she had been living out of her car for the past few weeks, when Don told her she could live rent-free at the warehouse, until she got back on her feet. He had sold his house that we all lived in during the show a few years back, so living there wasn't an option. When Don is in town, he usually stays at the warehouse in an RV. His two assistants were also living there temporarily, in a separate trailer. There was also another very large RV from an ice show, parked on the side of the property, along with a couple of trailers to tow his ice making equipment.

When I arrived, Don was in the back working in what looked like a junkyard. I was thinking he must not ever throw anything away, because there was so much ice making stuff scattered around everywhere. It was what many people might call an organized mess. The two young workers, who were supposed to be helping him, were still inside one of the trailers. They were a young couple in their twenties, about the same age as I used to be when I lived in Winter Haven in 1989. When they saw me, they were a little confused about who I was and what I was doing there.

Being back in this area again after almost 30 years was a bit surreal. The house Don, Carrie and I lived in during our show days was only 20 minutes from Don's warehouse. Before 2011, the park was still Cypress Gardens and not Legoland. Cypress Gardens was a rare and beautiful park with flowers and Cypress trees, and a beautiful lake for the water ski show. It was where I had proposed to Lisa almost three decades ago. Ironically, it was also the same place where Lisa hid the gun that she used to kill her stepfather. This was the first time I had been back in this area, since I first left for California in 1990, right after our show closed.

Many of the things I discovered about what happened with Lisa were swirling in my head, including several of my memories from the 14 months I lived in Winter Haven. Lisa was one of the main reasons that I didn't want to return over the years, but ironically, she was also the reason I eventually came back again. I had been as close as Orlando and Tampa Bay several times to visit Disney World, Universal Studios, and for skating competitions, but I never went back to Winter Haven again.

There were ghosts there from my past that I didn't want to confront. Lisa's spirit had haunted me for decades. Now, I was finally back again, and for a moment, it almost felt like I had never left. Many of the performers from Cypress Gardens still lived there but had obviously aged in the meantime. Surprisingly, some people were still performing not far from the park. Winter Haven is such a small town with a lot of locals and retired people. They didn't seem to venture out much to see the rest of the world. Don was probably one of the few people, who lived there for a long period of time, who had a life outside of this sleepy little corner of central Florida. If not for the Gardens, no one would ever know about Winter Haven, unless they had family who lived in the area.

While Don and I were talking, he told me that there was going to be a water ski show that evening in Winter Haven on Silver Lake. He said I should go with him to watch, along with Carrie and his two assistants. Sadly, there is no longer a water ski show at the park after the takeover, but the exhibition at the lake kept the tradition and spirit of Cypress Gardens' past glory alive. Some of the skiers, who previously performed at the Gardens, put on a show once a month for charity. Seeing the skiers again with familiar names and faces would feel like going back in time, so I decided to go. Almost 30 years later, these old pros didn't seem to miss a beat.

Pushing 60-years-old, Mark steered his hang-glider to the platform below with grace and skill, after being lifted into the air by a motorboat. Watching a man float above the earth in a kite, soaring like an eagle, is really something to witness. After the demonstration was over, our group went out for dinner and drinks. It felt comforting to be back among old friends, especially under the circumstances. It was a nice distraction from my recent painful experience with Lisa. We took photos, ate Buffalo wings, drank beer, and told stories from our past show days. It was really what I needed, but Lisa was still on my mind.

I was feeling a little calmer now, and more prepared to reengage with my arch-nemesis - Mademoiselle French. So, the next day I decided to call Lisa, because I wanted to see how she was doing, and to be honest - I missed her. When she answered the phone, she sounded very down and depressed, especially because she was stuck at home with her horrible parents, without a car. Her stepfather did manage to fix a pick-up truck they had on the property, so there was at least a usable vehicle to go somewhere in an emergency.

Lisa told me she was genuinely happy to hear from me, and sounded a little more cheerful, after we talked things out. She hoped there might still be a chance of getting the Jeep back, so she could leave the house occasionally. I was surprised that Lisa didn't insist on driving her Jeep when she was sent home from the beach. Legally, I believe she had the right to take it, even though she hadn't paid a cent for anything, including the insurance. Fortunately for me, it was one less battle I didn't have to fight with her at the time.

Lisa went through mood swings that I didn't really understand. For the moment, she seemed to be truly remorseful, and said she wanted to see me again. It was always challenging for me to know whether Lisa was being sincere or being manipulative. I still felt very guilty about breaking-up with her in the past, and I felt equally terrible about splitting-up with her again recently. If I had only spoken to Lisa the day after the night we broke-up, perhaps I could have changed the course of her future. If we had stayed together, it's possible that she might never have been arrested, nor had that terrible trucking accident. I might have been able to prevent a lot of the pain and suffering she went through in her life, if only we both made different choices in the past.

You almost never realize that one choice you make could have such an enormous impact on your life or the life of someone else in the future, until it's too late. It's profoundly disturbing to me to understand that my impulsive decision to break-up with Lisa had such a profoundly negative impact on her life, from that day forward. Therefore, I felt responsible for her life in the present.

However, in my mid-twenties, I'm not sure I would have had the courage to help Lisa deal with all her problems once she was arrested, because I was a different person then. Lisa and I were both so young in the eighties, but I was the only one who was naïve. When I found out about Lisa using cocaine and writing bad checks, I just wanted to run away from her. I didn't have the depth of understanding, nor the compassion that I needed to stand by her in the way that she should have expected of me. I should have at least given Lisa the chance to explain everything to me, instead of assuming the worst. This time, I told Lisa that I needed some time to think about what to do. I would be staying in Florida, while I thought about my decision. I didn't want to repeat the same mistake I made in the past, by not giving our relationship another chance.

Lisa's whole attitude and demeanor had softened during our conversations that followed. Her improved attitude could have been a ploy to take the Jeep back, but I felt she was sincerely sorry for the way she acted in St. Petersburg. It was probably the case that she just couldn't control her emotions any longer. Lisa's emotional state of mind could change on a dime, and her mood swings were just symptomatic of her mental illness. Someone who has 'Borderline Personality Disorder' has extreme mood swings, profound anxiety and fear of abandonment. It's a bit like being Bi-Polar but having several additional problems. I believe Lisa may have suffered from both. I felt sorry for her, and I still wanted to do what I could to help her, and not hurt her.

I just couldn't leave Florida without seeing and talking to Lisa again. I was afraid she might try to take her own life if I left and never spoke to her again, and that was exactly what I had been trying to prevent. Leaving without visiting Lisa was just not an option for me. I couldn't bring myself to abandon her again - not this time, and not this way. I really loved Lisa in the present in a way I never did in the past. I was in love with her before, but I never really loved her completely. I didn't do anything in the past to take care of her. Our past relationship was mainly about enjoying ourselves together.

The way I felt about Lisa at this time was entirely different. It was more real, whereas our relationship in the past was more like a fantasy. This time I knew all of Lisa's secrets, and I accepted and loved her, despite everything. In the past, it felt good being with Lisa all the time. However, when things went wrong, I bailed, instead of trying to work things out. I didn't have the patience before to put in the hard work to make our relationship better between us. I only wanted to be with Lisa for better, but not for worse. I suppose that was one reason why I put a two-year timeframe on our engagement. I knew I wasn't ready for a serious commitment just yet, but I was afraid of losing her when my show was cancelled. I was desperate to hold onto Lisa, but I let go of her anyway, because I assumed she didn't love me anymore - but that wasn't true.

Even though it was against my better judgement, and contrary to everything my friends had been telling me, I arranged to see Lisa again. I told her I would pick her up at her house, and we would discuss things over dinner the following day. She told me she was grateful to have this opportunity to make up for her behavior at the beach. I didn't care if she was being manipulative; I wanted to see her. Lisa deserved a better life than the one she had, and I was determined to do my best to see that she had a chance to be happy.

The next day, I drove to Lisa's house on Lake Buffum. She looked a little skittish when she first approached the Jeep. However, she seemed happy to see me, because she was smiling when she saw me drive up. Lisa had a certain type of impish expression that was both charming and devilish at the same time. When coupled with a glance, that only she could make, the combination was penetrating and irresistible. It was challenging to know exactly what was on her mind, but oftentimes she was thinking about sex. Whenever Lisa smiled this way, I could be certain that whatever she was thinking about was most likely mischievous.

The sound of Lisa's voice was also enticing to me. The pitch of her voice seemed to change drastically, depending on how she was feeling. At times, it could be a little raspy and sexy, but it could also be soft and soothing. Other times, her voice sounded sweet and flirtatious, but occasionally, it could also sound deep and forceful. It all depended on her mood. Lisa could manipulate her voice, as easily as she could manipulate men and women. If you added her good looks and personality to the pot, she had a mélange of highly seductive tools at her disposal, impossible to resist. Lisa was a lot like your favorite cocktail. Once you've tasted it, you can't put it down. As you continue to drink it, the more intoxicating it becomes.

Lisa had charisma and charm; beyond any woman I have ever met. It was impossible to ignore her magnetic personality and sexual fortitude. However, Lisa wasn't simply defined by her sex appeal. She was also clever, talented, and funny. She could do voice impressions of people and create characters using any number of foreign accents.

Lisa could have been a great actress, if she had decided to pursue that career path. She also had a tremendously versatile singing voice. Her favorite genre of music seemed to be bluesy country songs. Lisa loved to perform in front of a crowd and being on stage was second nature to her. She was born to be an entertainer, but unfortunately, her parents never recognized nor developed her numerous hidden talents. It's so important when children are young, to discover everything they are proficient at, so they are not limited in their pursuits later in life.

At age 23, Lisa's looks were stunning. She had the face and body of a supermodel. There were few women in the country at the time, who were more alluring. Now, at age 51, after decades of neglect and strain, Lisa's striking good looks had faded. Every experience she had been through in her life had damaged her body and broken her spirit. Lisa still had a charismatic personality, but even that was overshadowed by her mental illness. During her lifetime, Lisa had been close to death several times, but always survived and bounced back. Now, she just looked exhausted and defeated, and it broke my heart to see her this way. It was truly a miracle that she was still alive, but I feared her will to live was dying.

After everything Lisa had been through, including the drama at the beach, she was now sitting beside me with childlike exuberance. Her ability to persevere through life's greatest challenges was truly remarkable. Lisa was putting her life in my hands, but I wasn't sure if I was worthy of her confidence. It was an arduous responsibility to have to care for someone in her situation. Even though I loved her, I just didn't know if I could help her the way I wanted on my own. Lisa needed much more than love. She needed a safe, stress-free, clean environment to live. She also needed psychiatric help, a job, and to get away from her parents. I couldn't make all those things happen alone. I needed help, including cooperation from Lisa. Unfortunately, I didn't have many options, and Lisa kept putting obstacles in my way.

As Lisa and I drove away from the gate, which was put there to keep the horse on the property, I couldn't help but feel a heavy burden from the choices I would need to make. Lisa depended on me for everything, including her medical care. She had other people in her life, including her son, but I was her only real friend.

Lisa and I chose to go to Chili's restaurant to have lunch and talk. It wasn't far from her house or from where I was staying in Lake Wales. We talked about the things that happened at the beach, her current state of mind, and about the Jeep. I told Lisa that I still wasn't comfortable giving her back the keys to the car just yet. She didn't argue about it with me. Lisa accepted the situation and focused her attention on making a more positive impression. She behaved calmly, apologetically, and sweetly.

We also talked about things that were currently bothering her, including her struggle with drugs and alcohol. At the end of our conversation, I told Lisa that I wanted to spend a few more days together before I made up my mind. Lisa tried her best to be cooperative and to get along with me. I was in control of the Jeep, and I knew she wanted it back. However, I believed she sincerely wanted our relationship to improve.

"I'm staying just across the street," I said to Lisa. "Do you want to stay with me?"

"Yes Alex," Lisa said smiling.

"Okay then, let's go back to your house so you can get some clothes, and then we'll go to the hotel, okay?" I said.

"Okay baby," Lisa replied.

When we arrived at the hotel, Lisa explained to me that she had left her briefcase with all her articles and photos in the Uber car, while coming home from the beach. I was stunned, and extremely upset by this revelation. Lisa had left behind her entire life's history in that car!

"Will you help me get my stuff back Alex?" Lisa asked.

"Yes baby, as soon as possible," I replied.

I was planning to write her life's story with her help, so retrieving all her news articles was vitally important to both of us. Lisa had spent a great deal of time and effort over the years collecting and saving all those news stories about herself, and they had a lot of sentimental value to her and me. I didn't approve of her decision to bring them to the beach in the first place, but I understood why she did it. Lisa really wanted to share her life with me, and she brought the articles and photos with her for that reason. I couldn't be mad at her for wanting to feel close to me, so I had to conceal my annoyance at her careless mistake. All those memorabilia were too valuable to lose, so I was determined to retrieve it all.

Every day I spent with Lisa was painful to witness how desperate she needed to be loved. Now that I had a chance to think about it, this was likely the reason she was overtly affectionate in the past. Despite Lisa's tumultuous and notorious life, she was actually very proud of her fame, because it garnered the attention she desired. Perhaps, she subconsciously allowed herself to be caught for this reason. Lisa loved the spotlight because she equated the attention that came due to fame with love. A responsive audience gave her the impression that she was appreciated and adored. Attention was something Lisa craved her entire life, but she still found little satisfaction once the spotlight was turned off. The feeling she received from audiences and fans never lasted more than a few hours. It was like a drug wearing off; the highs became lows the instant she was alone.

I knew it was going to take some time to track down and retrieve Lisa's possessions. A few days had gone by, but Lisa still made no effort to secure her property. It was a good thing I stayed with her; otherwise, I don't think she would have ever recovered her things. Fortunately, Lisa still had the number of the Uber driver. When I called, I discovered the driver didn't speak English well. That made it more difficult for me to understand where to go to claim Lisa's belongings. However, I was able to find out that they were in a storage facility in Tampa, so Lisa and I decided to go there the following day. After much effort, we eventually found the place, and recovered all her things she had left behind. We were both exhausted by the time we finally accomplished our mission because it took us almost the entire day for the search and rescue effort.

As a result, we decided to stay in Tampa that night. We checked into the Safety Harbor Hotel, where I had stayed in the past and knew it was nice. While we were there, Lisa told me about her marriage. She said she married a man 20 years her senior around the year 2000, because she wanted to have another child, after losing her first baby to adoption. They had a son named Geoffrey. He had blonde hair and blue eyes and grew up to be a good-looking young man. Lisa's ex-husband Jeff was a real estate broker from Chicago, who owned property in central Florida. In fact, he used to own the land where Carmen and Dave were living, before relinquishing it to Lisa during their divorce.

Lisa told me that Jeff used to take her to extravagant parties, where he enjoyed showing her off as his trophy wife. What he may have thought was flattering was humiliating to her. He constantly put her down in front of strangers, making her feel badly about herself. Lisa said Jeff even made her clean toilets and perform maintenance work at one of the apartment complexes he owned on their wedding day. She also claimed that living with her ex-husband was constant emotional torture. Just two years into their marriage, Lisa couldn't take the abuse any longer and moved out. She began driving big-rig trucks in order to make a living, which she told me she loved because it gave her peace.

Due to their separation, Lisa now faced a custody battle for their son Geoffrey. She said Jeff would periodically threaten to take away her child completely by sending her back to prison if she resisted his demands. He eventually made good on his promise. One day, Jeff invited her over to his house, served her drinks, and deliberately caused a fight, according to Lisa. Jeff called the police and Lisa was charged with a parole violation. Lisa said Jeff bribed the judge, to make sure she served more time. It's not hard to believe that some judges from Chicago are corrupt, but Lisa's stories were not always reliable.

Ultimately, Lisa lost custody of Geoffrey, and she was forced to serve three more long years behind bars, separated from her son. Being segregated from a second child was unbearable for Lisa, and it took a profound toll on her sanity. I can't imagine how many nights she spent crying alone in her prison cell, missing her little boy. Lisa's incarceration, as well as her drug use, unfortunately had a lasting detrimental effect on her relationship with her son.

Growing up, Geoffrey must have been scarred emotionally from not having enough contact with his mother. By 2018, he was just becoming an adult. I watched Lisa occasionally try to communicate with her son via text message on SnapChat, because he didn't like talking to her directly. Lisa told me that Geoffrey almost never picked up the phone when she called him. Instead, they would send funny photos back and forth to each other occasionally, like teenage friends do. Their communication seemed more like a distant friendship than a true mother-son relationship.

Lisa loved her son with all her heart - more than she loved herself. It crushed her not to have the opportunity to spend more time with him. Geoffrey was clearly upset with his mom because she was not there for him growing up much of the time. Lisa talked to me about him constantly, which made her feel happy. However deep down, her separation and lack of communication with her boy was just another source of her pain. Lisa had terrible parental role models, so she never learned how to be a good mother herself. Despite that, she truly loved her son, and desperately missed Geoffrey and her daughter Joy. Lisa was truly heartbroken over losing both of her children. I saw it in her eyes each time I looked at her, whenever she spoke about them. I have never known a woman who had endured so much suffering in their lives, and it hurt me profoundly to see Lisa in such extreme agony.

The next day Lisa and I took a drive into Winter Haven to revisit the Gardens together. After we arrived, we changed our minds about going, because the park had changed so drastically when Legoland took over. The experience was not going to be what it might have been since the park had been altered so drastically. Instead, we decided to drive to the house on Bayhill drive, where I used to live with Don and Carrie. I remembered the address because the number has a connection to James Bond. I couldn't recall how to get there anymore, but thanks to my GPS, it was easy to find. It is a ranch house close to the park, and has a separate apartment connected to the main house. The times Lisa and I shared in that little apartment together were the ones that were the most memorable to me. So many days and nights, Lisa and I made love there. We had such intense passion for each other in those days.

Looking at the house, while remembering better times, made me feel sad and happy at the same time. I wished I could return to the past and relive those days - everything except our break-up. Unfortunately, Don sold the house in 2015, after holding onto it for over 25 years. It looked different because it had been newly painted. It seemed smaller from the outside for some reason. Once Lisa and I had our fill of reminiscing, we drove away after taking some photos of the house. I probably should have taken a selfie of us in front of the house, but my mind was preoccupied daydreaming.

Lisa and I were getting along very well, and I was starting to warm up to her again. We were really having a nice time together, and not fighting anymore over her drinking. It was hard not to feel the same way about Lisa, as I once did in the past, especially being together again in Winter Haven. It was really like we were living in the past. However, when Lisa drank, it often spoiled the peace between us. When she was in a good mood, there was no one I wanted to be with more than her. Unfortunately, I could never tell when her behavior was going to change. Lisa was so unpredictable, unlike my experience with her in the past. She and I never had this kind of time to spend together a long time ago, so perhaps that's the reason why I was unaware of her volatility. Lisa put a lot of effort into making a good impression on me when we were young. She had been through such terror during her childhood, and sadly it seemed like things had gone sour for her after we broke-up, and she spent time in prison for murder. Lisa's luck took another turn for the worse when she had that trucking accident. It was heartbreaking, because Lisa was such a uniquely talented and intelligent woman, and she had so much to offer the world.

I needed to leave Florida soon, but I wasn't ready to say goodbye to Lisa just yet. Then, I had one of my crazy impulsive ideas.

"How about instead of you dropping me at the airport tomorrow, we drive back to North Carolina together?" I asked Lisa.

"Really, can we?" Lisa asked.

"Yeah, why not?" I replied.

Lisa was very excited about my proposition because she was beginning to feel depressed knowing I planned to leave soon. At this time, a hurricane had just creamed the southeast coast. Many roads were flooded, and some flights were cancelled, including mine. I anticipated that we might have trouble driving back to Raleigh, due to the storm, but I wanted to stay with Lisa longer. I needed to get back home, but I still wasn't confident I could trust her with the Jeep. She and I were just beginning to hit our stride, and I didn't want to end our time together just yet. It had been almost 30 years since I last saw her, and something inside me felt scared to leave her again.

"Let's plan on leaving tomorrow, okay?" I said.

"Okay baby, I love you," Lisa replied.

As soon as we decided to go to North Carolina together, I started to have second thoughts. However, the dye was cast, and there was no turning back now.

12. The Trip North

Lisa needed to go back home to Fort Meade, to pack before we left for North Carolina. We drove back to her lake house, where she could gather her things to take with us. It may have been a crazy idea of mine to be stuck in a confined space with Lisa for a long time because her behavior was so unpredictable, but I decided to take the chance anyway. She would need to drive all the way back home again alone if I gave her back the Jeep, and she had already shown that she was incapable of driving 45 minutes from her home to Tampa by herself. That reason alone should have been enough to discard my plan. I don't know what I was thinking - I just didn't want to leave her.

It was an ill-conceived idea, but it allowed me to spend more time with Lisa. It was what I wanted, after the disastrous reunion we had at the beach. I really needed to get home soon for work, but I missed Lisa so much for so many years, and I just couldn't let her go before I felt ready. I could have flown back and left Lisa with the Jeep like I had planned in the first place, but I didn't want to do that anymore. If we hadn't had that dramatic scene at the beach, I might have felt better about leaving by myself.

Sometimes, I think I like to make my life more complicated on purpose, just to see what happens. I couldn't put my finger on it, but something compelled me to need to spend more time together. I chose to ignore the potential pitfalls of letting Lisa come with me. Perhaps, I was trying to make up for lost time and past mistakes. I admit that my motives for driving back home with Lisa were unclear in my mind. Lisa had been acting pleasantly and calmly the last few days, and we were really enjoying each other's company. She had a way of lulling me into a false sense of security, with her enchanting allure and flirtatious demeanor. I knew I needed to be on my guard, waiting for the other shoe to drop.

Kricket accompanied us most of the time we were together, but Lisa wanted to leave her behind again when we left for Raleigh, and that concerned me tremendously. We probably should have taken her with us as a precaution, but it would have been a lot of extra trouble, especially at any hotels. It was a double-edged sword, as was often the case with decisions regarding Lisa. Leaving Kricket home was certainly a risk I didn't really want to take, so it made me nervous when Lisa chose to leave her behind again.

The whole plan was starting to seem worse by the minute. After what I went through at the beach, I was afraid of what might happen during our trip up north. Despite my doubts, taking risks with Lisa was par for the course, if I wanted to spend time with her. I admit that my plan was laced with land mines, but I decided to go through with it anyway, against my own better judgement.

I decided to stop in Savannah overnight along the way, because there were still problems with the roads further north, due to the Hurricane. If the highway appeared to be clear the next day, we could continue, on our way to Raleigh. I had never been to Savannah, so I didn't know what to expect, but I had heard it was supposed to be interesting and quaint - like Charleston, South Carolina. I had high expectations for having a nice overnight stay. I looked for a place online along the waterfront, which had a bit of southern charm, and found a place I thought fit my expectations.

When we arrived in Savannah, we had to drive through downtown, which looked neglected, and crime ridden. The River Street Inn, where I had a reservation, seemed to be in a better location. The hotel itself appeared to be one of those very historic fancy southern gems, which was well preserved and updated. To our surprise, a film crew had set up to shoot a new version of 'Lady and the Tramp,' so that made things seem even more exciting. Apparently, the style and location of the hotel turned out to be a major factor pertaining to why it was chosen for the movie. I had chosen this hotel for the same reason.

It was close to dinnertime, after checking in and unpacking, but fortunately there were several restaurants around the hotel. We changed our clothes and freshened up before scouting out a place to eat. It was starting to get dark, so we looked for a place which we could walk to easily from the hotel. We chose a restaurant which was playing southern jazz and blues music. It was casual and a bit seedy but filled with people enjoying themselves. It also had a feel of local character, and a powerful aroma of fruits de mer. I could tell that the people in the tavern were mostly regulars, dressed in jeans and t-shirts. Lisa seemed attracted to the atmosphere, and she blended in perfectly with this type of hometown crowd. These were her kind of people, because they seemed down to earth and fun to be around. The piano player was prompting the audience to sing along, while the base player established the rhythm. I was waiting for Lisa to ask if she could sing with them, instead of sitting down with me. Her eyes always lit up whenever there was any opportunity to perform.

After Lisa and I were given a table, we noticed there were two young women in their late twenties or early thirties, sitting at the table next to us. One woman was particularly attractive. She was tall with long blonde hair, green eyes, and a slender body. She had on faded ripped jeans, beige knee-high boots, and a white lace short-sleeved blouse unbuttoned in the front, exposing her pink bra. The other woman was shorter with dark hair, brown eyes, and had a masculine disposition. She wore a simple navy-blue sleeveless t-shirt, which revealed a tattoo of a Bengal tiger on her right arm. I guessed they might be a couple, but I didn't want to assume. Lisa had the same impression as I did.

Not surprisingly, Lisa immediately started trying to attract the attention of the blonde woman. Her behavior didn't surprise me in the least, but I couldn't figure out what her game was this time. Lisa was clearly flirting and trying to elicit a reaction from me, and from the young woman. The blonde finally looked over in our direction and met eyes with Lisa's. They both smiled at each other, and then the young woman looked away, so that her date didn't notice. Lisa was not as tactful or discreet. I thought she may have been just trying to get a rise out of me, but I could never tell what Lisa was up to most of the time. I was afraid that if the dark-haired woman saw what Lisa was doing, she might become irritated, and I didn't want Lisa to become entangled in a bar room brawl. Lisa could be deliberately manipulative when she was bored or wasn't receiving enough attention, and it usually got her into trouble.

"What are you doing?" I asked Lisa.

"I wanted to make you jealous," Lisa replied.

"You don't need to make me jealous Vonnie," I said. "You already have my full attention."

"She's hot though, don't you think?" Lisa asked.

"Yes Vonnie, she's very attractive," I replied.

"I'm not interested in provoking a fight, and I'm a little too tired to have a ménage-a-trois this evening," I told Lisa. "Plus, I think the other woman isn't going to like it if you try and steal her girlfriend for the night."

"Who said I was planning on stealing her girlfriend?" Lisa replied. "Maybe I want her to join us instead of you."

"Very funny Vonnie," I said. "Don't forget I'm the one paying for the hotel room."

"Okay, you can watch then," Lisa replied teasingly.

Lisa was bi-sexual, so I knew she was half-serious, and not just fooling around. I also knew there were very few things that Lisa wouldn't do, especially if she found it thrilling. She had absolutely no inhibitions when it came to sex. In this arena, Lisa had complete confidence in her ability to seduce and satisfy any potential lover. However, she may have been feeling insecure about herself because she had put on so much weight over the past several years. Lisa may have been just trying to regain some self-confidence. If I asked her a question, my odds were 50-50 that she would tell me the truth. In this instance, I still wasn't certain what Lisa had on her mind, when she engaged the blonde in an amorous exchange.

Watching Lisa seduce another woman in front of me under these circumstances wasn't really a turn on, nor did I feel jealous - it was simply irritating. Reviving any further romantic relationship with Lisa at this point was not on my mind any longer, as much as changing her life. I tried to stay focused on my mission, and not allow Lisa to dissuade me with her childish exploits. In contrast, Lisa was determined to create distractions from her reality, instead of trying to manage her very serious problems. In any case, I just wanted to have a nice dinner without theatrics and drama for a change. Fortunately, we were able to finish our dinner peacefully, without further antics from my precocious circus clown.

After dinner, we walked outside along the riverfront. It must have been close to 9 o'clock in the evening. Night had fallen, and a full moon and gas-powered streetlamps illuminated the boardwalk, where several people were walking. There was an enormous white riverboat with decorative white lights, docked for tours during the day. Normally, I might say that it was a romantic atmosphere. However, there was something in the air that night, which didn't seem quite right, and it made me nervous. After we took some selfies in front of the riverboat, a man dressed in black walked up to us, with some flowers in his hand.

"Evenin' y'all; roses for the lady?" he asked.

"No thanks," I replied.

The man persisted, so we started to walk away, after I refused him two more times. Lisa was streetwise, and she noticed there were a few other men nearby watching us. It looked to her like they were positioning themselves around us in a circle. It could have been a bit of paranoia on her part, or maybe she was really onto something. I usually paid close attention whenever Lisa's radar perked up.

"Look Alex," Lisa said. "There are at least four of them, and they are closing the circle. We need to get out of here and back to the hotel now!"

"Okay Vonnie, let's go," I replied.

As we started to walk away, I looked over my shoulder and noticed one of them looked like he had started to pursue us. The other three were spreading out and were on the move. We weren't the only ones walking along the waterfront that evening, so I wasn't too anxious, but we kept moving in the direction of the hotel anyway. There were other people in the shops and restaurants, which gave us some sense of security. However, just because other people were around, didn't mean criminals wouldn't act. When they strike, they usually move with lightning speed, and flee the scene before others know what to do. I decided to play it safe just in case Lisa was right. When you're with someone, who has been to prison, you learn to trust their instincts, especially concerning crime on the street. As we began climbing the stairs, the four men appeared to break off their pursuit.

We didn't realize until later that there was a closer entrance to the hotel, just below the stairs off the boardwalk. It would have been easier to access. After we made it safely inside the hotel, we were still experiencing residual adrenaline from our ordeal on the riverfront. In a way, it was exhilarating - all my senses were on high alert. Whenever Lisa had nervous energy, her go to reaction was either to drink or have sex. So, she went down the hall to get ice to mix herself a vodka and coke.

Then, Lisa started talking about how hot the blonde was at dinner. Talking to me about the sexy young lady was an attempt on her part to put me in a romantic mood. While I was doing my best to ignore her drinking, I couldn't completely avoid her sexual advances. Lisa was a master of seduction, and she was never coy about making her intentions apparent, when it came to physical intimacy. Rejecting Lisa at any time for any reason was increasingly risky, based on her emotional fragility. It was always a balancing act trying to help Lisa, without becoming involved with her romantically. I did my best to find the right balance in our relationship, but she was always in control whenever she wanted something.

After Lisa finished her drink and with me, she and I took turns taking a shower and prepared for bed. When Lisa was done brushing her artificial teeth, she kissed me goodnight and put her head on the pillow. She fell asleep within just a few minutes, which she found difficult to do whenever she was alone. At home, she often felt full of anxiety and fought back pain. Whenever she was with me, she had access to a more supportive mattress, and usually slept soundly through the night. I tried my best to put Lisa's mind at ease before bedtime especially, so she would feel safe and relaxed. Occasionally, she would wake up for a little while and pour herself another drink, before going back to sleep.

The following day was going to be a long day because of the distance we still needed to drive to Raleigh. I closed my eyes reluctantly and hoped that everything would remain peaceful until morning. For a long time, my life had been predictable and stable. Being with Lisa again, turned all of that on its head, because spending time with her could often be chaotic, unnerving, and frustrating. It could be engaging, exhilarating and surprisingly pleasant as well. One thing I could be sure of was that life with her would always be unpredictable. In any case, sleeping together was usually a welcome break from all the daily drama. Each time I shut my eyes while next to Lisa; I never felt afraid.

The times Lisa and I spent together in our past were joyful memories for both of us. Each moment Lisa and I laid eyes on one another, we were always smiling and glad to see one another. Being together always made us both feel so good. Lisa and I had something special between us that seemed to fit together naturally. However, earning her trust again was another matter, after what happened in St. Petersburg. I realized that Lisa would never trust any man completely, after discovering what had happened with her stepfather during her childhood. Still, it was something that I knew I had to keep working on if I was going to make any progress. Time was not on my side. I knew Lisa needed help sooner than later, but she didn't intend to make it easy for me or surrender her freedom willingly.

It occurred to me that with all of Lisa's faults, she was still just a child inside her head. She was only trying to survive and get the attention and love she desperately needed. I swore to myself that nothing was going to keep me from continuing to try to help her. I understood just how monumental the task was going to be, especially because Lisa was so uncooperative. She also had no job or health insurance, and ironically the Affordable Health Care Act (ACA) was unaffordable, even though she was on Welfare. The ACA is clearly a useless program designed only to garner political capital, and doesn't help people like Lisa, who really needed medical care at low or no cost. In her case, the cost was over $600 dollars per month, and she received only $750 dollars a month from Welfare checks. That left her only $150 each month to buy food and to pay for other living expenses.

Lisa and I still had about a six-hour trip ahead of us in the morning, so I finally decided to turn my mind off and go to sleep. I reached for Lisa's hand, and put my head on her shoulder, before letting go of any further thoughts.

The next morning, there was a plethora of people surrounding the front of the hotel, because the movie crew was going to be filming again. I wanted to stick around and watch, but I needed to get back to North Carolina as soon as possible. In hindsight, I wish we would have decided to stay one more day to watch the acting. It wasn't often that I had an opportunity to see a movie being made. Once, while I was going to college in Buffalo, Robert Redford was in town to film the movie 'The Natural.' A friend of mine from school had a job as an Assistant Casting Director. I never asked him if he could sneak me in some place where I could watch, and perhaps meet some of the stars. It was just one more missed opportunity in my life. Standing so close to the set felt like we were right in the middle of the scene. It was both exciting and intimidating.

As we were checking out, Lisa said she had to go back to the room for something. She took a very long time, possibly because she went to sneak a drink. I knew I probably shouldn't disappear to fetch the car, because Lisa had such a great fear of abandonment. She might start to panic if she couldn't find me easily. I decided to go anyway because I was becoming impatient waiting for her to return. I wanted to put gas in the Jeep before our departure, so I took a chance and made a quick dash for the car. I did ask one of the hotel employees to tell Lisa that I would be right back and not to worry, but I figured that he probably wouldn't have the chance, and he didn't know what she looked like anyway.

When Lisa came back to the lobby and didn't see me standing there, she panicked as predicted. She thought I had left without her and began searching for me in desperation. Moments later, I pulled the Jeep around and parked near the front of the hotel. I tried to hurry to find Lisa because I knew she would be worried. As I walked expediently toward the front of the hotel, I spotted her walking outside looking for me in the crowd, gathered to view the filming. I could see Lisa had a worried look on her face, and it made me feel terrible that I caused her to become upset.

"Lisa, Lisa!" I shouted.

"Be quiet!" a film crewman yelled back at me. "We're trying to film here!"

"Sorry!" I replied.

When Lisa finally saw me, she smiled happily and scurried over toward me. She looked relieved, once she realized I hadn't left her behind.

"What happened to you baby?" Lisa said, using her funny voice. "I was 'scare' you left me. Don't do dat again Alex, okay?"

"Okay Vonnie, I'm sorry," I replied.

Lisa started using a cartoon-like voice periodically with me to break her nervous tension. She said she had never used this voice before in her life, but I found it hard to believe. It was one more skill of hers, which made me laugh. Lisa's ability to change her voice in various ways was something new that I hadn't experienced with her. I began noticing that she used humor to mask her fears and anxieties, and to hide her pain from her past. This tactic has become more recognized, after Robin Williams committed suicide. Lisa could really be hysterically funny when she wanted to be. Many professional comedians aren't as funny as she could be. Lisa should have been on a sitcom or done stand-up comedy because she had the ability to be amusingly animated, and entertaining.

Lisa had talents she didn't even recognize. She would periodically portray several different characters, during some of our phone conversations. One time during a call, she asked me to speak French to her, so she could hear my accent. Then she copied the tone of my voice and my accent, almost exactly - quite remarkably. Another time, she described what she imagined would happen in a nightclub in Paris, pretending to be a cocktail waitress talking to a customer. She had a better French accent than I do. I lived in France for almost a year, and I can speak the language well, but Lisa's accent was superior to mine.

I also asked her to mimic some other characters, and she did them flawlessly. Lisa could easily have had a career in acting if she had been given the opportunity. I believe she would have been a great success on stage or television. She was really one of the most multi-talented individuals that I have ever met in my life. She had abilities far beyond the average person, but she never understood that about herself, shamefully. Lisa told me that she considered herself to be a loser, and that took me by great surprise.

I have spent a lot of time around entertainers throughout my lifetime, due to my own professional experience on the ice. I have never met anyone more talented, more gifted, or more intelligent. Lisa had a special gift for performing, but sadly, many of her talents were overlooked and neglected. Unfortunately, Lisa simply couldn't see a positive future for herself, and never pursued a career that matched her abilities, outside of the circus. I don't think she ever had anyone in her life, who believed in her like I did. Most of the people around her were too busy trying to put her down or exploit her for their own purposes. Unfortunately, that happens to many entertainers like Michael Jackson, Elvis Presley, and Judy Garland.

I kissed Lisa to show her again that I was sorry for leaving her, without telling her where I was going. I put her things in the Jeep and continued our journey toward Raleigh. During the trip, Lisa couldn't sit still or stay quiet, because she became bored easily. Her instinct was always to find a way to be entertaining, whenever she had the chance. She didn't need a trapeze, a costume, or even a microphone to put on a show.

Since Lisa discovered that I liked her silly voice, she began using it to improvise an act while we were traveling, to pass the time. During this impromptu routine, Lisa began to describe her stepfather's sexual abuse, when she was still just a child. It was a bit bizarre, but I played along, because I understood that this might be one way Lisa dealt with her emotions. It was an improvement on her desire to drink. She prompted me to ask her probing questions, which she responded with provocative answers. The character Lisa created for herself was supposed to be a little girl, not more than about six-years-old.

"You know, when I was a little girl, my stepdaddy would come into my room after mommy tucked me in at night, because he said he wanted to read me a story," Lisa said.

"Really?" I asked.

"Yeah, uhuh; he would come in and lock the door, because he said he didn't want mommy to interrupt our story time," Lisa replied.

"What did he read to you?" I asked.

"Well, he had a book with him, but he never actually read me a story," Lisa replied.

"What did he do if he didn't read you a story?" I asked.

"Well, he told me to take off my jammies, before he would read to me, because he said I was going to be too hot." Lisa replied.

"What did you say to him?" I asked.

"I say no, I don't want to take off my jammies, because I will feel cold," Lisa replied.

"Then what happened?" I asked.

"Then he got mad at me, and he ripped my jammies and made me cry," Lisa replied.

"What happened next?" I asked.

"He made me kiss him and touch him, and that made me cry again," Lisa replied.

"How old were you when he first started doing story time with you?" I asked.

"I was only four years old," Lisa replied.

"How did he make you feel?" I asked.

"Oh, very bad, cuz he hurt me and made me cry, and caused me to be 'scare' of the dark," Lisa replied.

"I'm sorry he hurt you honey," I said.

Lisa looked at me, while tears formed in her eyes. I knew at that moment that there was no question that Lisa was telling the truth about the abuse she suffered as a child. I pulled the Jeep over to the side of the road, so that I could hold her, while she cried in my arms. We stayed parked, while Lisa wiped her eyes with a tissue that I gave to her. I kissed her and told her that she would always feel safe with me.

"I will protect you from now on Vonnie," I said. "I'm sorry I haven't been there for you in the past - I should have been."

"Thanks baby," Lisa said. "I love you."

"I love you too honey," I replied.

Lisa and I had kept the routine going for almost 45 minutes, before I had to stop the car. It would have been more pleasant to listen to her sing. In one respect, Lisa's spontaneous routine was very funny, but at the same time, it was extremely disturbing and made me uncomfortable. In a very twisted way, creating a comedy skit about her abuse helped her cope with her dark childhood experiences. It allowed her to bring her nightmares out into the open, while she felt safe to express herself. Lisa not only had a tremendous ability to entertain, but she also had an enormous capacity to cope with her circumstances, through performing and artistic expression. The part that wasn't advantageous was her propensity to drink excessively, to numb her sensitivities.

After we continued our journey, we came across a few detours due to heavy flooding, resulting from the hurricane. Ultimately, it took us two extra hours to get to Raleigh because of the road conditions. I did most of the driving, but Lisa still took the wheel for a couple of hours to give me some relief. She was actually a very good driver, when she wasn't under the influence of alcohol and drugs. I wasn't really surprised because she still had her commercial driver's license. However, in her present condition, the Jeep was really about all she could handle.

I could see that driving allowed Lisa the opportunity to relax, unwind and clear her mind. Being on the road and away from people, helped her to feel carefree, and escape from all of the pressure and drama of her turbulent life. Since Lisa had to concentrate on what was happening on the road, it kept her from thinking about her past. When Lisa was behind the wheel, her smile returned to her face, the glow reappeared in her eyes, and joy filled her heart. It almost made me cry to see her so happy.

The city lights of Raleigh were finally in sight. It almost seemed like I had been to another world and not just to another state. I didn't know how Lisa or I would react being together in my home environment. I hoped it would give her peace, but I thought it might make her more anxious and defensive. I really had no idea what to expect. I crossed my fingers and prayed for the best outcome.

13. Home Sweet Home

It felt good to be home, even though it took longer than it should have, due to the hurricane. Almost immediately, a sense of normality came over me. Lisa seemed calm and happy and began to smile more. She acted more relaxed than I had seen her for a while. Getting away from that horrible environment at home was something Lisa really needed. I looked forward to having a quiet dinner alone with her, watching some television, and going to sleep early. Lisa insisted on having a glass of wine with dinner, but that's all she drank, as far as I knew. I was grateful that she appeared to be trying to cut back on her alcohol consumption.

There were several things that I wanted to do with Lisa the next day, but unfortunately, there wasn't a lot of time before she needed to go back to Florida. I was still debating whether I was going to let her drive the Jeep back by herself or put her on a plane. The smart thing would have been to keep the Jeep and have her fly home. Lisa wasn't exactly ready for the responsibility of owning a new car or driving 12 hours back to Florida alone. However, I didn't want Lisa to be trapped in that house with her abusive and drug addicted parents. I didn't have the heart to do that to her. It was my deep regret that Lisa still had to continue to live with her parents awhile longer - at least until she could find a job and move out. Unfortunately, securing employment for Lisa was proving to be more challenging than I had expected.

I knew that Lisa's friendship circle included people who were bad influences. They were fellow drug addicts, alcoholics, and in some cases - former criminals. Lisa's friends and family were made up of people who did not have Lisa's best interests in mind. There was an occasion when a so-called friend of hers called to ask if he could have some of her prescription pain medication. The call came over the speakerphone in the Jeep. I told the guy to take a hike, and to stop asking Lisa to do something illegal. I'm sure he tried texting her back again later. This was the kind of pressure that Lisa constantly faced from her circle of influence. Unfortunately, she seemed to be as equally dependent on these degenerate people, as they were on her. I called it her 'circle of addiction.' Lisa seemed to need to be in constant contact with these types of people, except when she was decompressing in her pool at home after lunch.

I tried to put Lisa in touch with some of my friends - some of whom are doctors, lawyers and health care professionals. I was hoping it might give Lisa a chance to form better relationships. Most of my friends are very intelligent and successful people, who could give Lisa good advice, and wouldn't try to take advantage of her. The friends she currently had mainly created trouble for her and influenced her to continue to make poor choices. If Lisa had any chance of breaking away from her cycle of dependency, she would need to have a better circle of friends. Regardless of our personal relationship, I wanted Lisa to have a more peaceful and healthier life. Trying to achieve that goal was proving to be an extraordinarily ambitious endeavor. I knew that it was going to take many months or years to achieve, but time was a precious commodity, which seemed to be slipping away.

The next morning after breakfast, I wanted to start the day by trying to help Lisa feel better about herself. She wanted to have her hair colored and her nails done, so we went into town to find some shops, which had immediate openings. Lisa had been coloring her own hair for years because she didn't have enough money to get it done professionally. I didn't realize just how expensive it is to color women's hair, but it's not cheap. The cost didn't really matter because Lisa's happiness was more important to me. While Lisa was getting her hair cut and colored at the salon, she was very chatty as usual. I have seen many people in my time, who have a natural gift for charming people, but there was no one I had ever met quite like Lisa. She could be extremely delightful and loquacious, or she could be abrasive and intimidating. It all depended on how people treated her.

Several sensational articles and documentaries about Lisa have attempted to demonize and defame her character, but Lisa French was nothing like what she has been portrayed to be in the media or by Detective Ray. She was truly a caring and affectionate woman, who simply longed to be loved and treated with respect. If not for her horrible parents, Lisa would have likely become a superstar, loved by millions of people. She had undeniable magnetic appeal, along with an array of talents, which few individuals possessed. She had a way of connecting with people on a deeply personal level, which made it seem like a strong bond existed between her and someone she just met.

When Lisa was sufficiently pleased with her new look, we went out for lunch and talked about her future, instead of continuing to focus on her past. I tried to lay out a plan, which included opening a joint bank account, from which she could make car payments, and draw money from in an emergency. I wanted to be sure Lisa wasn't writing bad checks again, like she did in the past. It was risky trusting Lisa with money, but I was hoping she could be more responsible now at her age.

After making a trip to the bank, we arrived back home, so that Lisa could take her daily nap. It helped her to calm her mind and body from the stress she felt constantly. She had a relaxing morning, but Lisa carried with her decades of physical and emotional pain. She was trying desperately to get off the strong prescription medication she had been given by her doctor, but it was difficult and dangerous for her to stop taking it all at once. Her truck accident had been severe and caused substantial damage to her back and jaw. The impact of the crash should have killed her, but Lisa was a survivor. No matter what life threw at her, she somehow showed remarkable resilience and durability.

Despite her bad luck, Lisa was probably the biggest threat to herself. She should have enrolled in a rehabilitation facility, until she learned how to love and care for herself better, but she always fell short of following through doing it. Lisa didn't like to be confined or told what to do, so she resisted following my advice and the recommendations of her doctors to go back to a long-term care facility. So, the best I could do for her was to make sure she saw her primary care physician every month and try to keep her spirits up. Most of the time, I just felt helpless attempting to improve Lisa's life. The more I did for her, the more I saw how little impact it made overall.

As far as material things were concerned, Lisa didn't care about them. I think the only thing she really cared about was having someone in her life who didn't give up on her and loved her unconditionally. I tried very hard to give that kind of love to her this time, but Lisa was so jaded by her past and torn by her emotions, that she couldn't openly accept the love I tried to offer her. She could no longer trust anyone with her heart, after what her parents and her lover Pam had done to her. Ironically, Lisa never stopped trying to solicit love from her mother - something she would never truly experience in her lifetime.

Lisa and I only had just a couple of days left together before I had to decide if I was going to give her the Jeep back. In the past day or two, Lisa seemed very calm and relaxed, probably because of being away from the toxic environment at home. It seemed as if she was a different person entirely. The serenity of a peaceful home was what Lisa really needed on a permanent basis. Unfortunately, I was not able to offer it to her for more than a short time. When Lisa wasn't under any kind of pressure, she was a lot of fun, and I enjoyed her company tremendously. Even though Lisa still insisted on having a few drinks during the day, she drank less each day, and her mood swings appeared to be stabilizing. Overall, I felt better about letting her drive home alone. However, I was still very concerned that she wasn't ready to drive 12 hours by herself. So, I booked a hotel for her to rest and stay overnight near Charleston, South Carolina. It was difficult to know whether I was making the right decision, but I decided to hope for the best.

Lisa was a very complicated and volatile woman. She could become irate and defensive instantaneously if she felt pressured. I had to be careful with her because I could never predict what might set her off and cause her to become hysterical. Dealing with Lisa in the present was like I was walking on a high wire without a net. This was something Lisa could do with precision in the circus, but I didn't possess her talent. One little mistake on my part could be catastrophic, causing her to react impulsively and dangerously. Even though our interaction was more of a mental tightrope that I was treading, it could still have deadly consequences.

I was constantly reminded of the error that I made with her at the beach, which caused a meltdown of epic proportions. The environment that I took Lisa to in St. Petersburg had also been peaceful and relaxing, but I made the mistake of pressuring her about her drinking. I never really worried about myself when I was alone with Lisa, but it always concerned me that Lisa would do something to harm herself. For the moment, Lisa seemed in control, and I was very grateful that our time together in North Carolina had passed smoothly, without incident. Having a peaceful relationship was critical if I was going to help Lisa improve her life. If we weren't getting along, I couldn't do anything to help her.

Whenever Lisa felt worried, she usually listened to what I suggested, but she didn't always follow my advice. When she was alone, she would often make very poor decisions, which affected her in a negative way. Driving to the dealership in Tampa, likely under the influence of drugs and alcohol, is probably a good example. Some of these types of bad decisions became habit-forming. It was times like that, which caused me to have great concern about her driving home alone.

Lisa would often lie each time she thought she was going to be in trouble for something she did wrong - just like a child. She often spoke of how angry and abusive her first stepfather became, when she didn't perform to his satisfaction. As a result, she was afraid of facing severe consequences for the tiniest of infractions. During her life, Lisa was under constant threat from people, who were trying to exploit her for their own selfish desires. Lying was just how she addressed what she perceived as personal attacks against her. Occasionally, Lisa would lie to me about something, but later she would express remorse, say she was sorry and tell me the truth. I know she wanted to be honest with me. In fact, she longed to tell me everything about her life, but Lisa was often afraid of my reaction. However, this response was preconditioned.

To the average person, Lisa's bad habits might have appeared to be obvious character flaws. However, I knew that much of what Lisa did was often an attempt to protect herself, or a form of escape from her horrific reality. That didn't excuse her outbursts and actions, but knowing her history helped me to be more patient and understand her better.

In court, they don't want to hear much about what happened in your life before you committed a crime, as if that had nothing to do with it. I would say - it has everything to do with it. Sometimes, Lisa would also engage in behavior designed to punish herself. She didn't seem to mind these self-inflicted wounds because she felt she deserved to suffer. Ever since Lisa killed her stepfather, she endlessly engaged in self-destructive acts, which she knew would cause herself more trouble and anguish.

The day finally came when it was time for Lisa to go home. So, I decided I would trust her with the Jeep, knowing that it might be a huge mistake. Without having an opportunity to get away from her parents' house occasionally, Lisa might just give-up. I was afraid of what she might do under those circumstances, so I had to let her have the SUV back. I gave her some money for the trip, so she could buy gas and something to eat along the way. Then I hugged and kissed her goodbye, not knowing what might happen to her out on the long road home. I was hopeful things would be better for her, but I still worried that the worst would occur.

I felt a tear run down my cheek, as I watched her drive away, and I wondered if I would ever see Lisa again. It was finally the end of our reunion, which had become a mélange of bitter-sweet moments, laced with unpredictable adventures and turmoil. However, there were some very special and memorable moments as well - ones I will cherish and never forget. Lisa and I spent a little over two weeks together, except for those few days apart. It had been an extremely emotional rollercoaster ride for both of us. Events turned out nothing like I had imagined, but at least this time, we said goodbye on good terms. If all went well, I expected to see her again soon during the Holidays, but I told her I couldn't make any promises just yet.

Even though Lisa used to drive very large trucks for a living, she was much older now and in very poor health. However, she still should have been able to handle the Jeep if she didn't drink along the route. I kept thinking that bringing her to North Carolina and letting her drive all the way back home by herself was a colossal blunder, but it was too late to do anything about it now. I could only pray that it worked itself out.

I called Lisa several times during her trip to check on her progress, but she didn't always answer her phone. She seemed to be making slower progress than I expected. I imagined Lisa had taken time to stop for lunch, but perhaps she might have been drinking too, so that concerned me. Lisa loved people, and she often talked to everyone she met, so that might have slowed her down. I could imagine her just hanging-out and talking to strangers, whenever she stopped for gas or food. I don't know where it happened exactly, but one of the times she stopped for gas, while on the road with her big rig, she told me she met 'Kid Rock.' I tried to think of the best reasons why Lisa might be taking so long, instead of assuming the worst.

The times I was able to speak with Lisa, she said she was doing fine, so I tried not to worry. She claimed to be making progress, even though she didn't stick to the route the GPS was telling her to go. I reminded her to stay on the main highway, and to make sure the hotel destination was still set in the GPS, so that she didn't veer too far off course. I couldn't help but worry about her, and I had anxiety thinking about what a mistake I had made. Eventually, Lisa arrived at the hotel, but it wasn't until after 7 pm. She should have been there no later than 4 pm. Time meant nothing to Lisa; she always did things whenever she felt like it. Still, I was grateful that she arrived safely, and that she had a nice warm bed to sleep in for the night.

The next day was another fiasco. It seemed like Lisa had taken an enormous amount of time leaving the hotel and she refused to offer any explanation. It was almost noon, and she still hadn't left yet. I thought maybe Lisa drank a lot the night before, or perhaps first thing in the morning, and that's why she wasn't ready to drive yet. Maybe she was waiting until the effects of the alcohol began wearing off, before getting behind the wheel. I didn't really know what was happening, because Lisa refused to tell me anything, other than to say she slept late.

This is the problem with many alcoholics - drinking becomes the center of their world, and it interferes with virtually everything they need to do. It interferes with their job prospects, and their ability to keep their jobs. It also affects their personal relationships. Drug and alcohol abuse destroys people's ability to have happy and productive lives, probably more than anything else. The reason I think that many people self-medicate is because they are unwilling or unable to find the proper medical care they need. Psychiatric care is often not covered by most healthcare plans, for example.

The 'Affordable' Care Act has done absolutely nothing to solve challenging health care issues. In many respects, 'Obamacare' has made healthcare for many people in this country worse because millions of people lost their insurance, as a result. The new healthcare insurance often covers less than people's old plans and is usually more expensive. Premiums are higher now, and access to care is often more difficult. In Lisa's case, being on the government health care exchange would have eaten up most of her welfare check. It would have cost her more than paying for her monthly doctor visits out of pocket. It seems that no one who is on welfare can access healthcare, without having to pay a very high price.

It was close to 1 pm by the time Lisa finally hit the pavement. Inconceivably, by 7 pm, after starting from just outside of Charleston, Lisa was still in Georgia. I told her to stop for dinner, and that I would arrange for her to stay overnight again, to avoid driving in the dark. I booked another hotel for her near St. Augustine, Florida. When I asked Lisa why she was taking so long, she finally told me she didn't want to go home. I sympathized with how she felt, so I tried to be supportive, and not become upset with her for dragging her feet returning home.

Perhaps everything was moving too fast in her mind. Maybe she wasn't ready to be independent just yet. I should have known better, but I had confidence in Lisa's abilities - probably more than she did herself. I tried for months to encourage Lisa to seek help from a psychiatrist, and to go to a detox facility, but she kept putting it off. Even though she occasionally seemed like she might decide to go, she never did. She was too afraid to give up control over her life to a bunch of strangers, who had no love for her. So, the only thing I could do was to try to be supportive. However, that wasn't ever easy because Lisa often behaved with such hostility, whenever she felt frustrated. No matter what I did, it seemed like I was constantly fighting a losing battle - nothing I did was ever enough, it seemed.

Something must have happened either before or after Lisa crossed the state line into Florida, because her mood had changed drastically by the time she arrived at the next hotel. It seemed that the closer she approached her home in Fort Meade, the worse her mood became. Lisa became argumentative and belligerent again for no reason that I could understand. She must have been experiencing an enormous amount of anxiety, knowing she was going to be home soon. It must have felt like a punishment to her, after having such a nice time with me. It hurt me every time I knew she was suffering emotionally.

Carmen's husband Dave was verbally abusive and threatened Lisa and her mom whenever he was drunk. Unfortunately, Carmen never learned her lesson when it came to choosing men. Every man she ever brought into Lisa's life, proved to be a constant impediment to Lisa's happiness, health, and security. I understood why she didn't want to go back home.

Finally, around 5 pm on the third day, by some miracle, Lisa arrived at her parents' lake house. It took her twice as long to get there as it should have, but I was just so relieved she was finally there safe, without having had any accidents or tickets - none that I knew of anyway. However, my relief would not last for very long. It never took Lisa much time before she became involved in more drama again, and it always affected me in the worst possible way.

14. A Tangled Web

After Lisa arrived home, I didn't hear from her at all for several days. Each time I called her; it went to voicemail. When Lisa finally answered her phone toward the end of the week, she seemed depressed again. It was as if she had a brief period of happiness, being on vacation from her life, and then she was back to reality. Being alone again with her toxic parents in that filthy house again was taking a heavy toll on her spirit. Toward the end of October, she just went dark again, and wouldn't return any of my calls. I worried that something had happened to her. One afternoon when I called again, she finally answered, while on the road in the Jeep.

"Lisa, what's going on? Why haven't you answered your phone in over two weeks?" I asked.

Lisa was silent, while she was thinking up some lie to tell me. Then I heard a man's voice in the background. I reminded her that she was breaking our agreement that we made, not to let anyone else in the Jeep, which I was still paying for, other than her parents. She was obviously with a man. He was probably driving, even though he was not on the insurance. I wouldn't have minded if I wasn't paying for the car or didn't have my name on the registration and insurance. Somehow, she didn't seem to care that I was financially responsible if the Jeep was involved in an accident.

I helped her buy the Jeep for necessities like going to the doctor, to work, or to buy food. As long as I was still making the car payments and paying for the insurance, I felt I had the right to say how she used the car. I wasn't about to let Lisa get away with taking advantage of my generosity. Even though I was Lisa's friend more than her lover at this point, I didn't want that Jeep to be used to do anything illegal or have someone else driving it. I was already taking a big risk by allowing her to co-own the vehicle with me. I didn't want to increase my risk because of Lisa's irresponsible actions and bad choices.

Lisa attempted to come up with some lame excuse, as to why she was driving with someone other than her parents, but she was caught off guard, and didn't have anything believable to say. I could tell by the tone of her voice and her limited responses that she knew she had been caught doing something wrong. She also knew I was upset with her for several other reasons, including not answering her phone for several days. I had put an E-Z Pass sticker on the Jeep, so she didn't have to scramble looking for toll change. It had the added benefit of telling me exactly where and when she had gone through a toll. To some degree, it allowed me to know where she had taken the Jeep.

I was not as naive as Detective Ray when it came to dealing with Lisa. I knew what she was capable of, and I could often tell when she was lying. My love for her did not extend to becoming blind, deaf, and dumb. Once again, this demonstrated how poor her judgement was concerning the choices she made and the friends she kept. Apparently, the guy she was with is a former Green Beret soldier and lived somewhere near Vero Beach. I was certain that was where she had been, and why she didn't answer her phone. Instead of being someone who one might expect to be honorable, this guy was just another one of Lisa's low-life hook-ups, and a total loser.

One evening, while it was dark outside, Lisa said she slipped and fell on the concrete stairs of his apartment and cut and bruised her legs badly. Her friend did nothing to help her to care for her wounds, and they were left untreated for several days afterwards. She could have easily developed an infection because a couple of the abrasions were deep and not treated properly. Sometime later, Lisa said that soldier boy took the Jeep, without her permission, to go to court, while she was sleeping. He didn't even have his own means of transportation. It was hard for me to believe that a guy like this was ever allowed to put on a United States military uniform. He began blabbering, while Lisa and I were talking, in order to spew some profane threats, at which point I hung up the phone.

This incident made me determined to take the Jeep away from her. Knowing Lisa, he wasn't going to last two weeks with her anyway, so I didn't care about this stupid guy. I was certain soldier boy was in for more than he could handle with Lisa. I knew that I would outlast anyone else, because I was the only one who really cared about her. It was something that I was confident Lisa would realize eventually. I must confess that I had pushed Lisa away and terminated our romantic relationship by this time, due to her wild accusations. This brief relationship that she had formed with this man was simply a reaction to my rejection.

The problem for me was that I was liable for anything that happened, while someone else was driving that Jeep. The question was - what would be the best thing to do to protect myself, while still giving Lisa a chance to make a life for herself? There was no easy answer to this question. Lisa had really put me in a bind this time. I wasn't really surprised that she had created another mess for me to clean up. However, if Lisa was going to play this game with me, there were several things that I could do, including taking the Jeep away from her.

I could pull the insurance, at which point, the bank would contact us, and threaten to take the Jeep away. I could also stop making car payments, which would have the same effect. If Lisa was able to pick up the payments from now on, it would be better for me, but I doubted that would happen. I had a spare key to the Jeep, so if I found it, I could drive it away, and no one could stop me. However, there were downsides to pulling the payments and the insurance. Not making payments on time would hurt my credit and cancelling the insurance would expose me to liability if Lisa had an accident. Somehow, I was going to need to resolve the problem soon. I wasn't sure how just yet because the situation was complicated. I could try to take the Jeep, but the place where Lisa lived made it very difficult to get close, without being noticed. It was also hard to predict where she might be at any given time. It was really a no-win situation.

I began to realize that taking the car back was going to be a lot more complicated than I imagined. There just didn't seem to be any good options. Lisa would also be grounded again, and I didn't really want that to happen. I just wanted her to act responsibly. I had thought by age 51, she'd be more mature than she was in her twenties. Unfortunately, that wasn't the case. I had the Jeep under my control two separate times in the recent past, but I chose to give it back to her each time. My purpose in giving the car to her was so that she could get a job, move out of her parents' house, and start a new life for herself. However, Lisa had crossed the line this time, and my patience dealing with her antics was growing thin.

I needed to constantly remind myself why I was involved with her in the first place. I was trying to keep her from giving up on life and present her with an opportunity to be happy and create a better future for herself. Sometimes, it wasn't easy to stay focused on that goal. Lisa often made what I was trying to accomplish more challenging. Patience with her didn't come easy, but I knew I had to keep trying. When I agreed to help Lisa with transportation, she promised me she would get a job soon, make her car payments on time, and takeover paying for the insurance. I had confidence in her abilities and her personality, so I wasn't worried at first about her finding a job. However, Lisa's bad habits, along with her physical and mental condition were much worse than I realized in the beginning.

Lisa could have been successful doing any type of sales job, because she really had a gift for making people feel good. She seemed to be trying enthusiastically to find employment, but after a while, her energy and focus faded. I probably should have known that things weren't going to turn out the way I hoped they would. Lisa was making a mess of things, and it put me in the position of having to take care of everything for her. If I had thought it through, I probably should have bought her a used car, but I didn't want her to have expensive repair bills. I assumed that I could lease the Jeep and wouldn't have to buy it, but that didn't turn out well either.

The whole key to everything was for Lisa to find a job, and I worked very hard trying to help her find one. I asked several of my friends in Florida, including Don, to see if they could help her, but they were all skeptical about trusting her. I didn't blame them, and I was becoming frustrated with Lisa's belligerent attitude. She started being combative again, and it was wearing me down emotionally. Having a murder on your record, assault charges, drug, and alcohol use, and being unreliable, was not exactly a recipe for success. I continued to try to help Lisa anyway. I loved her, and I refused to give up trying to give her a new lease on life.

I could never quite anticipate how severe Lisa's reactions were going to be, if I did something that she perceived as pernicious. She would see trying to take the Jeep back as a betrayal. She might react aggressively, or it could cause her to become extremely depressed. I didn't want to see either of those things happen. Lisa trusted me, and that faith would be completely broken, if I took her Jeep away again. She would probably cut off our relationship entirely, and it might destroy any chance for me to continue to help her. I knew I couldn't solve the Jeep issue over the phone, which meant that I would have to go to see her again in Florida.

Several days went by, while I tried to calm down over Lisa's latest escapade. It gave me time to think about things from her perspective a bit more. Trying to get into Lisa's mind was a scary thing to attempt, but I tried very hard to understand her. I was still thinking of taking the Jeep back, but it would be necessary to speak with her face to face before I took any action. I knew that Lisa missed me, and she was hurt by the distance I was creating between us. I believed she was misbehaving because she was trying to get my attention. I admit that I was busy working and couldn't devote the kind of time Lisa needed from me.

I decided that the best thing to do was to go back down to Florida to spend more time with her. I thought perhaps that I had been too tough on her lately. What Lisa probably needed from me was to give her more attention and to be more understanding. Oftentimes, people don't need someone to solve their problems, as much as they need to feel supported and heard, without judgement. I decided to redirect my energy by treating Lisa with more patience and empathy. I knew we needed to break the cycle we were currently embroiled in. It was causing me a great deal of stress, and I wanted Lisa to have a better attitude.

I booked a flight to Orlando this time in early November, and asked Lisa to come and fetch me at the airport. As soon as I told Lisa about my plans, her whole demeanor changed. She was elated that I was coming to see her again. Sometimes Lisa couldn't articulate what she really wanted, but I should have known what she needed. She desired my love and attention, and she had been causing trouble, until I gave her what she wanted. I suppose that might be considered rewarding bad behavior, but Lisa really needed me, and I felt guilty that I couldn't stay with her for more than just a couple of weeks at a time. So, I left for the airport with my mission clearly in the front of my mind, which was to show Lisa how much I really loved her.

15. Rescue Mission

Lisa came to pick me up at the airport in Orlando, as promised. I could see the joy in her eyes and the glow on her face, as I opened the car door. She looked at me with a great big smile, and then she kissed me. Despite how upset and angry Lisa became at times, she still managed to produce an innocent, warm and cheerful expression, whenever she felt happy. It was clear that she missed me and wanted me back. I could sense her excitement that I was going to spend more time with her again. Lisa had abandonment issues, and like her little companion Kricket, she experienced separation anxiety, whenever we had to say goodbye. Lisa's full-time friend was lying in her little basket, curled up in a ball in the back seat.

"Hey baby," Lisa said cheerfully.

"Hi Vonnie, how are you?" I asked.

"I'm great because you're here," Lisa replied.

"Where are we going?" Lisa asked.

"I'll give you directions," I replied. "Hang on."

I rented a condominium at Champion's Gate, in between Orlando and Lake Wales. I wasn't sure how long I would be staying in Florida this time, which is why I took a one-way flight this time. Lisa's life was still extraordinarily complicated, and I needed to take as long as necessary, to see if I could solve more of her problems. One of my objectives for this trip was to try to see if I could help her find a job, so she could start paying for the Jeep, and move out of her parents' house. The place we were going to be staying was an apartment complex in a gated community. It had a restaurant, pool, hot-tub, and bar. It was also close to two major shopping plazas with plenty of restaurants and stores nearby. My plan was to eat and do laundry in the apartment, to save money and time. This place suited a dual purpose of providing Lisa with a safe and clean environment, where she could decompress from the constant stress that she was under at home. After we arrived and settled in, I noticed Lisa had open cuts and bruises on her legs.

"Lisa, what happened to your legs?" I asked.

"I fell down the stairs at the beach," Lisa replied.

"So why didn't you clean and dress your wounds or go to a hospital?" I asked.

"I don't know," Lisa replied.

"Those wounds are becoming infected." I said. "I gave you a first-aid kit and put it in your car. Didn't you remember that?" I asked.

"I forgot," Lisa replied.

"Well, we need to treat those wounds right away," I said. "I'm really upset that your stupid friend did nothing to take care of you. You really know how to pick men Lisa, just like your mother."

"Yeah, I know," Lisa replied. "He's a jerk."

I took the first-aid kit from the Jeep, after we put our things in the apartment. Then I spent some time cleaning and dressing the cuts on her legs. It made me angry that over a week had gone by and no one had addressed her injuries. It disturbed me that Lisa didn't seem to care what happened to her or how she was treated. She was just as guilty as anyone else for neglecting herself. It's something that she needed to be more aware of, and do something about in the near future.

Fortunately, the condominium was very nice. There were two bedrooms, a washer and dryer, a full kitchen, and a living and dining area. Lisa loved the apartment, and it made her think about having a place like it for herself. I thought this would be an ideal location for her to live because it wasn't a tourist area or overcrowded. It was only about 25 minutes from her parents' house, 15 minutes from Lake Buena Vista, and 30 minutes to commute to downtown Orlando. It was right in between lots of job opportunities, and not too far from her parents' home. The apartment was perfect for little Kricket too because she had more room to run around compared to a hotel room. Lisa took her almost everywhere, because Kricket was so portable and easy to manage. That little dog was a miracle worker when it came to keeping Lisa happy. She was the perfect misfit dog for an imperfect misfit girl.

Lisa had been used to relaxing in her pool at home in the afternoons to decompress. She called it "floaty time," because she lied on an air mattress and floated on top of the water. Normally, sitting around the house doing nothing except watching television is not particularly stressful for anyone. However, Lisa had to constantly put up with a negative environment created by both her parents each day. It was just after noon, by the time I finished cleaning Lisa's wounds. She wanted to go lie in the sun for a while by the pool, out of habit. Lisa couldn't go in the water however, because of the bandages I just put on her legs. It was going to take several days for her wounds to heal.

After Lisa had a chance to catch some sun, she couldn't resist going to the outdoor bar to have a drink. For Lisa, sucking a cocktail from a straw had the same effect as a baby's pacifier - it kept her calm when Kricket was not around to comfort her. In typical fashion, Lisa made small talk with everyone around us, including the bartender. She loved people and enjoyed being flirtatious, especially with women. I didn't mind because that was Lisa's natural character, and it never bothered me when she aroused attention to herself, because I was comfortable with how she felt about me. Lisa's friendliness was one thing that I had no interest in trying to change. When she was talking to people, she was happy. And, a happy Lisa was a calm Lisa, and a calm Lisa was much easier to deal with.

Lisa was someone who craved the limelight, and if you wanted to be with her, without driving yourself crazy, you had to accept that drawing attention to herself was part of her identity. You couldn't have a relationship with Lisa and be jealous of her flirtatiousness because you wouldn't last more than a week with her. Her approach to people was always very direct and engaging. She often spoke with a down to earth southern style, which warmed even the coldest hearts and the most rigid minds. It wasn't easy for people to take their eyes off her when she spoke to them, because she was so captivating.

Lisa's goal was to entertain and make people feel good. Most folks instantly liked her, because she had the ability to reach out and draw them in on a personal level, as if they were already close friends. However, it was really her eyes more than her words that held her audience's attention. I watched people whenever she engaged them in conversation, and their eyes never moved from her face. Lisa's stare was both penetrating and hypnotic. It was next to impossible not to be drawn in by her charms and sexual charisma.

This wasn't a pleasure trip for me. Lisa and I had a lot of work to do. When it was time for me to leave for home, I wanted to have completed several tasks, to improve her circumstances. One of the things I wanted to do was to put a resume together for her. I also wanted to visit some businesses in the Lake Wales/Winter Haven area, who were hiring. It would be good for Lisa to start working again, so she could earn some money and get out of the house. It would also allow her to interact with new people and make some better friends.

After we left the bar, Lisa and I went to work trying to piece her job history together. It wasn't easy because she never made a resume before, and we had to start from scratch. Despite this obstacle, Lisa did surprisingly well, helping me to finish it in just a couple of hours. She had a hard time remembering some dates, supervisors' names, and some details at first but overall, she did an excellent job. I was proud of Lisa for her effort. I assumed she would become frustrated or bored easily, but she stuck with it, until we finished. Now, she had something she could use when she applied for jobs.

Lisa was a highly intelligent woman, despite her lack of formal education. Doing a resume using a laptop wasn't exactly her forte. She was more comfortable applying for jobs by showing up in person and talking to the hiring manager. However, that's not how things are done anymore. At Disney for example, you must apply online - no one will talk to you otherwise. Most often, managers want to see a resume and a cover letter. If you don't have them, you aren't likely to be interviewed for a job. Lisa's obsolete approach was not going to be effective in most cases. If Lisa could get an interview, I was confident that most managers would like her enough to want to give her a job.

However, her biggest challenge was maneuvering around her criminal record, which followed her throughout her life. If she was offered a position, keeping her job might become something of a struggle. Over the years, Lisa had developed several bad habits, which could cause her to be fired. Drinking during the day was one of them and showing up on time was another. It also wasn't easy to predict if Lisa would have another meltdown, while at work. I sympathized with Lisa's frustration seeking employment.

I suggested to her to think about starting out doing volunteer work at an animal park, because it might help get her foot in the door. She told me she never thought of applying for work at a nature preserve or zoo, which was strange to me, because it's an obvious choice. Lisa didn't understand that having experience interacting with exotic wild animals was a unique skill. When we were finished with our work, she said felt tired and needed a nap. Finishing her resume was a little stressful for her, so I let her sleep for about an hour before waking her up for dinner.

Later that evening, we had a quiet meal at a nice Italian restaurant within the complex. I told Lisa it was a reward for her effort on her resume. I can't remember what we ordered, but I remember enjoying dinner very much because of the company. I wanted to give Lisa a pleasant evening, before we had to wake up the next morning and start looking for jobs. Lisa wasn't normally much of a wine drinker, but I tried to introduce her to some fine wines, hoping she would substitute it for vodka. I didn't want her to drink at all, but le vin rouge was an improvement over hard liquor. I was learning that Lisa needed to take baby steps, if she was ever going to make any progress. After dinner, we went back to the apartment to relax and take Kricket for a walk. Lisa was in a very good mood by the time we prepared to go to sleep. Having a peaceful day was not something that she experienced very often in her life. I was glad to be able to give her the opportunity to feel relaxed and happy for a change.

I think Lisa's life must have been a bit like Michael Jackson's, because they were both performing and touring, by the time they were only about six or seven years old. They didn't have many friends their age, nor did they have much playtime, because they spent their days rehearsing or on stage in front of an audience. Their lives were all about work and no play. When we think about entertainers' lives, we mainly focus on the glitz and glamour of show business. We don't often consider how much work goes into preparing for a show. Few people can imagine the sacrifices entertainers make every day of their lives. I know from my own show experience, being an entertainer is a very hard life, and it's filled with loneliness and isolation. When you mix in child sexual abuse, with the number of hours of rehearsal time, it's not a life you would wish on your worst enemy. However, Lisa endured everything in her life with a smile, and never let on how much suffering her life caused her.

Before bedtime, Lisa had to adjust her false teeth she wore after her accident. This was another source of discomfort and embarrassment for her. It was also a reminder to me of how much pain Lisa had to sustain during her miserable life. I told myself that I needed to try to be more patient and understanding with her, for that reason alone. Watching Lisa struggle brought me back to the reality of how badly damaged she had become, physically and emotionally. I really felt sorry for her, and I didn't want to do anything to add to her misery.

Almost everyone, who knew I was helping Lisa, didn't understand why I was spending so much of my time, money, and energy on her. However, when I looked at Lisa's face, and saw the anguish and desperation in her eyes, I knew exactly why I was trying to help her. I loved her and I didn't care what anyone else thought about it. I was willing to do anything in my power for her, including trading my life for hers.

When Lisa and I woke up the next morning, it seemed like she had a good night's sleep. She appeared to be in a good mood and asked me what I wanted for breakfast. Lisa made eggs because she knew Kricket loved to eat them. After breakfast, we dressed and went out to make copies of her resume. I planned to drive around to see how many places we could find that were hiring. It wasn't what Lisa preferred to do; however, she did show some enthusiasm about working again. She also seemed to be a lot more motivated to do things for herself because I was with her. The difficulty would come later, when she needed to follow-up on the jobs she applied for, after I left.

"Okay Lisa, you and I are going job hunting today," I said.

"Okay, okay!" Lisa replied using her funny voice. "Give me just one minute."

Lisa hurried to finish dressing and putting on her makeup. Armed with her new resume, I hoped we could make some progress finding a job. We went to several places in town - any place that seemed to be hiring. I let Lisa go in by herself to different stores, while I waited in the Jeep. She mentioned to me that she also wanted to apply to be a school bus driver. However, I didn't think she could stop drinking during the day, long enough to ensure children would be safe driving with her. Lisa was a skilled driver, but she was also an alcoholic, who couldn't stop drinking. I didn't want to discourage her, but I figured that driving a school bus wasn't likely to be the right job for her future.

I didn't understand why the police didn't charge Lisa with DUI, when she went to pick up the Jeep back in July. She could be extremely persuasive, so I assumed that's how she dodged having her license suspended. Unfortunately, I had to pay both of her fines, because she didn't escape receiving tickets for her offenses. If the tickets weren't paid, her license would have been revoked. Lisa told me she had taken sleeping pills by mistake and hadn't been drinking that morning. Her excuse was probably another one of her lies, but I couldn't prove it, so I had to give her the benefit of the doubt. It was possible that Lisa did take sleeping pills that day by accident, but I knew that Lisa usually drank every morning, when she woke up.

Lisa often lied about the smallest things sometimes and was honest about major events. However, it was hard to know when she was telling the truth and when she was lying, because her life was so unconventional. Her reality was so shocking, that most people would think the stories pertaining to her life were untrue - like the murder and child molestation. If I hadn't read the article in the newspaper, about her being responsible for the death of her stepfather, I never would have believed it. Lisa often fabricated the truth when she was under an immediate threat, or if she needed money for drugs or alcohol. Sadly, most of what she relayed about her life had a strong foundation in a dark reality. Lisa didn't realize if she only told me the truth, I would do my best to meet her needs, unless it had to do with something harmful or illegal.

Lisa and I spent the next few days running around town meeting with employers and handing out her resume. She really seemed liked she felt excited to work again. However, I started to see how easily tired Lisa became during the day. She needed to take several breaks and a nap, during the middle of the afternoon. Some of the reasons she became so fatigued were due to her weight and her afternoon alcohol habit. It was going to be a tough challenge for Lisa to stop drinking, especially if she felt stressed at work. Some of the drugs Lisa's doctor prescribed were also a factor concerning her energy and stamina. Her ability to work an eight-hour shift was in serious question. Despite these obstacles, we didn't give up the job search. I was very proud of her for making such a formidable effort.

I also wanted to update Lisa's membership at her gym that she joined recently. I hoped to find out if there were any classes that might be fun for her to take. Hopefully, she would enjoy herself, while trying to get back in shape. When we arrived, we met with the manager to pay off Lisa's current balance. He introduced us to one of the female trainers, who talked to her about some classes she was instructing. Not surprisingly, Lisa made an instant connection with her, and she appeared excited about the prospect of taking her classes. I thought this would be a great opportunity for her to meet new people, who would have a more positive and healthy influence on her life. After we finished our business at the gym, we headed back to the apartment.

When we arrived back at the apartment, Lisa needed to take a nap before dinner, but not before having another drink first. She said to me that she was grateful for all the time I was willing to spend helping her. Lisa also told me she'd probably be dead already, if not for my involvement in her life. After decades of abuse and neglect, it surprised me too that she was still alive. Lisa almost died several times over the years we were apart, but still managed to survive, so I'm not sure I deserved the compliment.

Lisa almost lost her life a minimum of five times. She almost broke her neck, after falling 10 feet in the air from the trapeze. Another time, she faced the death penalty for first degree murder. She almost died when she drove her 18-wheeler over an 80-foot embankment. She also experienced liver failure and expected to die alone in Hospice. She even tried to kill herself, by slitting her wrists, but fortunately she survived that experience as well.

In an indirect way, I felt partially responsible for what happened to Lisa after we broke-up. If I hadn't left her at a young age, there may have been a chance to keep her out of trouble and free from prison. I might have even been able to help her with her drug and alcohol addiction. There were many things I might have been able to do to make Lisa's life better, if I had only stayed with her, after we were engaged. The reason came down to the fact that I never gave her a chance to explain herself that night outside of the bar in Winter Haven. I simply asked for the engagement ring back and allowed her to walk out of my life. If we had stayed together, I might have been able to redirect the course of her life.

However, Lisa didn't always listen to my advice, but she did have a strong desire to please the people she loved. Since she loved me, she may have had a strong incentive to reboot her life, after we first met. It's hard to say for sure what would have happened. If I didn't have the power to change certain things concerning her fate, at least I could have been there to support her and give her encouragement. Lisa was not someone who could be controlled or tamed. She was as wild as the animals she worked with in the circus.

By age 23, Lisa had already formed many bad habits and several bad relationships, and they would have been hard to break. A number of those vices were cultivated, while trying to escape from her past. To deal effectively with her demons, Lisa needed professional counseling and medication, but she never received or accepted any aid. She really required a lot more assistance than I could offer her alone. I felt overwhelmed with the responsibility of trying to care for her, but I did my best.

Perhaps I felt guilt more than love - I'm not certain. Whatever it was, it motivated me to try to continue to help Lisa put her life back together again. In any case, I wasn't going to give up, even if it meant losing everything. I wasn't blind to the fact that helping Lisa was tearing my life apart, but it didn't matter to me. I cared more about saving her than anything else, and no one was going to stop me from trying - not even Lisa.

The following day, I took Lisa to see her doctor. I tried to impress upon him just how much she needed to see a psychiatrist. He had already been treating her for pain and anxiety, but he wasn't addressing Lisa's mental illness, her alcoholism, or her weight issues. Even though Lisa had been seeing this doctor for several years, it was unclear to me that he understood the nature of all her problems.

I had only been back in Lisa's life for about five or six months, and I already knew just about everything that was happening with her. Compared to her physician, I spent a lot more than 20 minutes with her each month, but I thought he should have been more aware of Lisa's mental illness. Unfortunately, he seemed to have very little clue and didn't know a thing about her sordid past. Lisa had also been seeing another medical professional named Donna. She and Lisa had formed a close friendship and spent time outside the office together. Donna should have known that Lisa needed more help, and tried harder to convince her to stop drinking, and seek psychiatric help. If she did, she was unsuccessful.

One of the reasons Lisa was seeing this primary care physician was because he was one of the few doctors nearby, who could prescribe opioids. I had a feeling she might have deliberately chosen to see him for that reason. Since Lisa was a drug addict, prescribing an addictive medication for her was probably a very bad thing to do. She had used cocaine, heroin, and any number of other drugs imaginable. It was going to be challenging for her to stop taking these addictive medications. Using opioids with a large quantity of alcohol can be deadly. I constantly reminded Lisa about this fact, but she didn't seem to care, and ignored my warnings. Lisa's doctor attempted to slowly take her off the painkillers he had prescribed. However, he gave her another addictive pain medicine, which if combined with alcohol, could be fatal.

The word painkiller is an appropriate name for what opioids can do to someone, especially an addict like Lisa. I asked her doctor if she could have an operation for her back, instead of having to take opioids indefinitely. I was disappointed that I didn't receive a satisfying answer to my question. It might have had to do with the fact that Lisa had no health insurance. Even if Lisa had been on 'Obamacare,' it was still going to cost her more than she or I could afford to obtain basic coverage. Lisa had suffered traumatic injuries during her trucking accident in Kansas. Her condition was so severe at the time, that she should have died from her injuries.

I didn't know what the best treatment for Lisa's pain should be at this point, but I didn't think opioids were the best solution. Instead, she needed to see an orthopedic surgeon. Unfortunately, Lisa was only being given addictive pills, which were doing nothing for her overall health and wellness. I also wanted Lisa to see a psychiatrist. However, whenever she went to see her primary care physician, she may have been putting on an act, so he may not have been aware of her emotional troubles. Perhaps, she didn't trust him enough to disclose all her problems to him, or she may have feared he might have institutionalized her - I didn't know the answer.

In any case, Lisa wasn't being treated well enough. If she had been more open, her doctor might have been able to help her better. However, she wasn't even truthful about the amount of alcohol she was consuming every day when she was asked. Doctors can't help you if you're not honest with them, or don't do what they tell you. I believed Lisa's physician cared about her, but he couldn't address her most pressing needs.

Time may have also been a factor, in terms of how much care Lisa received. Medical professionals usually spend only about 15 minutes with their patients, and then charge them around $300 dollars per hour for the visit. Lisa's doctor visits cost $125 dollars each month, out of pocket. That's about $1,500 dollars per year, for someone on welfare. Physicians are often preconditioned to run their practices like a business, instead of taking more time with each patient, to give them the best care. It's just how our system works, unfortunately. I experience the same thing when I see my doctors. I usually ask lots of questions, which forces them to spend a little more time with me. Patients need to come to their appointments armed with questions and should be prepared to give their doctors more information about themselves.

Before Lisa's visit ended, I felt reassured that her primary care doctor understood more about what Lisa had been going through. He gave me a list of therapists and rehabilitation centers to peruse. Lisa's drug abuse over many years was directly related to trying to self-medicate, in a failed attempt to forget her stepfather's abuse. She obviously did it to distract herself from all her painful memories. I was hoping that my support and encouragement would motivate her enough to try to put her life back together again - at least to the point where it became manageable and less stressful. I wanted Lisa to realize some level of happiness in her life, without all the daily drama. Perhaps it was just too late to bring about significant change.

I know I should have offered my help to Lisa in the past, instead of running away from her. I may have acted differently if I had known about her history sooner. I should have never abandoned her, and I regret that I did. I was painfully aware that Lisa was struggling in the present and holding onto her life and sanity by only a thread. She was overwhelmed, exhausted, and feeling defeated. Lisa put a lot of faith in me, but it seemed like she didn't believe anyone could help her at this point in her life. Ironically, she managed to be the biggest obstacle to giving herself the help she needed. Lisa refused to go to a rehabilitation center or make an appointment with a psychiatrist. She didn't trust doctors, and she had a deep fear of being institutionalized, without having the ability to stay in contact with people on the outside.

I had an impossible task ahead of me, but I wasn't about to give up without a fight. Caring for Lisa was a heavy burden, but if I didn't, no one else was willing to help her. It was probably Lisa's last chance to have a sustainable future. Her mother and stepfather only made matters worse, because of their own drug and alcohol abuse and the way they treated her. Their own intoxication contributed to the continual verbal abuse Lisa had to endure at home. I wished I had been able to have Lisa stay with me instead, but unfortunately, it wasn't possible. The best I could do was to spend time with her for a couple of weeks at a time and talk to her each day. I was doing everything I could think of to help Lisa have a more stable, peaceful, and healthy life, but nothing I did seemed to make a big enough impact.

Lisa kept telling me that she wanted to feel better, but her addictive habits seemed like they were never going to end, and she continued to refuse professional help. She didn't seem to want to stop drinking entirely, but she appeared to be trying very hard to cut down on the amount of hard liquor she drank during the day. I think she mainly wanted to be healthier for me, if for no other reason. Lisa often told everyone she was doing fine when her life was a complete mess. She could never relax, due to her parents' behavior and attitude. Her stepfather would often threaten to kick her out of the house, and she would call me crying after their fights. It broke my heart that I couldn't do more to help this desperate woman who I loved so much.

Lisa's life was nothing less than Hell on earth for most of her life. She might have been better off in prison. This was one of the reasons that I put up with so much trouble from her. Whatever difficulties I was going through with Lisa - she had it 100 times worse every day of her life. This was the woman, who at one time, I thought I wanted to be together with my entire life. Sadly, that dream was shattered, due to poor communication and a false impression. I abandoned my greatest lover, after one night of sheer stupidity.

Dealing with Lisa's stressful behavior in the present was insignificant penance to pay for the sins of my past. She deserved a better life - one that I should have given to her. Lisa French was really the most wonderful woman I had ever met in my life, and I was a fool to have let her go, without a fight. I believe I realized it at the time, but it only sank into my brain decades later. My goal at this point was to try to give Lisa back the life her parents stole from her, and the life I should have provided for her. However, I feared I had waited far too long to act on her behalf. I began to realize that I was fighting a losing battle and trying to relive a dream that I might never see come true. Lavonne's spirit had drifted out to sea, and I was drowning trying to chase it.

16. A Shocking Discovery

After Lisa's doctor appointment, she and I stopped by her house on the Lake to feed her parents' horse. The poor animal had been neglected and suffered from an open wound on its back. For three people with minimal cash flow, I found it interesting that they were living on 10 acres of prime real estate and could afford to own a horse. The view of the lake is extremely beautiful, especially during sunrise and sunset hours. It was a shame it was wasted on Lisa's parents.

A large part of Lisa's life was spent living in a trailer, but when she split with her husband, she acquired an option to buy land from her divorce settlement. However, her parents swindled the land from her, after she went back to prison, due to a fight between her and her ex-husband. After Lisa gave her parents power of attorney, they seized the opportunity to build a house on the land next to Lake Buffum and didn't put any of the property in Lisa's name. It didn't take long before they completely trashed the house and the property around it. It was shameful that this beautiful location was treated so badly and turned into a garbage dump.

While we were at the house, Lisa rummaged through a dresser in her bedroom and came across some baby pictures of her daughter.

"Look Alex, here's a picture of Joy!" Lisa said excitedly.

When I looked at the photos, I was stunned by what I saw. Lisa's little girl looked a lot like me when I was two or three years old. I was overwhelmed with emotion at the possibility that Lisa's little girl might be mine as well. She had these photographs of her daughter because the adoptive family agreed to send Lisa pictures and letters periodically. Unfortunately, she didn't have the letters handy to show me.

"Vonnie, your daughter looks an awful lot like I did when I was that age," I said.

"Really," Lisa replied.

"Yes, definitely," I said. "When I found out that you had given birth to a baby, I counted back the number of months since we had been together."

"How long had it been?" Lisa asked.

"It was approximately nine and a half to ten months," I replied. "Since you were with Rob right after me, I dismissed the notion that Joy was my child, and assumed she was his instead. Now that I'm looking at a photograph of your daughter, I think she could be mine."

"No way!" Lisa exclaimed.

"Yes way," I replied.

Lisa's eyes lit up and her face became flushed. Discovering that her baby could be ours 28 years later, seemed to make her surprisingly pleased.

"It never occurred to me that Joy might be your baby," Lisa said. "Rob and I never slept together. When my mom's boyfriend raped me and I got pregnant, I just assumed it was his. That happened soon after Rob and I broke up, which was not long after you and I were together for the last time."

"Well, do you think your child looks like your mom's boyfriend?" I asked.

"No, not at all," Lisa replied.

"Oh my God Alex, I think I had your baby!" Lisa exclaimed.

Lisa appeared to be very excited about the possibility that I could be her daughter's father. However, I wasn't convinced she was telling me the truth about Rob. I had an opportunity a few months later to contact him, so I could verify Lisa's story. He confirmed what she had told me saying he and Lisa were never intimate. Rob said he was certain that Joy wasn't his child.

"Did you have sex with any other guy during that time period?" I asked.

"No Alex, only my mom's boyfriend," Lisa replied.

"I suppose Carmen denies knowing about that too?" I asked.

"Of course, what do you expect from her?" Lisa replied.

At this time, I didn't recall reading that Lisa had been arrested at a boyfriend's place in Florida in 1991. The article from the Tampa Tribune didn't reveal his name, but I'm sure it wasn't Rob. Narrowing it down in the present, Lisa's daughter is most likely mine or this other ex-boyfriend's child. I was in shock over this new revelation. An array of emotions swirled through my head. If Joy was indeed our child, this would be something that connected our past to our present, and Joy would be a living product of our love. Still, I couldn't be sure I was her father, without finding Joy/Megan and taking DNA tests.

"You know Alex, everyone including my mother encouraged me to get an abortion," Lisa said. "I felt like I was being manipulated on all sides to do something that I didn't want to do. When I went to a clinic to have it done, suddenly I couldn't do it. So, I got the hell out of there, as fast as I could run. It was the best decision I ever made in my life. Now, I'm even happier knowing that Joy might be yours too."

"When I was ready for my baby to be born, I was taken out of prison in handcuffs and shackles to a hospital in Bartow," Lisa said. The police didn't even allow me to remove my restraints during the delivery. It was inhumane what the police forced me to do. I was crying most of the time, while I was in the delivery room. There was no one there to hold my hand or comfort me - not my mother, not any friends, and no boyfriend. No one was allowed to be in the room with me, except the doctor and nurses."

"Prior to the delivery, I was forced to sign adoption papers, promising to give Joy away," Lisa explained. "I begged my mom to take Joy before she was born, but she refused. I had to give up my first child because I was potentially facing the death penalty. Short of that happening, I was certain to go to prison for a long time. Mom just didn't want to raise another child. I don't think she really wanted to take care of me either. She's been more like a jealous older sister than a mother to me. I will never forgive her for making me give up my daughter. I was only 24 years old at the time; and it was such an emotional time for me. I was in Hell Alex, and I wanted to die!"

"After Joy was born, I pleaded with one of the nurses to hold my baby for just a few minutes," Lisa continued. "She felt sorry for me and gave Joy to me to hold for a little while. As I held my child in my arms and looked into her eyes, I told her that I loved her and promised she would never have to experience the kind of misery I had endured in my lifetime. Then I kissed her and said goodbye to her forever. It was the hardest thing I ever had to do."

I could see tears forming in Lisa's eyes, as she was telling me her heartbreaking story.

Finally, there was a moment of compassion from someone. It was a moment of pure joy, which was the reason Lisa decided to give that name to her child. Lisa wished her baby would have a better life than the one she had known growing up. She also prayed that her child would be loved in a way she had never experienced in her life.

It's unfortunate that journalists, who have attempted to write about Lisa's character, didn't know the first thing about her. Lisa had a heart of gold, and only wanted to love and to be loved. Instead, she was maligned by the press, and treated worse than a junkyard dog by almost everyone around her. Lisa had to constantly defend herself simply to survive, because there was no one else to protect her. I should have been the one to take on that role, but I was a coward in my youth.

"Vonnie, I'm very sorry that I wasn't there for you when you needed me," I said.

"It's okay Alex, but now we have to find Joy," Lisa replied.

"I agree," I said. "I want to try."

However, Lisa and I never took the opportunity to find Joy together during this visit, unfortunately. In hindsight, I wish I had gone to the adoption agency with Lisa the next day. At the time, I didn't consider it to be an urgent priority. Although Lisa and I wanted to find Joy/Megan, I wanted to accomplish other things first, which I felt were more important. At this time in November of 2018, Megan would have been 27 years old, since she was born in February of 1991. I hoped that searching for our child together might give Lisa a sense of purpose, and something she could look forward to doing soon. Discovering the truth about Joy was something I wanted to pursue also.

Several months later, I called the Catholic Charities adoption services in Lakeland Florida, but they refused to help me in any way.

They said they would record the information I gave them, but I was told they had no intention of contacting Joy's adoptive family. I would have been glad to provide any proof, including taking a DNA or blood test, but the woman I spoke to at the agency would not consider any type of assistance to help me find out if Joy was truly my daughter. They wouldn't even give the adoptive family an opportunity to make their own decision about whether they wanted to speak with me.

I believe that all adopted children have the right to know who their biological parents are. It's unconscionable to me that a Christian organization would choose to make no effort to be certain who is the true father of this child. That's the hypocrisy of many religious institutions, which have a long history of corruption and cover-ups. In New York State, the Governor recently opened all adoption records, and I was finally able to verify my own birth parents. Finding this information meant a great deal to me; and I will forever be grateful that I finally know my parents' names, as well as my own birth name. Unfortunately, I still don't know if Joy/Megan is my daughter, or how I can find her.

The main reason I went to Florida this time was to talk to Lisa about the Jeep, and to help her find a job. I tried to keep that in mind, while I was spending time with her. I really wanted to find out if I was Joy's father, but that wasn't my main priority. Perhaps, it should have been. It would be at least a couple of months before I would have another chance to see Lisa again, and I still needed to accomplish several things on my checklist before I departed. Lisa was still in a precarious position, and I wanted to help her achieve greater stability. So, I tried not to become side-tracked going on a wild goose chase.

I especially wanted Lisa to start feeling better. Her health and happiness were more important than anything else to me. However, keeping Lisa happy was an exhausting full-time job. I was really enjoying spending time with her again - she could be addictive. I wish I could have stayed with her permanently - it was something that I really wanted to do. My reasons for being in contact with Lisa were never exclusively about helping her. I loved her and I loved spending time with her. I was sincerely hoping that we might have a future together, since our past had been spoiled.

I was careful not to talk about the past too much at this time, because I feared Lisa's mind might still be very fragile. I wanted to ask her questions about the murder, her circus life, living in Chicago, and even about the rapes she endured as a child. However, I didn't think this was the right time to go into all of that. I could see how sensitive and delicate her mind had become, so I kept my curiosity at bay. I still wanted to pursue talking about her past, but only after she began therapy, and was under the care of a psychiatrist. Triggering old painful memories could push Lisa over the edge, and I wanted to avoid that happening at all costs. Instead, I tried to concentrate on Lisa's future, hoping I could make a difference in turning her life around. It might have been wishful-thinking or arrogance, believing that after 51 years on this earth, I could change her life. In any case, I was never going to give up trying. I felt like I owed it to Lisa to do whatever I could to make her life better. I loved her, and I couldn't bear to see Lisa suffer anymore. I was determined to improve her life, even if it killed me.

17. Letting Loose

Time was running out at the condo I reserved for the week, and I couldn't extend our stay there any longer, so I had to find another place for us to crash. I still hadn't accomplished everything that I wanted to on this trip yet. I managed to book another apartment suite, not far from where we had been staying. It was a little on the small side, compared to the last one, but it had everything we needed, including a kitchen.

This complex had an outdoor Karaoke bar, a pool, and a nice lake. It was going to be our new home base for the next few days. We had a little trouble at first getting Kricket approved to stay with us, until I showed the hotel manager a letter from Lisa's doctor, saying that she was an emotional support dog. One evening, they were going to be doing Karaoke and Lisa said she wanted to sing. I thought that would be a great thing to do, because it would help her to relax and put her in a good mood. We would both have fun together, and it would end my visit on a high note.

We left Kricket in the room that night and arrived a little after it started around 9:15 pm. Lisa's first move was to order a frozen margarita from the bar. We found a table and sat down to listen to the amateur acts on stage. I told Lisa that she better put her name on the list if she wanted to sing, which she did without hesitation. I can't remember the name of the song she chose, but it was some bluesy, country western song. Lisa could hardly wait to stand up in front of the audience and perform. I was anxious to hear her sing because she had never sung anything for me in the past. I was very curious to see whether she had talent as a vocalist.

"You want to sing too?" the DJ asked me.

"No thanks, I don't want to embarrass myself," I replied. "I'm not a singer - I'm an ice skater."

"Well, the only ice here is at the bar," the DJ replied.

When it was Lisa's turn, she put the microphone in her hand, while smiling enthusiastically. She was a natural performer, even though her core training was in the circus. However, I was about to learn that Lisa was more than just a talented trapeze artist. I knew that she loved an audience of any type, and a karaoke crowd at a bar was no exception. Lisa instinctively knew how to grab people's attention by the way she moved, along with her eye contact and sexual energy. She was really something to watch, as she began to belt out the lyrics like a pro. I was pleasantly surprised at how well Lisa could sing, demonstrating a remarkable range with her pitch. She received a big round of applause from the audience when she finished, which brought a glowing smile to her face. I could see Lisa was very pleased with herself, as she absorbed the energy from her new fans. The warm reception ignited her spirit and thirst for acclamation.

Lisa's demonstration made me realize that I didn't know her in the past, as well as I should have when we were both young. Spending so much time with her in the present made me appreciate just how many layers there were to this multi-talented woman. I couldn't understand why she didn't stick with performing during her life, instead of driving trucks. From an entertainment perspective, there seemed to be very little Lisa couldn't do. She could dance, sing, perform acrobatics, act, and mimic voices and foreign accents. She was amazingly talented, not to mention stunningly beautiful in her prime. Hollywood missed-out on a star. It's a shame that most people close to Lisa only wanted to take advantage of her, instead of helping her realize her potential. Perhaps they couldn't see all her natural gifts - I certainly missed many of them too. Lisa's parents seem to care very little about developing her career, unless it benefitted them. Giving children opportunities is what parents should do, not exploit them for personal gain.

"That was incredible Vonnie!" I said to her, as she sat down next to me.

"Thanks baby." Lisa replied, as she grabbed her drink with a smile.

I could see by the look on her face how satisfied Lisa was with herself. A young man stood up next to sing. He had just turned 21 and was having a birthday celebration. He turned out to be an extraordinarily good singer as well. It suddenly occurred to me that he and Lisa would be amazing singing together. So, I walked up to the guy after he finished singing and asked him if he would like to do a duet with Lisa.

"I enjoyed your performance," I said to him.

"How would you like to sing another song with my friend Lisa?" I asked.

"Sure, why not, that would be fun," he replied.

"Great, I will introduce you," I said.

I introduced him to Lisa, and we all went over to the DJ to request another song they could both sing together. They chose 'You're the One that I Want' by John Travolta and Olivia Newton John, from the movie 'Grease.' I thought to myself that their song choice might not be the right style for Lisa, because she seemed to be more of a country-blues singer. Her tone of voice sounded low and raspy, so I couldn't imagine her singing a pop song soprano.

"Lisa are you sure you can sing in a high key?" I asked.

"Don't worry babe; I can sing anything," Lisa replied.

I didn't have Lisa's confidence that she could sing in a completely different style and pitch, but it was her choice. I thought I should wait to hear her first before passing judgement. Several more acts finished before it was their turn to sing. Apparently, their performance was going to close the show. When the DJ announced their names, Lisa sprang up from her seat like a jack-in-the-box, and sprinted to the stage, mimicking a racehorse after the gates are opened. She was so excited to get back in front of the audience again, that she tripped, as she rose from her seat. From a distance, I could see the enthusiasm in her eyes, as she squeezed the microphone in her hand. I think if the DJ had given her the opportunity, she would have sung all night long. I could tell that Lisa didn't have another thought on her mind, other than performing. It made her forget about everything that was wrong with her life, if only for a few precious moments.

As the young man began to sing, he turned to face Lisa to play the part of Danny. This guy was extremely talented, and very good looking. He was tall, blonde with blue eyes, and had an athlete's body. He sang better than John Travolta, even though he is known better for his dancing ability. Then it was Lisa's turn to portray Sandy. Lisa sounded amazing and hit the high notes effortlessly! If she had gone to school, she could have made the lead in all the musicals. Perhaps, she could have even had a professional acting or singing career. I was extremely impressed with their performance - they both sounded like professionals. If you had heard them sing, you might believe they had been performing together for a long time, by the way they were taking cues from one another. Lisa was singing beautifully in a completely different style. I was so impressed with her versatility and range. It was such a shame Lisa's talents had been misdirected and underdeveloped for so many years.

Lisa was in her element when she was on stage. No one could ever guess this was the same woman who had been through so much pain and suffering in her life. Tonight, Lisa's flame was burning brightly, and she had only one thought in her head - playing to her audience. It was not only a sight to see, but it was also good therapy, and better medicine than any doctor could have prescribed for her. Lisa seemed so happy for a change and watching her perform almost made me cry. At this moment, nothing else mattered to her or to me.

Entertaining was just in Lisa's blood, and it showed. I was extremely proud of her, and I felt so pleased to see her smile. I couldn't help but sit back and enjoy the experience, because I didn't know when something like this would present itself again. On stage was the woman who I knew and loved so intimately with all my heart and soul. It had been almost 30 years since we split apart. Being together again felt like a dream - a dream I never wanted to end.

Their performance ended in enthusiastic applause and whistles from the crowd. I hadn't seen Lisa look so elated in such a long time. She seemed grateful for the audience's reaction, and she instinctively took a bow, along with her new friend. Their smiles lit up the shadowy stage, as the crowd kept applauding. When the cheers finally subsided, Lisa returned to our table. She hugged and kissed me and thanked me for encouraging her to sing.

"Thanks for knowing what I needed babe," Lisa said. "You're my hero!"

Those words were something Lisa said to me occasionally, and I felt appreciated when she complimented me in that way. It made my efforts seem like they were worthwhile. Ironically, in my mind, Lisa was my hero. This demonstrated how Lisa and I felt about one another. She and I have always had mutual respect and admiration for each other, which was the foundation upon which our love developed, and became stronger in the future.

Lisa had one final drink before we left the scene. We both felt a great sense of satisfaction and joy from the evening's festivities. Our spirits had become entwined in a way they hadn't been, since we were very young. Lisa put her arm around me and smiled, as we strolled back to the room together in unison. When Lisa and I were in harmony, no couple on the planet fit together more perfectly. This was one of the best times I spent with her, since we reunited. It took me back in time to when we were intensely in love in our youth.

Lisa felt so tired after all the excitement, that she fell asleep almost immediately. I felt so proud of her, as I watched her lie quietly at peace with her eyes closed. I wished she would have sweet dreams and wake up in the morning feeling as good as when she went to bed.

Trying to help Lisa was always so stressful, because her life turned out to be such a mess. Some days, I didn't know where to begin while attempting to fix all her broken parts. It made me realize that if it was challenging for me to be part of Lisa's life, it must be daunting for her to live it. No matter how much time I spent with her, or how much we accomplished during each week, there never seemed to be enough time to do everything she needed. It often felt like I was trying to take apart and rebuild her entire life in two weeks.

Overall, Lisa had been very cooperative and generally happy, while we were together this trip. However, things seemed to go downhill a little when Lisa started to think about me leaving again. Lisa had Kricket for emotional support, but she needed more than her four-legged friend to keep her happy. Unfortunately, I couldn't make a full-time job out of caring for Lisa. I had to go home and get some of my own work done. For me to help Lisa consistently, I would have to move to Florida. It was in the back of my mind, but it was not something I was ready to consider immediately. It would be very complicated, and I wasn't sure that it would help as much as I imagined. Perhaps I should have thought about this option more seriously, but I wasn't prepared to take that big of a risk - at least not yet.

I thought about bringing Lisa to North Carolina to live near me, but she still needed a job. Though it would have kept Lisa away from her parents, I wasn't convinced that having her move to North Carolina was the best solution. My current plan was to keep trying to help Lisa secure a job in Florida, so that she could live where her support system had been for most of her life. Unfortunately, Lisa's circle of friends and family were often the cause of many of her problems. The best I could do was to continue to try to support her as much as possible and talk to her every day.

When it was time for me to go home, Lisa dropped me back to the airport in Orlando. Before I exited the Jeep, I looked into Lisa's eyes, held her hands and kissed her to tell her goodbye. Tears were already forming in her eyes and running down her cheeks.

"I'll try to come back for Christmas or New Year's Eve, okay Vonnie," I said.

Lisa looked at me with her sad blue eyes; she put her arms around my neck and kissed me again.

"Okay baby, I love you!" Lisa replied. "Thanks for everything. I'm going to really miss you!"

"I love you too Vonnie," I said. "Try to take better care of yourself, okay baby."

"I'll try," Lisa replied. "I promise."

Lisa kissed me again and hugged me tightly with tremendous emotion. Then, I walked toward the terminal door. I turned around just long enough to see her blow me a kiss goodbye, as I watched her drive away. It was going to feel like a long plane ride home, even though it was only a two-hour flight. Every time Lisa and I had to go our separate ways, I felt sad too because I wondered whether I was going to see her again.

I couldn't predict what might happen to her in the future. The only thing I could be sure of was to expect plenty of surprises and drama. It made things seem even worse knowing the circumstances Lisa had to return to, without me. I felt guilty for having to leave her again. Even though I told her I would return soon, I think she still experienced a sense of abandonment. I was the only one who truly loved and cared for her. Now, Lisa was going to be alone again with her pain. I had to live with knowing about the despair and desperation she was feeling, while not being able to do much about it.

As the plane took off, I closed my eyes and prayed that God would watch over her.

18. Separation Anxiety

Once I had returned home, Lisa reengaged into her survival mode, and didn't call me back again for several days. She was obviously disturbed by my absence, after spending so much time with me recently. This was becoming a pattern whenever I left her. Lisa might have developed this habit in prison, while she was cut-off from the outside world. I thought to myself that I might be making matters worse rather than better, because she was becoming dependent on me for almost everything. When I wasn't there by her side, it was hard for her to cope with her life on her own. I finally heard from her almost a week later, but her attitude was combative and defensive.

I initially told Lisa that I would try to spend Christmas or New Years with her, but she was becoming so belligerent and nasty on the phone, that I decided not to go back down to Florida during the Holidays. I figured that her attitude was poor because she was unhappy that I left her again. Lisa knew that I needed to go, but that didn't make her feel any better. She was like a child who needed constant attention. I didn't blame her for how she felt, but I didn't want to reward her for behaving badly toward me either. Choosing not to see Lisa at Christmas time was a tough decision to make - I probably felt worse about it than she did. People who are depressed often become worse between November and January, and I was certain Lisa was no exception. Unfortunately, Lisa had become so hard for me to deal with that I told her I wasn't going to visit her until she started treating me better. I wanted Lisa to have a nice

Christmas, but I didn't feel like visiting her while she was acting so disrespectfully.

Instead of going to see Lisa during the Holidays, I sent her several gifts, including a bed for little Kricket. When I spoke with her on the phone, she told me that she never had a nice Christmas in her life, and this year would be no exception. It broke my heart to hear her say that, and it made me feel even worse than I did already. If she felt that way and wanted to see me, I wondered why she had been treating me so badly. Lisa was still pleased to receive the presents I sent her. I knew that it wasn't the same as being together with her. However, it was the best I could do under the circumstances. I still planned to go down to Florida to see her sometime soon, because I knew if I didn't, things between us would become even worse.

It hurt me to think about how bad Lisa's life had turned out during the years we were apart, but her life was equally horrible before we met. I felt terrible that her home environment was so deplorable while celebrating the holidays alone with her parents. A few weeks prior, Lisa told me she had planned to cook a couple of Cornish hens for Thanksgiving, hoping to have a nice family dinner. Unfortunately, Lisa wasn't in a very good mood on the day she cooked them because of her parents. So, she ended up going to bed early without eating because she was so upset. Crying herself to sleep was something Lisa had become accustomed to during her life. I went to bed myself feeling frustrated and upset, knowing that there was very little I could do to comfort her.

On Christmas Eve 2018, I happened to be in Charleston, South Carolina. Lisa called me around dinnertime, and we spoke for at least a half an hour. She said she felt sad, but happy to talk to me. I felt terrible that I wasn't with her, and I regretted making the decision not to see her. Lisa often acted like a child whenever she wanted attention. I don't remember her being like that when we were together in the past, so I assumed being in prison must have changed her demeanor significantly.

Lisa used to be so sweet and happy, whenever she was with me years ago. So many bad things must have happened to her since then. I should have considered that when I made my decision whether to visit her in December. Through her bad behavior, Lisa was trying to tell me that she needed me, and I responded by punishing her. Now, all I could do was to tell her that I loved her over the phone, and that I would try to see her as soon as possible. It was difficult for me not to cry, after hanging up the phone. I prayed that she would get through the holidays without incident. I prayed that I would have another opportunity soon to spend more time with her again.

I started to feel desperate that I couldn't do more to make her happy. I also felt guilty for not being with her when she needed me, throughout her life. I wasn't there when she was arrested, when she had her baby, when she was in prison, when she was in intensive care after her truck accident, or when she was in Hospice preparing to die, after having liver failure. I simply wasn't there for her. How is that love? Imagining Lisa's pain and suffering over decades was emotionally traumatizing for me. You never know when you end a relationship with someone, how their lives will be affected by your absence. My life was profoundly affected by Lisa's presence, as well as her absence. I tried very hard to ignore it over the years and bury my feelings for her, but I could never do it.

Sometimes people are better off apart, but other times, their lives become much worse without the influence of their lovers. I believe this was true about us. Lisa's life became so much worse without me looking out for her. I may have had a better life without Lisa, but I can't say I was happier. Living without her always caused me to feel that something was missing. I felt that she had filled a huge void in my soul at one time, but after we split up, the hole grew even larger. Losing Vonnie tormented me for decades after we broke-up.

I was beginning to think that no matter what I did to help Lisa, it wasn't making a lasting or deep enough impact. I kept thinking that I had waited too long to reconnect with her, and now it was too late. It was frustrating that Lisa often worked against all my efforts to help her. I understood that she had lost all trust and faith in most people and learned she could only count on herself.

When Pam betrayed Lisa in court, it was such a devastating blow to her. She cried throughout her testimony - I doubt Lisa ever recovered from it. After so many betrayals from everyone since then, I knew that she couldn't trust anyone anymore - not even me. I think it seemed to Lisa that no one would ever stand-by her, and no one would ever truly love her. This was the reason why it was so difficult for me to earn Lisa's confidence. In her mind, I had also let her down, and she was probably right.

Over the years, Lisa had developed many bad habits which became her daily routine. It was difficult for her to change once these rituals were formed. She was held captive by an unending loop of self-destruction, and for Lisa - there was no escape. She didn't seem to care about herself anymore because she believed no one loved her. Listening to the sound of her voice on the phone, I could hear by the tone of her voice that she felt totally alone. I saw first-hand how hard she tried to make people love her, especially her mother. However, all her efforts seemed to fall short of receiving the kind of true love and affection she desperately desired. The irony was that, even though I was crazy for Lisa in the past, I loved her more in the present, but she didn't seem to notice. Sadly, she couldn't love anyone any longer because she never learned how to love herself. Lisa was also hurt by the absence of her son and daughter in her life, and the lack of real love from her mother.

Lisa didn't receive much gratification from her ex-husband either. She wasn't married to him for more than a couple of years. Jeff was 20 years her senior, and she claimed he was very abusive. Lisa said she never felt any love from him at all and told me she only married him so she could have another child. However, Jeff took their son away from her after their divorce. Lisa and Carmen allowed themselves to be mistreated by men, most of their lives. This was a pattern they both created for themselves. I believe they viewed themselves to be unworthy of love and respect, allowing men and women alike, to treat them horribly.

Lisa had learned to associate abuse with love from a very young age. It was the only form of attention that she and her mom became accustomed to in their lives. Carmen was as much of a victim as Lisa, but she allowed herself to become an accomplice to her husbands' and boyfriends' crimes against her daughter. I asked Lisa one time why she hung around so many losers and people who mistreated her. Her response was that she saw herself as a loser too. I was shocked to hear her say that because in my eyes, Lisa was extraordinary - I idolized her.

After several days into the New Year, Lisa called me upset, and told me that her pain pills had been lost or stolen. I doubted she was telling me the truth. It was more likely that she had sold them to one of her friends and now needed more for herself. I'm not sure what she thought I could do about it. These were prescription opioids she was taking and were under strict regulation in Florida. In any case, no pharmacist nor her doctor were going to give her more, and there was nothing I could do to help her with her problem, even if she was telling the truth. This was likely another stunt of hers for attention and money. I knew that Lisa lied and manipulated whenever it suited her, so I wasn't about to fall for another one of her schemes.

Lisa wasn't a bad person in my eyes; she did what she felt was necessary to survive or receive satisfaction. It wasn't easy to know when Lisa was lying because some of her stories were plausible. Other times, her tales were simply unbelievable because they were so outrageous. Whenever Lisa had trouble answering straight forward questions, it was a safe bet that she wasn't being honest. Once, Lisa said that she had lost all the money she received from her welfare check, while buying a toy truck for her 18-year-old son, Geoffrey. I wondered why she was buying a child's toy for her son, instead of a more age-appropriate gift? He was going to college in Chicago, and really had no use for children's toys. These trucks apparently reminded Lisa of a time when Geoffrey was a small boy and used to play with these types of toys. She was likely buying them as souvenirs for herself because she missed her son terribly.

Perhaps Lisa thought having children would be her only chance to receive the love and attention she desired. Unfortunately, her children only brought her more pain because she couldn't be with them for more than a short period of time. Her daughter was severed from her life at birth, and her son was taken away by his father, after just a few years. Geoffrey unfortunately resented his mom, because Lisa had been absent from his life during much of his childhood. She mainly communicated with him on Snap-Chat when he grew up, and rarely answered her calls.

Lisa tried to tell me during her call, that while she was at a flea market, she became distracted by these children's toys and left her wallet on the table. She said someone must have walked off with it and the $750 dollars she received from Welfare. I thought to myself that she would never do something so foolish. I think she was hoping I was going to send her the money she lost, but I wasn't buying her tall tale. In this case, her story was so ridiculous that I knew she was lying to me. If Lisa had told me the truth, I might have helped her, but she was already costing me a small fortune, and I was annoyed that she was trying to con me into giving her more money. I didn't mind helping her, but I became angry when she tried to take advantage of my generosity.

It had been a very long time since Lisa and I had been so close. However, she was vastly different from the young woman I used to know in 1989. When Lisa and I first met, I thought she was the sweetest, sexiest, most talented woman I had ever met. I don't remember her ever being angry with me in the past, causing trouble or arguing about anything. She was always happy and excited to be with me. Sadly, the experiences Lisa had after her arrest must have altered her mind dramatically. At age 51, Lisa seemed damaged beyond repair. If I hadn't left her, perhaps that wouldn't have happened. She was a shadow of the way she used to be in the past when she was around me in the present. However, she was still flirtatious, adventurous, and entertaining. Those things were in her blood permanently, but her spirit had been broken.

Lisa and I continued to communicate just about every day, despite her elaborate anecdotes. She was becoming more exhausting to deal with by the day, and my patience was wearing thin. Some days, I just needed a break from all her drama, but there was never an intermission between acts. I think it was her mood swings that caused me the most stress. When Lisa was cheerful, she could be entertaining and pleasant to talk to. Our relationship endured because of those moments. However, whenever Lisa was upset, she could be abusive and hurtful, and I didn't know how much more of it I could take. Her moods didn't simply change from one day to the next - they changed from one minute to the next. She could be like a box of Cracker Jacks sometimes - sweet and a little nutty, with a surprise waiting for you.

No matter how Lisa made me feel, I was still obligated to stay in contact with her. I wanted to continue to try to help her and keep her spirits uplifted. However, sometimes, Lisa made me so upset, that I couldn't always be delicate when I responded to her. I felt bad about it afterwards and kept telling myself that I should try harder to ignore her provocative insults and threats. Lisa knew exactly what to say to hurt me and make me angry. It was difficult not to react to her when she tried to push my buttons.

The biggest problem I had with her was that I was emotionally involved with her, which made helping her so much more challenging. I understood that my emotional attachment to her could be dangerous to both of us, but it was even more perilous for her, if I wasn't involved in her life at all. I hated being in the position of being Lisa's lover and caregiver at the same time. However, I didn't know what else to do other than to convince her to see a psychiatrist.

It had been about two months since I had been with her last. I knew I should make plans to go see her again soon. It was very difficult to separate business from pleasure with her, but I tried my best to focus on my mission. Perhaps I shouldn't have tried to take such a sterile approach with her, because what she needed most was to feel loved. Unfortunately, because of all the problems Lisa created, I often neglected to show her enough affection and tell her how much I loved her. She was critically important to me in so many ways, and I often failed to convey this to her. The situation that presented itself was such a double-edged sword. No matter how I played her game, any mistakes I made would likely have dire consequences. I needed a new strategy - I needed a miracle.

19. Back in the Saddle

After the New Year in January of 2019, Lisa called me to tell me that both of her parents had to go to the hospital soon for operations. Her mother was going in first for hip surgery, and her stepfather was going to be in a different hospital a week later for his heart condition. Carmen's surgery may have had something to do with her fall in September. She claimed that she had slipped on the kitchen tile floor, while coming inside from the pool. At least that was the story Carmen told Lisa, while we were in St. Petersburg. Carmen's injury could have been domestic violence, for all we knew. If that was the case, it may have been the reason Dave never called for an ambulance and left his wife bleeding on the floor. In any case, Carmen was going to be in the hospital for a few days, and then transferred to a rehabilitation healthcare facility.

Lisa sounded anxious on the phone when she broke the news to me. Not only was her mom going to be away from home for a couple of weeks, but she would also be stuck at home alone with Dave, until it was time for him to leave for the hospital. Lisa told me she was afraid to be alone with Dave and asked me if I would come to Florida to stay with her. I was still feeling guilty about leaving Lisa alone for the holidays, so I told Lisa that I would come down to keep her company, while her mom was away.

I asked Lisa if she would agree to exchange cars with me when I came down to see her. I planned to give her my 2010 Audi A-3 in exchange for the Jeep. That way, Lisa would no longer need to be stressed over making car payments, and it would also release me from liability, if she were to cause an accident. I told her that the car would be thoroughly inspected, have all necessary repairs made, and I would put new tires on the car. The Audi had only 45,000 miles on it at the time, so it was still in excellent condition. Even though it was an older model, it drove like a dream. I loved my car, and I didn't want to give it up, but I needed to do this for both of us.

Due to Lisa's erratic and petulant behavior and recent accident record, I thought it was best not to have both of our names on her car registration. If anything happened currently, I would be on the hook for any damage or injuries she caused. I told Lisa that she wouldn't have to make any car payments until she secured a job, and that she would have five years to pay me back. My car was one third of the value of the Jeep, so it would be relatively easy to pay me for the car over five years. I knew that I would probably never see any money from her, but I was willing to make the sacrifice to give both of us peace of mind. It was not ideal, but at the time, it seemed like the best thing to do.

Each time I went down to Florida to see Lisa, I had to spend a lot of money. I couldn't stay at her house because of her stepfather and the condition the house was in. I usually needed to spend at least two weeks with her each time I went to see her, to help her with everything she needed to have accomplished. Unfortunately, she didn't seem to be motivated enough to do much on her own without my help. I booked a place for several days, not far from Lake Buena Vista. This time I needed to drive down with my car, since Lisa agreed to make the vehicle exchange. If I drove straight through without stopping, it would take me between 11 and 12 hours. I wanted to arrive in Florida as fast as possible, because Lisa was becoming increasingly anxious about her mom leaving for the hospital.

There was so much more that needed to be accomplished on this third trip, and it was going to take a lot of time to complete all the tasks. We needed to take care of legal matters, go to the DMV to switch the car registration, change the car insurance, clean her house, and visit her mother in the nursing home. It overwhelmed me just thinking about everything, especially since Lisa didn't have much stamina, and had to take naps during the day. There was no one else in a position to help Lisa, so it was all up to me to take care of her.

I had decided that I couldn't allow Lisa to continue to suffer. She had a torturous existence, and I knew she had been thinking that it was a life not worth living anymore. Not only was Lisa extremely unhappy, but she didn't do much, other than drink, watch television, take drugs and sleep. If she had any chance of having a better life, her habits needed to change, and she needed to find a job. Every day, I had to live with the thought that Lisa could die at any minute, and I needed to do my best to prevent it from happening. Every time that I spoke with her, she seemed more desperate and anxious. She cried almost every day that I spoke to her.

"Alex, I need you to hurry up and get here," Lisa said. "Dave is driving me crazy, and I need to get away from him."

"I'm coming baby," I replied. "Just hang on okay - I will be there as fast as I can."

I told Lisa that I would drive all day, so we could be together sooner. Then we could exchange cars, after I helped her get away from that Hell hole. It took me a little over 11 hours, but I finally made it to Winter Haven. I was exhausted when I arrived and didn't have enough strength to go see Lisa until the following morning. The minute I arrived, I called to tell her where to meet me in the morning. I decided it would be prudent to have a good night's sleep and then have the car rechecked at Firestone, before giving it to Lisa. I wanted them to perform a complete diagnostic, to make sure everything was running perfectly.

I called Lisa the next morning to tell her to meet me around noon at the Dollar Store in Lake Wales, so we could have lunch and go to the DMV together. After finishing at Firestone, I went to meet her at the plaza. I was there waiting awhile when I saw her green Jeep pull up in the parking lot. Kricket was in the back seat curled up in her bed. As Lisa opened her car door, she saw me waiting for her, and began to smile brightly. She always seemed very excited to see me each time I came to visit her.

Lisa was naturally a very happy person, but her mood was often spoiled by people who mistreated her. Despite her terrible circumstances, Lisa had an innocent glow about her whenever she felt happy. It was accentuated whenever she was around animals, or people who treated her well. She was just a child inside her mind, and always carried with her the warmth of the sun and a spirit of enthusiasm. Unfortunately, the men associated with her mother and people who were jealous of her often eclipsed her brilliant light.

"Hey baby," Lisa said excitedly, as she walked Kricket in my direction.

"Hi Vonnie, how are you and Kricket?" I asked.

Lisa put her arm around me tightly and kissed me. She was very glad to see me.

"Are you hungry?" I asked.

"Starvin," Lisa replied.

"Let's have something to eat first, and then head over to the DMV," I said. "Okay?"

"Okay, okay!" Lisa replied in her funny voice.

Whenever Lisa spoke to me with that squeaky voice, it always made me laugh. After lunch, we drove over to the DMV to complete the car registration paperwork. In hindsight, I wished I would have consulted an attorney before handing my car over to her, because it was going to become an issue later. I planned to give Lisa the title to my car, so that she could register the Audi in her name, releasing me from any liability. I wrote up an agreement that she signed, but unfortunately there was more I needed to do to protect my investment.

The agreement that Lisa and I made did not require her to make monthly payments or start paying me back right away. Until Lisa found a job and a new place to live, I wasn't going to pressure her for money anymore, since all the payments for the Audi had already been made. I was hoping to help Lisa still have a car to drive, while at the same time, relieving myself of any liability. The Jeep had become a source of tension, and I wanted to diffuse the pressure it had caused between us. I also wanted Lisa to have a chance to regain control over her life, so she could rediscover a sense of freedom and happiness.

Another thing Lisa and I needed to accomplish was reversing the power of attorney Lisa granted to her mother and stepfather. We needed to stop at a bank to have a document notarized, saying that she was revoking the power of attorney from her parents. When Lisa went back to prison, Carmen and Dave took advantage of the situation by manipulating Lisa into giving them power of attorney. They used it to exercise an option to buy the land by Lake Buffum, which was part of Lisa's divorce settlement. The land was supposed to remain in Lisa's possession, but Carmen and Dave put it in their names and cut Lisa out of her property rights.

Lisa told me she wanted to regain control over her life. So, after we finished at the DMV, I took Lisa over to SunTrust Bank to notarize a document, which took power of attorney away from her parents, and put it solely back into Lisa's hands again. I could have asked Lisa to grant me power of attorney, which she would have agreed to, but I thought it was best for Lisa to have sole control over her life. I didn't want Lisa to have any reason to worry that I would take advantage of her the same way her parents did. I just wanted Lisa to have her life back again. Lisa also wanted to have power of attorney over her mother, so she could stop Dave from putting Carmen away somewhere. She also wanted to keep him from having sole control over the property in Fort Meade. We had to wait until we could see Carmen to have her sign paperwork, which wouldn't be until after she was transferred to the rehabilitation center.

The place that Lisa's mom would be transferred to was southeast of Lake Wales near Sebring, which was a lot further south. When the time came for Carmen to leave the hospital, we would need to move closer to where she was relocating, so that it would be easier for Lisa to see her. Our current hotel reservation was north of Winter Haven because there were more places which had full kitchens there, and I had no idea where Carmen would be after she was released from the hospital. After we finished all our business for that day, Lisa and I went to the apartment complex where we were staying. It was dinnertime, so after we were settled in, I brought Lisa out to grab something to eat nearby. As we approached some restaurants near Lake Buena Vista, she began to experience hallucinations and suffer from extreme anxiety.

"Alex, where are we?" Lisa asked in a desperate voice. "What are we doing here? I want to go home."

"Don't worry Lisa; we are just arriving at some restaurants, so we can have something to eat," I replied.

Lisa began to press her hands and face against the car window. She appeared to be having an anxiety attack and started to cry. I had to stop the car in the parking lot, to reassure her. Because of Lisa's emotional condition, I decided it was better not to go inside any restaurant. Instead, I chose to go to a Taco Bell drive through, so we could eat in the car. After I ordered some food for us and Lisa started eating, she seemed to calm down. It was a very bizarre experience, and a reminder to me that I was dealing with a mentally ill woman.

"I'm sorry Alex," Lisa said.

"Don't be sorry Vonnie," I replied. "Everything's going to be all right, okay?"

"Okay," Lisa replied, still looking worried.

"Can we go back home now?" Lisa asked, referring to the apartment.

"Sure baby," I replied. "We'll go back and take Kricket for a walk, okay?"

"Okay," Lisa replied in a child-like voice.

It had been a long day and Lisa and I were exhausted. We took showers and got ready for bed, after walking Kricket. Spending time with Lisa always broke my heart because it was a first-hand reminder how much her life had been torn apart over the years.

"Thanks for coming Alex," Lisa said.

"You're welcome Vonnie; I'm happy to be with you," I replied.

We took the elevator to our floor, after Kricket finished her business. I was a little concerned that we were on a high floor again, not just because of Lisa - I don't like heights. Lisa had her ritual drink before going to bed, and then she kissed me goodnight and slipped under the covers. Lisa usually dozed off first, and I often watched her while she was sleeping, to make sure she was resting peacefully.

It always made me a little bit nervous closing my eyes, while lying next to Lisa, but I was never scared. It was possible her sleep might be invaded by nightmares from her childhood, so there was always the chance she could wake up frightened. I never knew what to expect when I slept next to her, but I was generally more concerned about her doing something harmful to herself, than I was about her reacting to a nightmare. Lisa's mind was clouded with anger, fear, and paranoia. However, I was confident that if something happened while she slept, everything would be all right once she woke up. Her daily life had been plagued by emotional turmoil, but I still had hope that her dreams would be more pleasant. If Lisa couldn't avoid dreaming about her childhood, she would have no escape from her pain, except through death. This was the thought that bothered me the most, whenever she laid her head down on the pillow and closed her eyes.

As I was thinking, I decided that perhaps it might put Lisa in the right frame of mind, if we spent the next day at Disney's Animal Kingdom. Lisa told me she had never been there before, which I found surprising. I hoped that taking her there might inspire her enough to try to find a job working with wild exotic animals again. I knew that Lisa would really enjoy the park, and it would be good exercise for both of us. I thought it might help her to relax and unwind and take her mind off all the things that were causing her so much anxiety.

Lisa had extensive experience working with wild animals, having traveled with the circus for most of her childhood. If it weren't for her run-ins with the law and her erratic behavior, Lisa would be a perfect fit working at Animal Kingdom. She had worked with lions, tigers, bears and elephants for over 15 years. Lisa didn't fear any dangerous animal. She had greater trepidation of men, which is why she took so many women as lovers. One time, Lisa told me that she had put her head in a lion's mouth, but that didn't even scare her. The only time she felt afraid of an animal was when she was swarmed by a Kookaburra bird, which she said went crazy and attacked her.

Thinking about going to the park gave me a feeling that I could still inspire Lisa to live her life again with enthusiasm, and hope for the future. As I slowly drifted off to sleep, I tried to remember how things used to be in our past. Life with Lisa was so wonderful when we were both young. I may have been naïve to everything Lisa had been through before we met, but perhaps not knowing kept my thoughts about her pure and untainted.

If only Lisa had confided in me about her past, I might have been more understanding, and chose to stay together with her. I may have been spooked by the knowledge that she had killed someone, but I might not have abandoned her if I knew the reason for her actions. Lisa was probably too scared to tell me the truth for fear of losing me or being caught. I'm sure that's why she never said anything to me three decades ago. However, she was here with me now, and I felt grateful that we were together again.

Lisa began the day with a drink the minute she woke up. After we dressed, we went across the street to Denny's for breakfast. She loved pancakes and waffles with lots of whipped cream and syrup, along with a cup of coffee. She didn't seem to be worried about her weight, and if eating a delicious breakfast made her happy, I didn't want to object. After we began eating, I told Lisa about what I had planned for the day.

"How would you like to go to Animal Kingdom today Vonnie?" I asked.

"Wow, really?" Lisa replied.

"Sure, why not?" I said.

"That would be great baby, "Lisa replied.

So, after breakfast we took Kricket outside for her walk, and then we hopped into the Jeep to drive to Disney. We couldn't be gone too long, because Kricket would need to go outside again for another bathroom break. I figured four or five hours would be okay to be away. When we arrived at the first checkpoint, we told the guard we were there for an interview, so he let us through, without asking us to pay for parking. We planned to go to the Human Resources office first, even though we didn't have an appointment.

Lisa and I took the tram from the parking area and walked to one of the guest services windows. Then, we asked if we could talk to the hiring manager. We were told that all applications had to be completed online, and we couldn't see anyone in person, until that was accomplished. I should have known better; I was still living in the past when it came to current hiring practices. Everything is done online these days, making everyone's experience so impersonal. I'm not convinced technology is bringing us closer together, more than it's pulling us all apart.

Since Lisa couldn't get an interview that day or even fill out a job application, we entered the park and went on a few rides, while reminiscing about our Cypress Gardens days. Lisa smiled all morning long, and it felt good to see her so happy. By lunchtime, Lisa and I located a restaurant close to where we had been walking that served lobster sandwiches. Normally, park food isn't very appetizing, but this meal was exceptionally fresh and tasted delicious. I don't think I have ever had such a fantastic lunch at a theme park. Disney has exceptional attention to details in general, but their food that afternoon raised the bar for theme parks, in terms of culinary quality. It was a bit of a challenge finding a table, but we managed to grab one when some people stood up to leave.

Lisa almost changed her mind about going to the park earlier, because she didn't think she was going to be able to buy alcohol there. She said she couldn't last four hours without drinking, which is not a good thing if you plan to work an eight-hour day. This was how dependent Lisa was on drinking every day. She didn't seem to trust me when I told her that Disney sold alcoholic drinks. We hadn't walked very far after finishing lunch, before she saw a place to stop for a margarita. She wanted two because she said they were small. I wanted to have an enjoyable day, so I didn't argue with her. I drank some of hers deliberately so she wouldn't drink as much.

Afterwards, we went on more rides and racked up plenty of steps, while walking around the park. It was such a beautifully clear day with no clouds in sight. We tried to stay out of the sun as much as possible, since it was very hot, even for January. Being in the park together appeared to take Lisa's mind off her problems, which was so important to her mental health. I kept thinking to myself that it was a shame that we never took the opportunity to do anything like this when we were young. We were both just so busy and our schedules didn't line up, but if we had wanted to, we could have taken a day off to go to the beach together or something. I guess when you already work in a theme park, it's the last place you want to go on your day off. It was a crazy time, and we were crazy kids. We assumed we had our whole lives ahead of us to spend together. We never realized just what precious little time we had left.

One of the last things we did that day was to go on the African safari ride. Lisa obviously loved seeing all the African and Asian wildlife. We had fun taking photographs and talking about her circus days. I could tell that she really missed being around them every day. Animals were Lisa's friends, unlike humans, who had mostly mistreated her. In contrast, wild creatures had always shown Lisa affection and calmed her restless spirit. She really felt at ease among jungle beasts. They added an element of danger and distracted her from her painful memories. Lisa seemed to thrive on the adrenalin from interacting with them. She enjoyed watching horror movies for the same reason.

Lisa was really a product of the jungle, and not of the civilized world. She didn't really fit into society with all its rules, responsibilities, and restrictions. She felt freer traveling with the circus. Working among natural predators at Animal Kingdom or a zoo was where Lisa would feel most comfortable. She slept near them as a child, ate among them, and cared for them like family. Unfortunately, just like her feline friends, Lisa would wind up in a cage too and was labeled a dangerous killer. She was truly like one of these ferocious cats - beautiful, but deadly. These powerful predators were her protectors and confidents - not threats to her. They gave her the love and joy she never received from humans. Lisa never understood the concept between right and wrong - how could she? Like an animal, all she knew was about survival. The big top was her classroom, and the jungle beasts were her teachers.

Lisa's whole world at one time was the circus, and the only law she knew how to live by was the law of the jungle. Outsiders were seen as either foreigners or fans. Unfortunately, this was how Lisa's stepfather got away with abusing her, while she was still a child. If anyone knew of any wrongdoing in the circus, no one would ever think of going to the police. It just wasn't done because anyone who betrayed another circus member would be blacklisted. So, Lisa couldn't even rely on her own mother or fellow co-workers to keep her safe from harm. She had to rely completely on herself. However, a young girl barely old enough to ride a bicycle, much less an elephant, wasn't well equipped to defend herself from her stepfather.

After Lisa and I finished the safari ride, she smiled enthusiastically, because seeing all those animals had ignited her spirit and brought back memories of her circus days.

"I would love to work here," Lisa said to me. "I don't know why I didn't think about it before."

"I'm glad you enjoyed your day Vonnie," I replied.

Lisa gave me a big hug, which nearly took my breath away, and then she kissed me.

"I love you baby," Lisa said.

"I love you too Vonnie," I replied.

It was getting close to 5 o'clock, so it was time for us to ride the tram back to the Jeep. We needed to let Kricket outside for her walk, since she had been cooped-up in the room for most of the day. My feet were starting to hurt from all the walking we had been doing, so I was glad to be going back to the hotel. The best part was that we both spent an enjoyable afternoon together. Days like this didn't happen very often, especially for Lisa.

More than seven years of Lisa's life had been spent in a cage. However, her parent's home wasn't much of an improvement over prison. It was never clean, there were constant arguments at home, and it was miles from the nearest gas station. I knew that Lisa appreciated having this kind of quality time with me, and the thought of having to go back to live with her parents again weighed heavily on her mind.

Lisa must have thought to herself - "If only days like this could last forever. If only I could go home to a peaceful clean house, where no one attacked me. If only by some miracle, I could finally be free from all my pain and suffering. If only I had a chance to be happy. God must be punishing me for the sin of my birth. I must be a bad person. I must deserve this life he gave me."

It was heart-breaking to realize the tragic life Lisa had endured for over 50 years. Lisa was really a child of God, and not the Devil, as some people have portrayed her to be. In my eyes, she was a beacon of light in the darkness, which threatened to extinguish her flame. Lisa Yvonne French was an angel among demons. I prayed that one day, she would finally be lifted above the Hellish life she was born into. I hoped she would be rewarded for her courage and perseverance in Heaven.

20. Panicked

The next day, we needed to move further south because Carmen was getting out of the hospital soon. I had to find another place for us to stay, so we could be closer to the lake house, and to where Lisa's mom would be rehabilitating. I don't remember what caused it, but Lisa was becoming belligerent again. She was really driving me crazy, and I was losing my patience with her. Lisa became so anxious thinking about her mom's condition, but that was no excuse for how she was acting. I wasn't sure what else it could be, but she woke up in a very bad frame of mind, and her stress level was through the roof, for no apparent reason.

I decided that I ought to leave Lisa alone for a while and prepare to leave the hotel. So, I went downstairs and put my luggage in the Jeep, to give her a little space and time to calm down. I called her doctor's office to see if I could make an appointment that day to address her anxiety. Lisa was still in the room becoming more nervous by the minute. She must have noticed that all my things were gone, and that I took nothing of hers with me. She started to panic because she thought I planned to leave her at the hotel. Lisa must not have been able to find her key, so she made sure she could reenter the room by using the deadbolt to keep the door from locking. She left Kricket behind, instead of bringing her, when she came down to look for me.

While the phone was still ringing, I saw Lisa come out of the front door of the hotel, as I stood behind the Jeep. From a distance, I could see a look of fear and anxiety on her face. She was scared, like she was in Savannah, thinking once again that I had left her. Her fear of abandonment was real, and a symptom of her BPD. I hung up the phone before anyone picked-up, and I shouted at Lisa. She didn't have any of her things with her. She must have left everything in the room to come look for me. When Lisa saw me, she hurried over toward me with tears in her eyes.

"I thought you left me," Lisa cried.

"I would never do that honey," I replied. "I love you, and no matter how crazy you are making me; I would never leave you and Kricket stranded far from home - okay?"

"Okay," Lisa replied. "You make me 'scare.'"

I put my arms around her to let her know everything was all right. Gradually, she became calmer, and her breathing slowed down to a normal rhythm. Lisa gave me a little smile as she looked up at me endearingly, relieved that I was still there with her. She took my arm and we walked back to the room together. She still had a tear or two in her eyes and a worried look on her face. I have never seen another human being look so helpless in all my life.

We still had to retrieve her things along with her dog, who must have been having a little anxiety attack of her own. Kricket mirrored her master in many ways. She seemed helpless and fragile, needing lots of love and attention. After putting Lisa's luggage and her faithful companion in the Jeep, we drove down south toward Lake Wales. Lisa was still feeling extremely anxious, as we headed toward our next destination.

Lisa ended up falling asleep in the Jeep from emotional exhaustion, even though it was only about a 35-minute ride. I felt badly for Lisa, and I wanted her to get immediate help, so I phoned her doctor's office again, while she was still sleeping. I secured an appointment about an hour from when I called, but it had to be with another doctor. In the meantime, I wanted to stop by a rehabilitation clinic to ask some questions about their program and collect some reading materials. I was curious to see if this place would be a good fit for Lisa to recover from her alcohol dependency and emotional distress.

As we arrived, Lisa woke up and discovered where I had brought her. Apparently, she had been there before. She panicked again and acted defensively because she thought I was trying to commit her. I tried to reassure her that we were only there for information, and that I had no intention of leaving her there alone. I had to give Lisa my keys to the Jeep, so she would remain calm and hoped she wouldn't drive away. She was still apprehensive when I went inside the facility. I spoke with someone at the counter who gave me some promotional materials and answered my questions. I didn't want to take too long because I knew that Lisa was still nervous, while waiting for me outside. At least she had Kricket in the car to help her stay calm.

When I returned, Lisa was in the driver's seat, because she was paranoid that people from inside were going to come out and forcibly commit her against her will. I didn't blame her for feeling that way, because everyone close to her had betrayed her several times in the past. Trust remained an obstacle with her, and I just had to work around it. When Lisa realized that nothing was going to happen to her, she calmed down and moved over so that I could drive.

"Lisa, you don't have to be scared," I said. "I'm not going to put you in here against your will. I would never do that. I just wanted to ask for information about this place in case you decide to come here."

At first, Lisa didn't respond. She was still looking at me like she didn't trust what I was saying.

"I've been here before," Lisa replied. "I know what they do there, and I'm not going back again. They take your cell phone away from you, and I won't be able to talk to anyone, including you."

"Don't worry baby," I said. "If you don't want to stay here, you don't have to. I just want you to have options, which will help you recover."

Lisa didn't say anything. She clearly considered the rehabilitation center to be like prison. She must have remembered what she had gone through in the past and didn't like it. She appeared to be flustered and began to cry. She kept clawing at the passenger side window, as if she was trying to escape. I worried about her level of anxiety, so I tried to hurry to her doctor's office. On the way there, Lisa fell asleep again, tired from feeling stressed out.

When we arrived, she woke up and became agitated all over again. Lisa thought I brought her to the doctor's office to leave her there. Her fear of abandonment seemed to be on high alert all day. This time, she was afraid I was trying to have her doctor put her in a psychiatric facility. Truthfully, that's where she probably belonged, but I had no desire to force her to go. I wanted Lisa to make that decision on her own, without pressure from me or anyone else. I tried to tell her that I brought her to see a doctor because I was worried about her anxiety. I told her I wanted to see if he could prescribe something to calm her nerves. Lisa didn't seem to believe me and became hysterical. She opened the car door and walked away toward the plaza, shouting vociferously, so that everyone in the doctor's office could hear her. Lisa became apoplectic, while continuing to repeat the same accusation.

"You lied to me!" she shouted. "You betrayed me!"

"Lisa, come back; I'm trying to help you!" I shouted.

Lisa wouldn't listen, and she just kept walking toward the Winn-Dixie grocery store. I didn't know what to do next, except to go inside and tell the receptionist that I had brought Lisa for her appointment, but she was refusing to come inside. After hearing all the commotion in the parking lot, Lisa's doctor called the police. Perhaps he did it because he thought Lisa might hurt herself or because she was disturbing the other patients. She was capable of violence if she felt threatened, so calling law enforcement was the prudent thing to do. Although these days, some on the Left would have demanded a social worker be called instead. Realistically, Lisa could have easily hurt someone without a weapon if she was provoked. Then we might have had a dead social worker on our hands. When Lisa felt anxious, she caused everyone around her to react to her antics. It could be exhausting at times. I never saw Lisa act so volatile or dramatic when we were together in the past. If she was like that with other people, I never witnessed it.

Lisa told me one time that some psychiatrists believe that if someone experiences emotional trauma at a very young age, from that point on their emotional development slows down or stops. I believe the clinical term is called 'Developmental Arrest.' In her case, I would say this condition was apparent. She often acted as if she was only seven or eight years old. Her behavior likely evolved or rather, didn't develop, due to her sexual abuse. Strangely enough, When Lisa was around me at 23 years of age, she was sweet, affectionate, pleasant to be around and self-confident. She seemed to have all the hallmarks of being a happy and well-adjusted young lady. She must have concealed her torment from me to allow our relationship to develop. I believe she was further traumatized while in prison, and her ability to control her emotions must have been shattered. Twenty-eight years later, Lisa was not the same woman anymore. She was emotionally and physically broken, and all the king's horsemen and all the king's men wouldn't be able to put Lisa back together again.

When the police finally arrived, Lisa had walked back in front of the doctor's office and was pacing back and forth in the parking lot. A male and a female officer questioned both of us separately. I spoke to the male officer, and she spoke to the policewoman. This was becoming a recurring habit with the police having to come every time Lisa caused a disturbance. While being questioned, she skillfully changed her demeanor and calmed down, as she had done before in St. Petersburg. Lisa had many encounters with the police in the past and knew exactly how to talk to them.

After I explained the situation to the male officer, he asked me if I could take Lisa home. I told him that I wouldn't put her back in the Jeep in her present state of mind. Instead, I insisted she see her doctor. In my view, Lisa was at risk for jumping out of the car while it was in motion. I told the police officer that I would not allow her to have an opportunity to hurt herself, but he was welcome to take Lisa home himself. I wasn't about to put her back in the Jeep unless she agreed to see her doctor.

After several minutes of coaxing, the police and I finally convinced Lisa to go inside. I took little Kricket out of the back seat and brought her with us. Lisa was calmer now, but she was still suffering from severe anxiety. I could see that her face was still flushed, her eyes were bloodshot, and she was perspiring around her neck and forehead. I was glad she was finally going to be evaluated by one of the physicians because she really needed help. I held her hand, so she knew I was there to support her. It was going to cost me more money out of pocket, but that was the least of my concern. I could see that Lisa still felt scared because she had a desperate look in her eyes.

"Don't leave me here alone Alex," Lisa said.

"Don't worry baby; I won't leave you here," I replied. "I promise - it's going to be okay."

"Okay," Lisa said, as she looked at me with the expression of a small child.

I felt sad and concerned for Lisa. I was hopeful that this doctor's visit would help, but it wasn't going to solve her long-term problems. I felt that she needed to be institutionalized, but Lisa had to decide to commit herself of her own free will. I think her primary care doctor would have referred her to a psychiatrist years ago if he had known more about her psychological condition. I doubt he knew just how bad she was, until I brought it to his attention. Lisa often put on a good act in front of people. However, on this visit, there was no hiding her behavior. I had the impression that Lisa never shared her history, which may have been why her physician was in the dark.

When it was Lisa's turn to be seen, I went in with her again. This new doctor seemed to be very kind and patient. I filled him in as best as I could concerning Lisa's history. I told him that she was an alcoholic and that I would like him to help her to stop drinking. I also wanted him to wean her off the addictive and dangerous medicines she was taking. Lisa tried to say that she only had a few drinks each day, but I made sure he knew that she had been consuming at least eight vodka drinks every day. I told the doctor that I was concerned about her drinking habit, not only because of the medications she was on, but also because she almost died from liver failure. It was dangerous for her to drink, while she was still taking opioids. I also told him that Lisa suffered many years from child abuse, so that he understood that she needed psychiatric care as well.

I wanted to go to the Jeep to get some things Lisa needed, so that she felt more comfortable. She was still fearful that I was going to leave her, so she asked me to leave some of my things behind. When I returned, Lisa looked relieved. She convinced herself that I might not come back. I told the doctor that I thought Lisa might be bi-polar or something along those lines. At this point, she should have been referred for an immediate psychiatric evaluation. However, because he was seeing her for the first time, it wasn't something he was prepared to do. Instead, he prescribed a two-day supply of anxiety medicine and told Lisa to call him in two days to testify how she was doing. This doctor was very caring, and I appreciated the extra time he spent with her.

I thought that I should have asked her doctor for some anxiety medicine for myself, after everything Lisa put me through. Her behavior was really stressing me out, and I didn't know how much longer I could tolerate her outbursts. She really drove me crazy sometimes, and it became increasingly more difficult for me to understand how to help her. Lisa really needed more assistance than she was receiving, and it was going to be challenging to find affordable quality psychiatric care for her.

Afterwards, Lisa and I went to the Winn-Dixie to have her prescription filled. While we were waiting for her medication, I found a place to stay on the internet, close to her parents' house. It had a full kitchen, so we could cook dinner and eat alone. We didn't accomplish much that day, but at least Lisa was feeling better. I was just glad the day was almost over, and that we could have dinner soon and go to sleep. It was another day that I just felt frustrated and helpless. However, I had no intention of giving up. I was going to see this through, even if it killed me.

Spending time with Lisa was always an adventure, but it wasn't always fun. It felt something like being a detective in a real-life murder mystery - always one step behind the suspect. Ironically, Lisa had already survived her own horror story. According to Detective Ray, she was the villain and not the victim, but I knew better. His ego couldn't handle the fact that Lisa had made a complete fool out of him.

As we drove to the hotel, I wondered what was in store for us next. Little did I realize; we were about to experience something that would frighten me as much as Lisa.

21. The Creepy Hotel

On this trip, Lisa and I ended up moving around a lot more than the last time I visited. We needed to be closer to Lisa's house to feed her horse, grab some clean clothes, and check the mail. Somehow, we ended up at an old retreat house, which rested next to a lake. Originally, we planned to only stay one night, but the person at the front desk talked me into booking two nights. It wasn't too expensive, and it was in a good location with a kitchen, so I thought it would be fine. It seemed peaceful enough during the daytime, but at night it felt spooky, especially with the mist coming off the lake. It looked like a scene from a Scooby-Doo movie, where monsters emerge from a murky swamp.

The hotel itself looked like a converted old farmhouse, more like a bed and breakfast place, but without the breakfast. It appeared run down and neglected and gave us the impression that it was either haunted or something nefarious was going on there. Additionally, it was in a secluded location, and very few guests seemed to be staying there. Nothing in the place looked like it had ever been repaired or updated since it was first built. On the inside, it reminded me of someone's grandparents' farmhouse. It just had a creepy vibe to it and made Lisa and I feel uncomfortable. The room we were given was large enough but dated. There weren't that many rooms to begin with, but I didn't see more than two other cars in the parking lot. It was ironic that Lisa had a reputation for being a dangerous criminal, but around me, she often acted scared. Whenever Lisa became nervous, she sometimes used humor and her funny voice to settle her anxiety.

"Alex, how did you find this place?" Lisa asked.

"You gonna make me 'scare!'" Lisa said. "Someone gonna come here and try to kill us!"

"Don't worry Lisa," I said. "They don't know who they're dealing with."

"You gonna protect me?" Lisa asked.

"No Lisa, you're going to defend me; you're the one who went to prison for taking down a bad guy," I replied.

"Oh yeah, that's right," Lisa said. "No one better try and attack us, cuz I will snap their neck like a twig."

We both laughed, and it lightened the mood. I had no doubt that Lisa was more than capable of killing any man, once she wrapped her arms around his neck and squeezed. She was powerful and had a grip like a boa-constrictor. I knew first-hand because she showed me once what she could do. That was an experience I never wanted to repeat.

I called down to the front desk to see if they had a corkscrew to open a bottle of wine we bought, before going out to buy some food for dinner. I was hoping that if we had some wine together, Lisa wouldn't be tempted to drink the vodka she brought with us. The lady who answered the phone said there wasn't any in the building. At that time, she didn't mention anything else concerning alcohol. She even suggested looking for one at Publix, which was just down the road at the corner plaza. I thought that would be perfect because we could buy some food there at the same time. After we finished shopping and returned to the hotel, Lisa said she wanted to make chicken parmesan, which sounded delicious. As she started cooking, I scanned the room more carefully, and discovered an unusual sign. It read:

"THERE WILL BE A $200 FINE FOR ANYONE CAUGHT DRINKING ALCOHOL ON THE PROPERTY!"

I was shocked! As I read further, I realized that we must have stumbled into a religious retreat sanctuary, which had strict rules concerning drinking. I felt like we were in a 'Twilight Zone' movie. This place was getting creepier by the minute.

"Hey Lisa, check this out," I said.

"What's that baby," Lisa replied.

"There is no alcohol allowed here," I said. "We're going to get in trouble for drinking if they catch us. We can't stay another night in this place. We must get out of here by tomorrow. I was incensed that the lady at the front desk didn't say anything about drinking there."

"Oh my Gosh Alex, what are we going to do?" Lisa asked.

"We can still drink the wine, but we can't leave the bottle in the trash, and we should leave in the morning." I replied.

Lisa felt nervous again after hearing the news about the alcohol ban. She couldn't stand the thought of not being able to drink for more than two hours, much less two days. I couldn't stand the thought of having to pay a $200 fine. I felt like we had hit a time warp, and we were back in the 1920s, during prohibition.

Lisa continued to cook dinner, but now she seemed distracted. She was excited to be making dinner for both of us again, because it made her feel like we were a normal married couple. She dreamed of having a peaceful life, and often talked about what would make her happy in the future. In that moment, it almost felt like we were living the life we were meant to have together - a life that had slipped away through our fingers and left a scar. Occasionally, Lisa would write my last name next to hers. She liked to daydream about us finally getting married, after I first asked her almost three decades ago. The life we both wanted to share together had been interrupted by a cruel twist of fate, as if by providence. Our relationship felt like it had been sabotaged. Evil had brought darkness into our lives, and eclipsed our love for each other, but I was trying to fight back.

Perhaps it was not our fate to be reunited. I couldn't shake the feeling that there was going to be a heavy price to pay. It was almost as if I had made a deal with the devil to be together with her again. It seemed cruel to have been torn apart and destined to live our lives without one another. I think deep down, Lisa knew she could never have a happy life. Too much water had passed under the bridge. Her life seemed to be caught in a horrifying tide of wickedness, which prohibited her from setting foot on dry land. She had been cursed from the day she was born, and there was no hope for a better future, despite my best efforts.

The chicken parmesan didn't turn out exactly as Lisa hoped. She was a little frustrated that she had over-cooked the chicken. So, she poured herself a glass of wine, to soften her disappointment in her culinary skills. I had the impression that Lisa was thinking she couldn't do anything right. When I noticed how she seemed to be feeling, I gave her a hug and told her that it didn't matter if dinner wasn't perfect.

While we were eating, Lisa continued to talk about the life she wanted for herself and for us. In her mind, her future included being together, along with little Kricket. I wanted Lisa to be motivated to change her life, and I wasn't about to discourage her aspirations. Lisa smiled all through dinner because she had hope that her life was going to change soon. It was encouraging, and it made me feel good that she wanted a chance for a better life. She was pleased we were together again. I must admit, the idea of being together permanently was appealing to me as well. It seemed like Lisa was beginning to think about a future for herself for the first time, which didn't include her mother. She wanted to experience living in a happy environment, free from arguments, stress, and abuse. Lisa was imagining having a place of her own that she could be proud of, instead of the garbage dump where she was currently living.

It was a shame, because in the right hands, their property next to Lake Buffum could have been worth close to $750,000 dollars. Instead, Carmen and Dave would be lucky to get $200,000 in its present condition, if they sold it during their divorce. If Lisa's parents hadn't stolen her land from her, she could have sold it and used the money to buy a condominium for herself. Instead, Lisa was completely broke and didn't have a job. She couldn't even afford to rent a place yet. I knew I was going to have to spend more time during this visit trying to help her find work, so that she could move out on her own. If Lisa was going to have any future at all, she needed to find and hold a decent job.

Nighttime at this hotel felt even more eerie than it did during the day. After 8 pm, the staff had all left for the night. There was a number to call in an emergency, but no staff stayed in the hotel after hours. I discovered too late that the cable television wasn't working. I tried to see if I could find someone to help us, but after calling the main number and talking to one of the staff on the phone, I realized nothing was going to happen until morning. We weren't going to be watching TV that night. We had to figure out something else to keep ourselves occupied and entertained.

I knew what Lisa had in mind, whenever she was bored - drinking and sex. That was all she ever thought about. It was great when we were younger, but she never moved too far beyond that mentality in 28 years. Unfortunately, Lisa didn't look anything like she did in the past. It wasn't because of her age - it was due to her alcohol consumption and poor eating habits. Lately, sex had taken a back seat to a bottle of vodka. That was hard for me to swallow, based on our past. She rarely drank in front of me before, but always wanted to have sex. She said to me recently that making love with me in our youth was exciting. It was a big compliment coming from a woman who used to be as hot as Raquel Welch, in her prime. At least, we still had Kricket to entertain us, and Lisa was still determined to finish the bottle of wine. Anytime Lisa knew she was doing something wrong, it turned her on. I knew it was going to be a long, but potentially memorable night.

I needed to go to the Jeep to get something before bedtime; and it was also time for Kricket's walk. I noticed when we went out the front door, it hadn't been locked. It made me think that the door to the hotel wasn't secured at night. This revelation only added to the list of things that made us feel uncomfortable about staying there. Anyone could access the building from the outside without having a key or card. On our way back inside, I locked the front door, but I wasn't confident it was going to remain that way throughout the night. When we went upstairs, I tried locking the door to our room, but then Lisa discovered she was still able to push it open from the corridor. Not only was the front door not securely locked, but now we couldn't even bolt the door to our room. We couldn't call anyone to come and fix it either because it was so late. I thought to myself that we weren't safe in this place, and I didn't want to stay the night, but we had no choice.

"What the Hell!" Lisa exclaimed.

"Oh my God Lisa, someone could easily come into our room, while we are sleeping." I said.

"Oh no Alex, I scare!" Lisa replied, in her funny voice. "We gonna die!"

We were both very disturbed by our predicament, especially since there wasn't anything we could do about it.

"Help me push the couch in front of the door Lisa," I said.

"Okay, but it's heavy," Lisa replied.

"How you find this place Alex?" Lisa asked.

"On the internet," I replied. "I had no idea it was going to be like this. Next time, we will stick to mainstream hotels. I'm sorry Vonnie."

"Dat's okay baby," Lisa replied.

This place couldn't get any creepier unless a ghost started floating through the hallway with chains rattling. I had the feeling that we were going to be up all night, and not just because we were going to be having sex. Kricket was not much of a watchdog and couldn't alert us to intruders. If someone were to come into our room, she wouldn't even bark. She would just stay curled up sleeping in her bed. I'm surprised Lisa didn't choose to have a German shepherd or a Rottweiler, instead of a lap dog. Lisa wasn't a light sleeper either. When she fell asleep, she was out cold - nothing could wake her up after she closed her eyes. I decided to tease Lisa to break the tension.

"What if there's a murderer in this place?" I asked Lisa.

"There already is baby - me!" Lisa replied. "People better not mess with us or else!"

We both had a good laugh over that one. Lisa could be so funny sometimes. I was appreciative of the times she made me laugh because a lot of the time, Lisa made me want to cry. We eventually fell asleep after our midnight tryst, but we woke up early to the sound of crickets. I think it was around 7 am when I opened my eyes. I was thankful that we were both still alive, and grateful no one tried to force open our door. As far as we could tell, no one had been murdered the night before, but we couldn't possibly stay in that place one more night. We couldn't wait to get out of there.

The lady at the front desk tried to make us pay for the extra night, so I told her that Lisa's mother had just been transferred to the nursing home, and that we needed to move closer to her. I had mentioned that to the concierge when we first checked in, but she was being stubborn and uncooperative. It was necessary to get a hold of the owner and talk him into giving us a refund. I practically had to threaten him, but he finally agreed to remove the charge. Lisa's mom was about to leave the hospital, but not until the following day, so I told a little white lie. The truth was that this hotel made our skin crawl. It seemed like a religious cult hotel since no one was allowed to drink. I didn't want Lisa to consume alcohol, but I knew she would do it anyway. Then I would be stuck paying a $200 dollar fine. I was just glad to get away from there finally.

We needed to find another place to stay closer to the nursing home in Sebring. Visiting Carmen was supposed to be relaxing, but instead, I was about to glimpse into Lisa's dark destiny - and my eternal nightmare.

22. Deadly Omen

Carmen had recently left the hospital and had transferred to the rehabilitation center in Sebring. We decided to travel further south and stay in town there, so Lisa could see her mom every day easily. Despite how badly Carmen had treated her daughter over the years, Lisa still loved her mom religiously, and felt responsible for taking care of her. It showed me just how desperate Lisa was for her mother's love.

There was a lot I didn't know about Carmen in the past, even though I used to work with her every day during our show 'Classical Ice' at Cypress Gardens. She always seemed to be a stable hard worker, who stayed out of trouble. She mainly kept to herself, and didn't create drama, unlike her daughter, who had a completely different personality. Lisa was extremely intelligent, overtly expressive, confident, and a risk taker. Carmen was simple minded, submissive, and non-confrontational. She often tried to hide her emotions, while Lisa usually wore her emotions on her sleeve.

What Lisa and her mom had most in common was their strong need for attention and praise. Carmen was one of those women who kept her family's secrets close to her chest. Like her daughter Lisa, she was a woman who seemed to live in fear of the men she brought into her life. However, she consistently chose abusive despicable men to be around her and her daughter. Lisa told me that most of the men in her life, not including me, had mistreated her - especially her mother's lovers.

Carmen, at age 70 had become emaciated and frail. I felt a little sorry for her, but every time I thought about what she allowed Lisa to endure, that feeling quickly faded away. Unfortunately, many victims of abuse become abusers themselves. This was true about Lisa's mother. Whether it's verbal, physical, or emotional abuse, it's still all harmful. Despite Carmen's failure as a mother, Lisa still had an unyielding devotion toward her, which was difficult for me to understand. She and I usually got along, but she could be two-faced at times. I didn't care what she said about me, so I let her know how displeased I felt about Lisa's current circumstances, and how badly I thought she had treated her daughter throughout her life. Carmen looked at me in disbelief, when I told her how bad a caretaker I thought she had been. This was a woman who was in serious denial of her fitness as a guardian.

Lisa and I were living day to day out of a suitcase, the same as when we were touring in our past lives. In a way, it almost felt like we were in our twenties again, roaming around the country and living spontaneously. Occasionally, it felt like a fun adventure, but it was often stressful too. When I was with Lisa, everything was unpredictable, except that I could count on periodic drama. While searching for a place to stay near the nursing home, to my surprise, I happened to find a nostalgic historic European style hotel called 'Le Chateau Elan,' right next to a Formula 1 race car track. I thought that staying there would be more fun than staying at a chain hotel, so I booked it for a couple of nights. I was a little apprehensive at first, breaking my promise to stay in chain hotels, after our strange experience at the creepy hotel in Lake Wales. However, I decided to take a chance on this one anyway, because it looked so enticing.

After checking in at the front desk, we entered our room and were able to look out of our window to see one of the Formula 1 drivers practicing in a white sports car. We could hear the blistering sound of the powerful engine, as he lapped the track. I had been to a Daytona 400 race once, but I wasn't as close to the track then as we were now.

Fortunately, we didn't have to worry about crowd noise from people cheering in the stands, because this was only a practice run. Seeing an actual race might have been more exciting, but this experience was sufficiently thrilling. This hotel was in the middle of a very small town, where nothing much went on except for these car races. It was interesting to look at some of the old black and white photographs on the walls of people who attended the spectacles years ago. Anyway, it was an enormous improvement from the hotel where we just stayed the other night.

One way Formula 1 races differ from 'Indy-car' is that Formula 1 tracks have lots of twists and right turns, instead of following a counterclockwise oval track. This pattern forces the drivers to slow down considerably, and then speed up again along the route. If a driver takes a turn too fast, he'll drive off the track and crash. It takes tremendous concentration and skill to navigate this type of speedway. This track reminded me of the route leading to and from Lisa's parents' house. The pathway near her home had long stretches of road followed by a series of sharp turns. The speed limit by her house is a maximum of 35 miles per hour. Not many people traveled that route. It's a remote area in the backwoods, where there are few homes, traffic lights, and stop signs. It's more likely that someone will hit a tree than another car if they are speeding along the route.

Lisa and I stared out of the hotel room window, while watching the white colored Formula 1 car zigzagging around the speedway. As the driver rounded the curves and reached the straightaways, he must have reached speeds over 120 miles per hour. It was mesmerizing to watch. I could imagine Lisa driving a car like that when she was younger. She was a daredevil, who had few fears, other than spiders and Kookaburras. Not long afterwards, a black car entered the arena and gave chase. Now there were two moving targets. It almost seemed like we were watching a video game, as we glared through the window at the moving targets. I was thinking about the risk, while Lisa was contemplating the thrill. This was an example of how Lisa and I were different, despite being so much alike. She was someone who was attracted to danger, while I had a healthy fear of it.

"This is so cool Alex," Lisa said. "I want to drive one of those cars because the experience of moving at that speed would be exhilarating. I think driving that fast would give me a similar sensation to when I performed on the Cloud Swing in the circus. I would love to feel that rush of adrenaline again!"

"It looks scarier than fun to me," I replied. "It's certainly exciting to watch."

"I'd like to drive that black car and put my foot to the floor," Lisa said.

"Wouldn't you be afraid of crashing, after what you went through in your truck?" I asked her.

"No, I'm not afraid to die," Lisa replied.

"I don't want you to die Vonnie," I said. "I want you to be happy."

"Thanks babe," Lisa replied. "However, you only live once."

The Formula 1 cars made me ponder being in a race against time - a race I had no hope of winning. As we continued to stare through the glass, I couldn't help but feel that I was watching the future play out in front of my eyes - one that had deadly consequences. I sensed a chill running through me, as the room seemed to turn cold. As I looked up, the sky appeared to be turning from blue to grey, and I sensed a terrific storm coming.

Then, like a flash flood, rain began pouring down, and the black car's tires began to hydroplane, causing it to spin out of control. Water flew into the air creating a wave, which hid the car from our view, for just a moment. The driver slammed on his brakes and his car helicoptered into a lamppost. Lisa and I heard the crash from our room, just as a bolt of lightning lit up the dark sky. The driver managed to slow the car down just enough, so that the impact was buffered. The man in the white car maneuvered over to see if the other driver was injured. The guy in the black sports car was shaken from the incident, and his body was draped over the steering wheel. Lisa and I heard the crackle of thunder, just as his car door flew open. He was dragged from his front seat by the other driver, as he slowly gained consciousness, and stood on his own two feet.

I had an eerie feeling that dark forces were at work. I couldn't help but stare at the two cars parked so close to one another - one white one black. It reminded me of life and death - when someone I love might be taken away from me in an instant. I took Lisa's hand and looked into her eyes, which appeared to be grey now. I didn't say a word, but she knew what I was thinking. I felt like I was staring death in the face. She squeezed my hand to reassure me. I wanted to look to see what was happening outside, but I couldn't turn away from her gaze.

"It's okay Alex," Lisa said finally. "You won't need to worry about me anymore. I know where I'm going, and you won't be able to follow me. I will be alright. I'm going to go where no one can hurt me. Just don't forget about me, okay?"

I put my arms around her and held her tightly. Tears began to stream down my cheeks. As I closed my eyes, Lisa could feel my body trembling against hers, as she gently caressed my neck and whispered in my ear to be brave. I knew exactly what Lisa was suggesting. She wasn't signaling that she was moving out of Florida. The expression on her face and the sadness in her eyes revealed her intentions to me. The look she gave me touched my soul in a profound and agonizing way. It made me feel like crying at her feet with my arms clenched around her bare ankles. I felt completely helpless and at her mercy. The rain continued to pour down outside, as the wind picked up and lightning continued to illuminate the black sky.

"I love you Vonnie; I'm not ready to let you leave me just yet," I said.

"I know baby; don't cry," Lisa replied.

I felt exhausted after this, so Lisa and I took a brief nap together. In the afternoon, we went over to the rehabilitation facility to see her mother. Carmen was in bed when we arrived, not feeling well. The nurse said she might have caught a flu virus, which could be contagious. Lisa put on a mask and gloves so she could hug her mom, while I kept my distance in the doorway. I noticed by Carmen's bed table that she had brought a bunch of photos of herself from home. She was showing them off to the medical staff and bragging about herself. The whole thing struck me as odd. Most mothers keep photos of their children and boast about them - not themselves. I was surprised to see that Carmen didn't have one photo of her daughter with her. I thought to myself - how strange is that? What a narcissist!

Carmen was like a self-centered child who never grew up - just like her daughter, except more selfish and a lot more callous. Overall, Carmen seemed to be in good spirits. She said she was glad to be away from her abusive husband and hoped he wouldn't visit before he had to go to the hospital for surgery. Dave seemed to be putting off his operation for several days, for some reason. I didn't care what he did, as long as I didn't have to see him. Unfortunately, the worst thing happened. Dave tried to visit his wife at the center, even though the front desk staff was told not to give him Carmen's room number. Fortunately, Lisa and I were not there when he arrived. Dave must have been drunk at the time. The head nurse told us he became aggressive and boisterous, cursing and threatening the staff. He even spit in her face, to make matters even worse. Dave also attempted to have Carmen released before she was finished with her therapy. The head nurse eventually called the police, after he continued his obnoxious behavior.

Dave finally left, before the police arrived to arrest him for disturbing the peace. He was subsequently banned from returning to the center, which was a relief to everyone. The front desk had orders to call the police the minute they saw him again. How Carmen could tolerate a man like that for 27 years was beyond my imagination. Dave was obviously not much of an improvement from Lisa's first stepfather. He is a horrible, vile excuse for a human being, who left his wife bleeding on the kitchen floor back in September, while we were at the beach. He didn't call an ambulance, go with her to the hospital, or even pick her up when she was ready to come home.

Dave is an alcoholic and a drug addict. He has mistreated his animals and he's abusive toward everyone. His home looks worse than a crack house, with cat feces left on his bed and puke on his bedroom floor. The man is simply disgusting and repulsive in every way imaginable. I was thankful that I never ran into him face to face. I did speak to him once on a video call, when I thought he was serious about selling his house. That was one time I had the displeasure of interacting with him. It was before I knew what he was really like.

In contrast, the people at the rehabilitation center were very gracious and considerate. I was not technically family, but they allowed me unfettered access to the facility, since I was with Lisa, and had good manners. The rules of the center allowed us to take Carmen out for lunch, so we took her to a Chinese restaurant across the street one afternoon. When Lisa went to the bathroom, I took the opportunity to let Carmen know how I felt about her role in her daughter's miserable life.

"You know Carmen," I said. "I believe that you think you love your daughter, but you're not a good mother. Lisa is a mess physically and emotionally, and you haven't done much to help her over her lifetime. You are to blame for much of what's happened to her."

Carmen didn't say a word at first. She just stared at me, looking completely shocked and confused. She was giving me the deer in headlights look with her jaw wide open. I don't think she was being coy with me either. Carmen simply had no clue just how bad of a parent she had been to Lisa. Deep down, she must have known what I was talking about. However, she was in denial and didn't want to take any responsibility for her daughter's condition.

"Don't tell me you didn't know about the abuse Lisa suffered as a child," I said. "You can deny it all you want to Lisa, but I'm not stupid - I can see through your facade. Something like that just doesn't happen for 14 years, without you knowing about it - especially since you two are so close."

Carmen's face began to look distressed, as she shrank in her seat. She put both of her hands on her head with her elbows on the table and looked down, without responding. She may not have known how much Lisa told me over the past several months, but I knew plenty. Lisa and I had talked just about every day for several hours since we reconnected, and we spent about two weeks at a time together, whenever I visited her. It almost seemed like I had spent more time with Lisa in the present versus the past. Over several months, Lisa had disclosed many secrets to me that I never knew before. Some of the things she told me would curl the hair on the back of your neck. She described things that people might only see or hear about in a horror movie or psychiatric ward. The stories Lisa told me were emotionally overwhelming at times. I couldn't begin to imagine how she endured such abuse throughout her life.

"Why didn't you show up for Lisa's trial?" I asked Carmen. "She was on trial for her life for God's sake! You couldn't be bothered to be there for even one day. What's wrong with you? What kind of a mother abandons her child like that?"

"I couldn't go Alex!" Carmen replied. "What do you want from me?"

"I want the truth Carmen," I said.

"Why didn't you visit your daughter more than twice, while she was in prison for seven years?" I asked.

"I couldn't go Alex," she repeated. "I couldn't go, okay!"

"No, it's not okay," I replied. "That's not good enough Carmen! That's not even close to being good enough!"

I don't care how many years people have spent with Lisa. I knew her mind, as well, if not better than anyone. I didn't know about everything she had experienced in her life, but I knew quite a lot. I understood how Lisa's mind worked. I understood how profoundly she had been impacted by her cruel challenges, and how those experiences affected her thoughts and actions. Lisa was really a very sensitive and fragile woman, whose formidable reactions were a defensive response to being constantly threatened. Her family, her lovers, the police, and the media all attacked her at one time or another. She had no one on her side throughout most of her life. I should have been there to defend her.

I wasn't blind to Lisa's faults. I was aware of most of them. I'm not trying to make excuses for her actions. She was no saint, and she would tell anyone the same thing. Lisa may have been a victim of child abuse, but she chose to deal with her abuser by killing him, and then abusing herself. She understood she could have chosen a different path; however, she didn't have many roads from which to choose.

She dealt with poverty by stealing, which many people do. However, it wasn't always the case that she needed what she stole. Sometimes, she took things because she was bored, or wanted to give something of value to someone she loved, or simply for the thrill.

Lisa did bad things to survive and to feel loved and satisfied, and occasionally because it was exciting. Most of the time, she realized what she was doing was wrong. However, Lisa was a woman without many options or morals. She never went to Catholic school like I did, nor did she have good parents to keep her in line.

Most of us can't imagine what it was like to walk in Lisa's shoes because the path she treaded was so treacherous. No one would want to know what it was like to lead her life because it was so painful and heartbreaking. There was a lot about Lisa and her life that was broken, and she felt like her mind and spirit was beyond repair. She told me she wanted to change and live a better life, but she just didn't know how to do it. The people around her were making it very difficult for any changes to occur because they were such bad influences. Lisa was trapped in a world that was destroying her from the inside and outside, and there was very little she thought could do about it on her own. She was forced to succumb to the deadly grip her demons had around her neck.

Lisa didn't seem to want me to fix her problems, as much as she needed to feel loved by me. It's often a mistake men make with women. We want to jump in and solve their problems, instead of just being supportive and caregiving. Sometimes it's hard to love someone who is abusive toward you or themselves, and Lisa could be very cruel at times. She knew how to hurt me, whenever she wanted to. However, when it came to her mother, Lisa somehow found a way to love the only person who never showed her any real love in return.

In the present, I came to understand Lisa much better than I ever did before. I knew more about her past, and more about how her mind worked. I also understood more about the complexities of her emotions. Lisa's mother may have known a lot about things that Lisa went through in her life, but I think I understood what was going on inside Lisa's head better than anyone else. Carmen often said she didn't understand her daughter, which was somewhat ironic, because she and Lisa were so much alike, in certain ways. Their biggest differences concerned courage and compassion. Carmen was a coward and unempathetic, while Lisa was courageous, truly loved her mother, and cared about other people.

When I first met Lisa, I felt like we were a perfect match for each other, and that we were destined to be together forever. What I didn't realize for a long time was that the deck was stacked against us. In the past, Lisa and I had an extremely intimate physical and emotional relationship, but our interactions were often sexually indulgent. We never used to share our deepest thoughts with each other. In contrast, our relationship became more meaningful in the present, and less sexual. I also tried very hard to take care of her as much as possible this time, which I didn't do before. At present, I was spending an enormous amount of time focusing on Lisa's needs and talking to her about things that really mattered.

She and I weren't ready for the responsibilities of marriage back in 1989, even though we didn't plan on making the commitment for another two years after our engagement. That would have been 1991. As fate would have it, that was the same year of Lisa's arrest and when she had her baby. That year, I was only 27 years old, and Lisa was just 25. Neither one of us was ready to become a parent and have a family.

Our lives were so up in the air back then, and our futures - so uncertain. Lisa especially wasn't prepared for what happened to her when she was arrested. I happened to be in France doing another ice show. I didn't have the slightest clue what was happening to Lisa back in America. Despite our past mistakes, my priority in the present was to help her financially and emotionally, as well as try to take care of her health.

When I spoke with Lisa about her life, she trusted me enough to answer all my questions, as openly and honestly as she knew how.

She had no reason to lie to me about anything anymore. Lisa didn't seem to mind revealing her secrets to me, whenever she thought she had nothing to lose. Even though it was extraordinarily difficult dealing with her attitude and behavior, I understood why she turned out the way she did. The closest people in her life used and abused her shamelessly.

When Lisa finally returned from the bathroom, I tried to change the subject.

"What are you guys talking about?" Lisa asked.

"You, of course; who else," I replied.

"I hope it was something good," Lisa said.

"Don't worry Vonnie; it wasn't," I replied smiling.

Lisa laughed.

"Well, I hope you at least saved me some food," Lisa said.

"Oh, there's plenty to eat here honey," I replied. "However, some of it may be a little hard to swallow."

Carmen was noticeably quiet during our lunch. She had been blind-sided by my criticism, but I didn't care. She ruined Lisa's life, and I wanted to make sure that she knew that I was angry with her. After we finished eating, we took Carmen to buy some new clothes she needed, before taking her back to the rehabilitation center. Then Lisa and I drove back to our hotel. Lisa and I sat by the bar for a bit, so we could talk more without her mother present.

"I told your mom what a bad mother I thought she had been to you," I said to Lisa.

"You did, really?" Lisa replied.

"Yes, I did," I said.

"Oh my God, what did she say?" Lisa asked. "Did she admit that she knew about my stepfather raping me?"

"She didn't say much, and she didn't admit to anything," I replied.

"I'm not surprised," Lisa said. "She's never apologized to me for any of it."

"Finish your drink and we'll go upstairs," I said.

"Okay baby, thanks for sticking up for me," Lisa replied.

"Anytime honey; you know I love you," I said.

"I love you too," Lisa replied.

I paid the waitress for the drinks, then we took the elevator to our room holding hands. Lisa managed to give me that seductive and flirtatious look that she trademarked, as we ascended to our floor. I see that same expression sometimes from women, who are excited about being on a first date. It's a look that's very innocent and pure, but suggestive, at the same time.

Whenever her mood allowed, Lisa could be so sweet, loving, and affectionate, despite her Dr. Jekyll and Mrs. Hyde personality. She could also act nasty and verbally abusive for no apparent reason. I knew that when Lisa was angry; her vitriol was not actually directed at me. She frequently acted badly, due to the pain in her body and the firestorm in her mind. Whenever I spent time with her in the present, I was either in Heaven or Hell. Unfortunately, Hell was the only place Lisa experienced for most of her tortured life. No matter how much I tried to help her, it seemed that her story had already been written and sealed.

23. The House on the Lake

It was still not possible for Lisa and me to stay at the house on Buffum Lake, even though Dave finally had to go into the hospital for his heart surgery. We couldn't sleep there because the house was still so disgustingly dirty, and it wasn't secure. There was a problem with the windows closing and with one of the locks. Their horse still needed to be given food every day, so Lisa and I had to stop by the house to feed him. I also noticed that the poor animal had an untreated, open wound on its back. Lisa's parents should have called a veterinarian, but I don't think they wanted to spend the money. Lisa told me that she wasn't sure what the horse's injury was caused by, but she thought it might have been from a cougar. She said it had been living on or near their property for months. There was absolutely a deadly cougar on their property, but I wasn't convinced yet that it had four legs.

"What are you talking about Lisa? I asked. "What cougar?"

"Florida has cougars Alex," Lisa replied. "Don't you know that? There was one on our property for a while, but I think it's gone now."

"You can't be serious!" I said.

"Oh, I'm serious alright," Lisa replied.

"Why the hell didn't you tell me?" I asked.

"You never asked," Lisa replied.

"Who would ever think of asking whether someone had a mountain lion on their property?" I asked.

"Oh, I don't know, maybe someone who didn't want to get mauled while trespassing," Lisa replied sarcastically.

The thought of being confronted by a panther at home frightened me, since I grew up near a city. Being confronted by a dangerous wild animal was the last thing someone should have to worry about when they're coming home from a long day at work. Having a relationship of any kind with Lisa was a hazardous occupation. Being surrounded by danger might have been second nature to Lisa, but it certainly wasn't something I could ever get used to. Where I grew up, we only had to worry about cars driving by our house, while playing street hockey or touch football. I've only seen a cougar in an old Lincoln/Mercury commercial or at the zoo. I'm not a hunter either, so being on guard from savage predators was not something that I ever had to think about.

"Oh, by the way, don't worry about the dog, he won't hurt you, but watch out for the mountain lion, because it might kill you," I thought to myself.

"We used to have an elephant here too at one time," Lisa said. "We had elephant rides for locals and tourists up north in Maine during the summer. We made a lot of money doing that, until the elephant died, and our cash flow dried up."

Dave mistreated that animal too, and that's why it died prematurely. Lisa blamed all their animals' poor care on Dave, who had been in trouble in the past several times for animal cruelty.

Lisa talked about owning these exotic animals so casually, as if it was no big deal, and a normal thing that happened in everyone's family. This was how closed off she was from the rest of society, where people like me only saw these types of animals in the circus or at the zoo. Lisa grew up in the circus, so being around wild animals from Asia and Africa was second nature to her. She wasn't afraid of a panther living near her home at all - in fact, she felt thrilled by it. The difference was that this four-legged beast was a dangerous predator and unpredictable, and not a trained circus performer. Lisa did not seem to be afraid of things that most people would completely lose their minds over. Instead, she had tremendous anxiety concerning normal things, like not being able to find me, wondering if I had left her somewhere.

Lisa Yvonne French was an extremely complex and complicated woman, but somehow, I understood her better than anyone. She and I were very much alike, which is why I could relate to her easily. The times when Lisa reacted in a negative, spontaneous manner were more difficult for me to anticipate. However, I slowly learned what not to do around her, which made the situation worse. I began to understand why she felt so vexed about certain things, but her extreme behavior still caught me off guard, occasionally. I tried very hard to put myself in her place; but how could I comprehend what it was like to live Lisa's life? Most times, I was able to understand how her mind worked, because she and I often had the same thoughts and saw things the same way. However, the hardest thing for me to understand was why she kept sabotaging herself and putting herself down. I did appreciate the fact that ever since Lisa killed her stepfather, she thought she had become a despicable person, and developed a death wish.

The media certainly portrayed Lisa as an evil genius, but there was nothing evil about her. Even though it was close to 30 years ago, Lisa still never overcame her self-loathing and didn't think she deserved to be happy. It was partially for this reason, that no matter what she did or how badly she acted, I still loved her, because she was unable to love herself. I didn't care what other people thought about Lisa or what people thought about me for loving her. I only knew that I did, and no one was going to change that. I knew my relationship with Lisa was hurting me in the eyes of others, but it didn't matter. I was prepared to stand by her this time, through any type of criticism that came our way. Before I decided to reconnect with Lisa, I had to ask myself only one crucial question:

"Did Lisa tell the truth about the 14-year long rapes since she was just a child, or did she make it all up to escape the death penalty?"

It could have been a lie just to gain sympathy from the jury. I often wondered why she never told me about it in the past. If she didn't tell the truth about what happened during her childhood, then perhaps she was a manipulative sociopath, who could fool anyone with only a smile and a glance. If she wasn't lying about the abuse, then she was not the cold-blooded killer the media continuously portrayed her to be. In that case, she was a courageous victim and not a murderer. If that was true, then I told myself that I should try to do everything in my power to help her. It took me several weeks to think about this fundamental question. I finally decided that Lisa must have been telling the truth, and that's why I ultimately contacted her. As it turned out, I was right to believe her, but if I had been wrong, I wouldn't have been able to close my eyes and fall asleep next to her, without fearing for my life.

Even when I witnessed Lisa at her highest peak of anger, I was still never afraid of her. I knew that her anger and frustration wasn't directed toward me. I just happened to be with her sometimes when she exploded. Lisa was not a psycho-killer or a sociopath. She was a child inside of a woman's body, who had been under constant assault during her life, from people she should have been able to trust. Lisa was just a little girl who was at the end of her rope, which had been prepared by her parents to put around her neck. She was in tremendous pain emotionally and physically, and desperately needed help. Most of all, Lisa needed someone who truly loved her, and to be involved in her life. I kept thinking that I was too late coming to her aid, but I wasn't about to give up. I couldn't shake the feeling however, that I was digging in quicksand, and that time was running out.

Even though I had been to Lisa's house before, I could barely look at it now because it was so deplorable. The pool area had junk and trash everywhere. Inside the house you could barely see the floor, because there was dirt several inches thick, liquor bottles, clothes, garbage, and empty food bags everywhere.

The kitchen looked like it hadn't been cleaned in years. Dirty dishes and pans were in the sink and on the counter tops. The center island, which was quite long, was littered with pots, pans, and other junk. It was unusable to prepare food on because of the clutter. The refrigerator in the kitchen was a filthy vile mess. You couldn't put anything good to eat in there. When I opened the refrigerator door, the food left inside was inedible because it had been rotting for months and mold was growing around it. There were liquids of various kinds spilled everywhere inside, and the stench was unbearable. Rats would not eat anything in that refrigerator - it was that disgusting.

I couldn't imagine how long Lisa was living like this, but I couldn't spend one day there without getting sick to my stomach. This was not poverty - this was pure neglect from degenerate people, who were constantly taking drugs, drinking alcohol, and sleeping during the day. Their home should have been declared unlivable by a health inspector because it was so vile.

There was no hot water in two out of the three bathrooms, and hardly any edible food in the pantry, except for the cat and dog. Lisa would not have been much worse off if she had been living on the street, which she had done before. When I opened the front closet in the living room, there were no coats and no shoes or any place to put them. There were only more pots, pans, and other things for the kitchen, in a pile on the floor. One bedroom was three feet high in nothing but junk, most of which could never be used for anything.

In the family room, there were Christmas lights laced around an old coffee table, even though it was almost February, and the floor was littered with dirt and empty liquor bottles. The carpets in all the rooms were stained and filthy. They looked like they had never been cleaned or vacuumed in months, if not years. There was a hole in one of the walls where Lisa said she tripped and put her head through it. Recessed lights were out all over the house, especially in the dining area, which overlooked the pool. The windows in most of the rooms were jammed in an open position. When it rained, the water and dirt came in from the outside, creating mold and mildew along the windowsills. It also allowed the house to be vulnerable to intruders.

Lisa, her mother, and stepfather all slept in separate rooms in this four bedroom, three bath ranch house. In Lisa's room, there were dead bugs everywhere on the carpet, and it was cold and damp because the window wasn't shut. Her bed was in such poor shape that it seemed like it would collapse under her weight. Her mattress and sheets were soiled and hadn't been washed in months. Lisa's bathroom was really a guest bathroom, off the dining room, which had no hot water.

In Dave's room, he had left an opening in the sliding glass door, so that a stray cat could get inside. However, no food or water was left for it when he left the house. Cat feces were left on his bed, which had soiled the comforter, which attracted flies and caused a sickening odor. I couldn't see the floor in his room, due to all the dirty clothes and liquor bottles spread around everywhere. The bathroom floor was a mess with used towels and dirty clothes, just like the other two bathrooms in the house. Dave's shower and the other two tubs looked like they were never cleaned. There was an open peanut butter jar on his nightstand, along with dirty cereal bowls, and open bags of chips.

Carmen's bedroom was equally filthy and neglected. Clothes were all over the floor and on the bed. The bathroom was dirty and cluttered, and her mattress and box spring were on the floor with no bed frame. Lampshades and lightbulbs were missing from the lamps, and an assortment of wigs were tossed about in various places. It was difficult to open the door to any of the bedrooms, due to all the mess. I decided we would not consider touching the junk room, the pool area or Carmen and Dave's bedrooms. However, we would clean Carmen's bathroom, and take the clothes off her bed, since she would be coming home from the rehabilitation facility soon. She would require a clean bathroom and place to sleep. We probably should have washed her sheets too, but there wasn't time.

The house looked like it hadn't been cleaned in years. The inside looked like something you might see in a horror film. There was so much work to do that I just wanted to call a cleaning company and pay to have it professionally scrubbed and decluttered. I thought that most companies might turn down the work or charge triple the normal price to do the job. The house was in such disarray that it was going to take a couple of weeks to clean the entire house, but I only had three days. I had never seen any place that was anywhere near this messy or dirty, and I sold real estate for a living. The whole project made me feel depressed, just thinking about the amount of work that needed to be done.

Instead of hiring a team, I thought it would be a better idea if Lisa and I did the work ourselves. So, I told Lisa that we were going to spend the next few days cleaning her house. I planned to close the windows, lock the doors, and tackle the areas she had to use, so that she didn't have to continue living in an unsecure filthy home any longer. I told her that if she did a good job helping me, I was going to buy her a new bed to sleep on. Ironically, when Lisa and I first made contact, she told me she was too busy to talk because she was cleaning other people's homes to make money. However, that turned out not to be true. In any case, she needed to clean her own house.

Perhaps afterwards, she could slowly begin the process of putting her life back together again.

I began to appreciate more how Lisa must have been feeling, living in this pigpen every day. I didn't want to leave Florida again, knowing that she had to continue to live in these deplorable conditions. Their home was unlivable by any standard. There wasn't hot water anywhere in the house including the kitchen, except for in Dave's bathroom, because he was such a selfish bastard. He kept the master bedroom for himself, and Carmen had one of the smaller rooms - at least it had an en-suite. In good condition, the property might have been worth around $700,000 dollars, but in its present state, they would be lucky to receive $200,000 dollars for it.

When I first contacted Lisa in May of 2018, I also spoke to Dave on a video call. He said he and Carmen were getting a divorce and were planning to list the house for sale. They were all living on welfare and weren't going to be able to keep up with the mortgage payments and taxes. The plan was for Dave and Carmen to split the money from the sale of the house and go their separate ways. Carmen had filed for divorce over two years ago, but Dave had been doing everything in his power to obstruct the process. I was practicing real estate at that time, so I referred Lisa to a local real estate company to receive a referral fee. However, Dave changed his mind and decided that he didn't want to sell the house any longer or even get divorced. Carmen still wanted the divorce. However, each time there was a court date, Dave refused to show up, causing further delays.

The last thing I needed to do before leaving Florida would be to leave Lisa my Audi and drive the Jeep home. That way, she could have a good car, without feeling pressured to make payments immediately. Having the Jeep in my possession would allow me not to have to worry about being liable for an accident Lisa might cause. By the time I was finished with everything that I needed to do for her this trip, she would have taken back power of attorney from her parents and gained power of attorney over her mother. She would also have a clean house, a good car with no payments for a while, good food to eat from a clean refrigerator, have a current paid membership at a local gym, and perhaps even a few offers for a job.

I was also hoping to find Lisa a good psychiatrist or rehabilitation center, which was affordable and agreeable to her. Taking care of Lisa's basic needs often distracted me from focusing on her mental health plan, but those things needed to be taken care of as well. I was hoping her primary care doctor would do more to help with Lisa's mental health, but he really didn't do much in that regard, except to give me a list of psychiatrists' numbers to call.

"Let's get to work, okay Lisa," I said.

"Yes baby, I'm ready," Lisa replied.

It was going to take at least three or four days to clean the areas on my list. Surprisingly, they had a good washer and dryer, but it seemed like it was rarely used. We needed to collect all the trash and put it in the dozen large garbage cans that were outside in the yard. Once that was finished, I wanted Lisa to help me put all the trash in the back of Dave's pick-up truck, so they could be taken to the curb. It was going to be a lot of work, but I was determined to do it, if Lisa helped me. Part of my plan was to create a dramatic display for Dave to see, in addition to making it easier to take away all the garbage that had accumulated.

The first day, Lisa did a good job helping me to clean the kitchen. It was the hardest job because of the condition of the refrigerator. It took us all day just to finish cleaning that area of the house. Unfortunately, after the kitchen was finally usable, Lisa did less and less every day to help me. She would only pitch-in a little at a time, and then she would take a break and lie down on the recliner in front of the television. She would have a drink and then take a nap, after watching Dr. Phil or some other program like it. It allowed her to listen to other people, who had equally messed up lives. I think it helped her feel like she was not alone in her misery. Lisa appeared on Dr. Phil, sometime after getting out of prison in 1995. If you ever watched his show, you might think that some of those people are actors because their lives are so unbelievable. It's hard to imagine the turmoil and the drama in their lives is real. Lisa's life was as bad, if not worse than most of the people who appeared on his show.

By the nineties, Lisa had become quite infamous, especially in central Florida. She made national news when she appeared on a show called 'Hard Copy,' which was a television detective series, highlighting notorious killers like Lisa. She was also invited to be on talk shows hosted by Geraldo Rivera, Maury Povich, and others. She said there was also an article written about her in Vanity Fair. Lisa also posed nude for Gallery magazine. Penthouse wanted her to do a spread for them as well. However, the photo shoot with Penthouse never materialized because Lisa was arrested before contracts could be signed. Despite all the negative publicity, she loved all of this attention. Whether it was good or bad, Lisa craved to be in the spotlight. She welcomed the notoriety, even if it painted a picture of her dark side. She was very proud of everything she did that made her famous.

Strangely enough, I was very proud of my relationship with Lisa. I have never felt ashamed of her, unlike her ex-husband Jeff. I felt privileged that she and I had such a close relationship and deep love affair. My life has been enormously enriched because of that circus girl, and I feel lucky to have known her so intimately. She made many bad choices in her life, but she was only reacting to her guardians and environment. Lisa was a beautiful and caring human being, and I loved her for the woman I knew she could be.

While Lisa watched television during her breaks, she would drink, get tired and then fall asleep. She would be unconscious for at least an hour or two, while I was still busy cleaning. When Lisa woke up, she would go straight to the refrigerator and pour herself another drink. At least by this time she had stopped drinking vodka. Instead, she drank some strawberry drink with five percent alcohol content. Then she would come to help me clean for about 30 minutes. Afterwards, the pattern would repeat itself. Lisa became less and less helpful as time went on. At a certain point, I was doing all the work and it made me angry.

I finally became fed-up with Lisa drinking constantly and not getting any work done. I wanted her to get off her butt and come help me - after all, it was her house. It wasn't easy for me to understand Lisa's mental and emotional state of mind. I couldn't relate to what she had been through, or what she was still going through. Her experiences were intensely frightening. I have never been faced with anything like what she experienced, so I didn't want to judge her too harshly. At times, she seemed to have lots of energy, and acted like everyone else. Sometimes, I forgot about the pain she had been suffering through during her life. Perhaps this task was overwhelming for her, but I was still losing my patience. It might have been because I was becoming physically exhausted from doing everything myself.

Lisa's mind occasionally seemed normal, and her mood was often cheerful. Other times, she was an emotional train wreck, completely out of control. It was clear to me that Lisa desperately needed more help than I could offer her alone. However, she convinced herself that she was beyond salvation and could not recover from her past. When Lisa refused to help clean more and continued to drink, I became extremely annoyed.

I would have liked to have more time to finish what I wanted to do and take more breaks myself, but I was feeling pressure to reach my goal before Dave returned. I wanted to rest, but I didn't have much choice, except to keep pressing on. I had already stayed almost a week longer than I anticipated. However, I didn't want to leave until I knew Lisa had a better living environment. I couldn't do much about her mentally ill, drug addicted and abusive parents, but at least Lisa's surroundings would be more comfortable for her, until she could move out.

By noon on the fourth day, everything I wanted accomplished at the house was completed. We even had time to pop over to the furniture store to buy a new mattress, box spring, and bed frame. Since I finally finished cleaning, I asked Lisa if she was ready to go have her fingerprinting done for the school bus driving job. She must have been annoyed regarding my criticism of her housework efforts, so she refused to go. This was the job she said she really wanted, and now she didn't want to complete her application. I lost my patience again and it sparked another argument.

When I'm rested and feel energetic, I have greater capacity to be patient with Lisa. However, when I'm tired and frustrated, I'm not as tolerant of her belligerent behavior. Taking on the house cleaning alone and dealing with Lisa's poor attitude brought me to my breaking point. I told Lisa, if she didn't want to have her fingerprinting done, I was going to go back home, even though I planned to stay one more night.

As I was leaving, I took the keys to the Jeep. For some reason, Lisa must have thought I also grabbed the keys to the Audi because she couldn't find them. However, they were still hung up on the key hook that I had put on her bedroom wall. She became flustered and accused me of taking them. She began shouting to her neighbor to come and help her. I thought there was a good chance he might be dangerous, knowing the kind of people she and her parents associated with, so I rushed to leave. Lisa followed me out of the house, as the situation escalated and became increasingly confrontational. I tried to calm her down and change her frame of mind, but my efforts proved to be futile. I asked her again if she wanted to go have her fingerprinting done. At first, she said yes, and put some of her things in the Jeep, including her medicine bag. Then, she changed her mind and refused to go. I pleaded with her to reconsider, but she ignored me.

At this point, my patience had disappeared completely. So, I hopped into the Jeep and started to drive away. Lisa stood in front of my path, which forced me to back-up. I couldn't understand why she was trying to stop me from leaving. Then she circled around behind the Jeep, causing me to stop again. As I drove forward, Lisa screamed at me about something. I couldn't understand what she was trying to say. Then I realized that I still had some things of hers in the back of the Jeep, including all her medicine. That must have been what she was trying to tell me. Lisa became exhausted trying to run after me and I got scared. She was out of shape and became easily winded. She probably had a heart condition, due to her weight, and everything she put her body through. So, I stopped the car to prevent her from having a medical emergency. I felt bad and tried talking to her calmly again.

"I'm sorry Lisa," I said. "I didn't remember that I still had your medicine in the car."

Lisa didn't reply and sauntered to the back of the Jeep. I opened the trunk and handed her everything that belonged to her. I tried one last time to ask her if she would calm down and go with me to complete her application. It didn't matter to me if she didn't get the job, as long as she kept trying to put her life together again.

"Lisa, won't you please go with me to have your fingerprinting done?" I asked.

"No!" Lisa replied defiantly.

That was it for me; I was done with Lisa for this visit. I climbed back in the Jeep and started to drive away. I didn't know how far I was going to go this time, nor did I know if I would ever see Lisa again. I should have realized that she needed me to stay, and to try to be more patient with her. However, I felt so frustrated. I was also physically and mentally exhausted. Dave was coming back home at any minute, and I needed to leave with or without her. I was so disappointed with myself for allowing my emotions to spin out of control. This was the problem of being emotionally involved with someone you're trying to help. I knew there were risks, but I didn't know what else to do. Despite all my efforts, I felt I had failed in my quest.

At least I had possession of the Jeep again, but that wasn't as important to me as Lisa's health and happiness. Sadly, I had messed everything up again. I should have never left her, without trying harder to change her mood, or without giving her a hug - I regret not doing that. I should have just asked Lisa if she wanted to go to lunch with me and end the day on a positive note. Instead, I left for home, feeling very unsettled in my mind and in my heart. Leaving Lisa like this was something I knew I would regret in the future. I should have gone back or at least called her before I left town, but I allowed my emotions to cloud my judgement again.

The only comfort I had was that Lisa had a cleaner place to live, a car to drive, and a new bed that was coming in a day or two. She also had food to eat in a clean kitchen and her little dog Kricket to comfort her. At least Lisa would have no toxic parents to bother her nor me either, for at least one more night. Perhaps being alone was the best thing for her state of mind. On the other hand, it might have deadly consequences. As I was driving, I kept thinking that maybe I should just stop somewhere and cool down. However, I just kept going, until I crossed the border into South Carolina. Lisa called me soon after I arrived at the hotel I stopped at for the night.

"Hi Alex, where are you now?" Lisa asked. "Did you leave Florida already?"

"Yes, I'm in South Carolina," I replied. "I will drive the rest of the way home tomorrow."

"Oh, okay," Lisa said. "I'm sorry; you know."

"I'm sorry too Lisa," I said. "I love you; I just want you to feel safe and happy."

"Thanks baby," Lisa replied.

I could tell Lisa was disappointed that I wasn't coming back; she probably felt demoralized. She always became intensely depressed whenever I left her. This time it seemed worse because we split up on bad terms. Lisa had calmed down a lot since I left. I could tell by the tone of her voice that she was hoping I would change my mind and come back. However, I had already spent more time with her than I had planned, and I really needed to go home. Lisa's mother and stepfather were going to be coming home the next morning, so I thought there was no sense in returning. I felt guilty about how I left, and I knew that Lisa felt badly too. It always broke my heart knowing how sad she became when I couldn't be with her anymore. I knew that Lisa really had a hard time managing her behavior, and I was upset with myself for losing control of the situation.

"Lisa, I'm really sorry, but I need to go home," I said. "I promise I'll come back for your birthday in April, okay?"

"Okay," Lisa replied sadly. "Drive safely - I love you."

"I love you too Vonnie," I replied. "Take care of yourself."

After I hung up the phone, I felt terrible, so I went to sleep early. The next morning, I didn't call Lisa before I left. I just hopped in the Jeep and drove the rest of the way home. I didn't speak to her again until the following day. She was noticeably distraught when we spoke. Her emotions were like a pinball - constantly unpredictable. Lisa had the capacity to bounce back at any moment because she was conditioned to be resilient. She was a survivor; and no matter how many bad things happened to her, or how much pain and suffering she had to endure, she always found ways to cope. Lisa knew I was always there for her in spirit; and I'm sure she knew I intended to keep my promise to see her again. Unfortunately, Lisa dealt with her emotional distress by being self-destructive, and that always concerned me. It sometimes seemed like visiting her made things worse, instead of better. She had such a hard time readjusting to my absence, but what else could I do. I couldn't have her live with me - at least not yet.

A few days later, after I was back in North Carolina, the bed I bought for Lisa finally arrived. I had also bought her new sheets and expensive pillows, in addition to sending a nice comforter. I wanted her to have something supportive and comfortable to sleep on, so she wouldn't be in so much pain, due to her back injury. I was hoping that it would help her to sleep better at night. After receiving the new mattress and bedding, Lisa gave me a call.

"Alex, guess what," Lisa said excitedly. "I got my new bed!"

"That's great honey," I replied. "I'm glad."

"I love it, I really love it!" Lisa exclaimed. "It's so comfortable! I'm going to be able to sleep so much better now. Thank you so much Alex - I love you!"

"You're welcome Vonnie," I replied.

Lisa seemed so happy now, and I felt pleased that she was grateful that I helped her to feel better. I wished that I had bought it sooner, but I never realized she needed it. She never mentioned to me before that her bed was in such poor condition. Little by little, I felt that Lisa's life had been improving over the nine-month period that we were in contact. I hoped that she could find a job soon and address her mental health issues with a physician, as soon as possible.

I just wanted her to get her life back on track and finally move out of her parents' house. Lisa was never going to be able to recover and have a happy life if she had to continue living with Dave and Carmen. She was still emotionally attached to her mother, but living with her parents was pushing her off a cliff. I knew that Lisa wanted to live with me instead, but that was something I wasn't prepared to entertain at the time. The best I could offer her was my love and support. I wished I could have told her that we would live happily ever after, but that kind of ending only exists in fairy tales.

24. A Cry for Help

It was February 12, 2018, when I received a call from Lisa during the day. She was hysterical, screaming and crying. However, this time it felt different. Lisa was extremely angry. She told me she had a knife and wanted to kill her mother with it. Lisa said her mother was ungrateful and refused to apologize for the years of suffering that she endured. It was hard to anticipate what Lisa would do because her behavior was so unpredictable. She had killed one of her parents before and could easily do it again. I had no doubt that Lisa could be dangerous if she was pushed too far. I had always been cognizant of this fact, whenever I spent time with her. Generally, I was confident that Lisa would only hurt someone if she felt threatened, but this time, I wasn't so sure.

"Would you ever hurt or kill anyone again?" I asked Lisa one time.

"No Alex; if I ever felt like killing anyone again, I would probably kill myself," Lisa replied.

I never forgot those words she spoke to me. I thought about what she had told me while we were talking on the phone that day. I started to think that, instead of posing a threat to her mother, Lisa might be suicidal. Her mental state had completely broken down. Until now, Lisa displayed an unusual and misdirected devotion toward protecting and taking care of her mother. Now, Lisa seemed like she had finally woken up to the reality that her mom had done irreparable harm to her. I was responsible for helping Lisa to see the truth, and I knew Carmen didn't like it.

The truth was that Lisa's mom had exploited her daughter throughout her lifetime. As a young child, Lisa was told to stand on a high wire by age seven, without using a safety net. Lisa was allowed to roam freely around dangerous, wild animals unsupervised, and she was not provided with a safe and clean environment. Carmen allowed her husband to rape her daughter for years. I believe she convinced Lisa to kill her second husband and persuaded one of her boyfriends to take semi-nude photographs of her daughter for money, and then he raped her. Carmen and her third husband Dave also stole Lisa's land from her while she was in prison. Lisa's mom also chose to let her daughter grow-up without an education, and without a decent place to live. Lisa deserved much better treatment and care.

Lisa's entire life had been one long miserable and tormented existence, and Carmen was at the center of it all. Lisa was finally beginning to see that her mother never really loved her in the way a good parent should. Her relationship with her mom had finally reached a breaking point, and the conflict between them was boiling over toward an epic climax. Lisa was in terrible pain emotionally at this moment. Her mind was in fragments and her desire for retribution was burning a hole in her soul. Lisa's life had been one long nightmare from which she could never wake-up. She had been under constant threat from everyone around her, and she felt exhausted from fighting back. Despite all my efforts, I sensed that Lisa just didn't want to keep fighting anymore. She had enough of the constant struggle, torment, sorrow, and disappointment. Mentally, Lisa was stronger now and she was ready to take control of her life again. She was determined to end her pain.

When I first met Lisa, she was living in an old mobile home near Winter Haven, Florida. I visited her there occasionally when we were working for Cypress Gardens. The way Lisa had been living didn't really have any impact on me at that time. However, if I had thought about it, I would have asked her to live with me, instead of allowing her to continue to exist in that horrible trailer. While I was doing another show in Virginia in 1985, I also lived in a trailer for a short period of time, so I didn't think it was unusual for an entertainer. After so many years of living on the road, Lisa and Carmen finally had a decent home and a beautiful place to settle. Unfortunately, she and Dave didn't take care of it, and turned their property into a junkyard.

Entertainers are people who love to perform and travel. Our lifestyle is more about our freedom and sense of adventure than stability. Performers of all types often have 'Peter Pan Syndrome' - people who never want to grow up. They live their lives in a bubble, removed from the rest of the civilized world. Especially for people in Lisa's circle, societal norms and rules don't exist. Circus people, and many other show performers often live like gypsies - roaming from place to place, never settling down. They live their lives on their own terms, often outside of the law. It's because of this lifestyle, that drifters often do things that polite society would not find acceptable. In Lisa's case, her stories of rape, incest and murder seemed to have been tolerated and kept secret by her society.

It seems that an innocent child had to pay a heavy price for a handful of despicable individuals, who tolerated incest, pedophilia, and injustice. It's not always the perpetrator of the crime who is the only guilty party. It's often the case that the people who protect these criminals and keep their secrets are also responsible and should be punished, as well. If not for the people around them, the Jeffrey Epsteins and the Alvin Johnsons of the world would have been put in prison the moment they committed their first crime. It's not only the men who circle the wagons around these predators, but it's also women like Carmen and Ghislaine, who support and defend these monsters.

As Lisa and I continued our conversation on the phone, she said something truly alarming to me.

"I don't believe that I belong on this earth," Lisa said.

"What are you talking about Lisa?" I replied.

"I just don't belong here," Lisa repeated.

"Don't say that Lisa," I replied.

I knew at that moment Lisa was contemplating suicide, but it wasn't to attract attention from me. I knew she was serious, and it scared me. I spoke to her for several minutes after she made that statement to try to comfort her. I succeeded in helping her decompress for the moment, but I knew the minute I hung up the phone, she and her mom would likely start fighting again. I tried to give Lisa some words of encouragement before we ended the call.

"Everything's going to be okay Lisa," I said. "Try to get out of the house for a while. I need you to trust me. I love you, and I'm going to get help for you."

"Okay." Lisa replied. "Thanks; I love you too."

Lisa had a way of changing the tone of her voice during a conversation, which sometimes made it seem like I was speaking with a half dozen different people at the same time. When she first started talking to me, her voice had a deep, penetrating, and frightening pitch, which sounded that way whenever she was angry. Her tone was harsh and full of fire because she was furious with her mother. Before we hung up, Lisa's voice gradually became softer, sweeter, and slower - almost like a child, who desperately needed her mother to hold her and keep her safe from harm.

Unfortunately, Lisa didn't have a mother who protected her - she only had me. I couldn't be with her all the time. However, I was still Lisa's caregiver, her financier, her confidant, and her lover, but most of all - I was her best friend. It was a vital role to fill - the responsibility was overwhelming. I was dealing with a 51-year-old woman, who had the emotions of a five-year-old child. Although, this adolescent had a mind like Cat Woman and a kiss like Poison Ivy - a powerful cocktail of intellect and passion.

Lisa was beyond my ability to help her psychologically, but she refused to seek help from professionals. She needed to have 24-hour care. However, without her cooperation, I couldn't provide her with what she needed, to become healthier. For the moment, it seemed Lisa had her sights targeted on her mother. I would be lying if I said I wasn't afraid of what might happen. In hindsight, I wish I had taken a plane and flown down there the same day. Instead, as soon as I hung up the phone, I called Lisa's primary care doctor to ask for help. I didn't know what else to do.

Apparently, the protocol in Florida is to contact the police - so that's what her doctor did. Before they arrived at Lisa's house, a female officer called me. I told her about the conversation I had with Lisa. I explained to the policewoman that Lisa had a volatile personality, and if frightened, she could be dangerous. I warned the officer not to approach Lisa with aggression or make her feel threatened, because she might retaliate in an unpredictable way. Despite my warning, the police showed up at Lisa's house with their lights flashing and sirens blazing, according to Lisa. This was not the way they should have entered the property. I didn't report to the police that she had threatened her mother with a knife because I didn't want Lisa to be harmed or arrested. Fortunately, they found her outside her home, crying in the black Audi.

Lisa was distraught and alone, except for Kricket. Apparently, the police decided to put her in handcuffs, and then questioned her and her parents. Unfortunately, they released her after their interview, rather than take her to a mental institution to be evaluated by a psychiatrist. It was a huge mistake and misguided protocol to release a woman who is suicidal. Apparently in Florida, there is no such law requiring that a person suspected of suicide to be temporarily institutionalized, which I think is highly irresponsible.

After the incident, Lisa texted me and told me what happened. I made the mistake of not calling her back directly. She made me aware by text message that her doctor had called and spoke with her after the police left. Lisa conveyed to me that she was tired of the police, tired of doctors, and tired of everything. I should have realized what she meant by that, but I didn't read between the lines. Then, Lisa texted me these words:

"LOSE MY NUMBER!"

I thought to myself, if that's what she wanted, I would leave her alone for the time-being. However, I was still determined not to allow anything to happen to her, and that's why I called her doctor right away. I told Lisa that I didn't care if she was upset with me for doing it. For the moment, I understood that Lisa would likely refuse further help from anyone, including me - she just wanted to be left alone. However, I misunderstood what Lisa was trying to say to me. She was telling me that she wanted to end her life!

Lisa had a way of wearing me down with the drama she created. At this point, I felt mentally and emotionally exhausted. I didn't know what to do anymore - I was totally burned out. I knew that I was losing the war, after being defeated in so many battles. Lisa always seemed to be in control of everything, even though I had the illusion of being in the driver's seat. It was pure madness on my part, thinking that I had any power over her, or could influence any of her decisions. Lisa must have felt completely alone and simply tired of the struggle. I'm sure she just wanted to let all her pain evaporate into thin air.

Lisa had spent her lifetime fighting spiritual demons and human monsters, while never experiencing true love. Sadly, she never stopped wishing for her mother's love, while ignoring what I had to offer her. Most people in Lisa's life were just out to see what they could take from her and gave nothing back. The same thing happened to Elvis Presley, Michael Jackson, and Judy Garland. The people around these superstars systematically sucked the life out of them like parasites.

Lisa had nothing left to give anymore, and her heart could not absorb more disappointment. She was a woman who searched for love her entire life, but never found it. Ironically, I loved Lisa more in the present than I ever did in the past. Unfortunately, by this time, Lisa had lost her faith, and she was exhausted waiting for someone to love her unconditionally. In Lisa's mind, love was just a series of broken promises and empty words.

I found Lisa's reckless and self-destructive habits to be extremely disheartening. I finally realized that our relationship could never make a full recovery from the state we left it in 1990. Almost 30 years in the past, I had abandoned our relationship over a false perception, pride, and stupidity. In the present, I was desperate to correct my catastrophic mistake. Unfortunately, it was probably too late. It seemed like Lisa had finally given up, after decades of struggle and heartbreak. I anguished over the notion that there was nothing more I could do to save her. I sensed things were about to implode, and it made me afraid.

In my youth, Lisa was like the sun, which projected warmth and vitality into my life and everyone around her. On this day, February 12, 2019, I felt the cold chill of winter touch my soul, as I imagined there being a solar eclipse on the horizon. Lisa's bright shining light would soon go out for eternity, and leave me alone in the darkness, separated from her fiery spirit - forever.

25. The Phone Call

It was the afternoon of February 16, 2019, just four days after I last communicated with Lisa. I didn't call her on Valentine's Day, to my grand regret. I assumed she was still upset with me for calling her doctor, forcing the police to arrive at her house. It sometimes took Lisa a day or two to calm down after an episode, but she still hadn't contacted me. I thought, perhaps she might have been waiting for me to call her first. I decided to text Lisa a couple of times, but I received no reply. I tried to ask her if she was all right, and if she appreciated everything that I tried to do for her. I expressed disappointment and regret that we were on bad terms again.

I couldn't understand why Lisa was angry with me for trying to save her life. Maybe she wasn't blaming me for her current misery, but just frustrated about her life and her current circumstances. At least she had a new bed to sleep in, a nice car to drive, and a much cleaner house with fresh food in her refrigerator. Lisa didn't need to worry about her doctor bills or car payments for now, due to my help. I had done everything I could think of to improve her life, short of staying with her every day. Suddenly, a call came in from Lisa's phone. I hurried to pick it up, but I was surprised when I didn't hear her voice on the other end of the line.

"Alex, this is Carmen," she said. "Lisa is dead!"

"No, no, no, oh no!" I screamed.

I started to cry, and I couldn't catch my breath. I was overwhelmed with grief. My legs felt weak, and in an instant, I was on my knees on the floor. When I was finally able to speak, I asked Carmen what happened.

"Lisa was in an accident with the car; Kricket is dead too," Carmen said.

"When did this happen?" I asked.

"Lisa was found by the police after midnight, not far from the house on Valentine's Day," Carmen said. "She was on her way to Karaoke."

Carmen had waited a day and a half to tell me the news. Despite my emotional state, I thought to myself that the story didn't make any sense.

"Why would Lisa go out so late at night with Kricket on Valentine's Day?" I thought. "She wouldn't go to a bar with her dog, even if she was allowed in with her."

The Audi I gave her was made of solid steel and had airbags. It was in perfect condition with new top-grade tires. If she was wearing a seatbelt and driving the speed limit, it would have been impossible for her to have a fatal accident, even if she had been drinking. The story Carmen was trying to feed me didn't satisfy my appetite for the truth. She simply wasn't being straight with me. I prayed that Carmen was lying about Lisa's death. My heart and spirit were inconsolably crushed. People close to me had died before, but I never felt this devastated by their passing. The pain in my heart was unbearable. I should have been prepared all along for something like this to happen, but I still felt completely blindsided. It was the timing of this tragedy that caught me by surprise.

Lisa's quality of life had greatly improved because of the help and attention I had given her. All she had to do was to follow through finding a job and making an appointment with a psychiatrist. Then she could move out of her parents' house and restart her life in a more peaceful environment. I just couldn't accept that this was the time when she decided to throw her life away. Lisa had cheated death so many times in the past, only to end it all now. Why?

"I don't understand, Carmen, how could this have happened?" I asked.

"I don't know Alex," Carmen replied.

"Will you let me know when you know anything else, okay?" I asked.

"Okay Alex," Carmen replied.

I wasn't satisfied with Carmen's story. As I hung up the phone, I began to cry again. I just sat on the floor for what seemed like hours, until it became dark outside. All I could think of was that Lisa was gone forever, and I never bothered to call her on the day she died. Whatever happened to her was no accident. I was sure that Lisa committed suicide, and she chose to kill herself in my car on Valentine's Day. I believe Lisa might have intended to send a message to her mother and me - one that we would remember every February 14th. Lisa said to me that if something happened to her, she wanted me to take care of her four-legged baby. So, it surprised me that she chose to put Kricket in the car to die along with her - Egyptian style. Perhaps she wanted to have her companion with her in the Afterlife.

I was so distraught that I didn't want to do anything except go to bed. I had already cried for several hours, while huddled on the floor of my first-floor guest room. I was emotionally worn out, so I went upstairs, got undressed, turned off the light, and went to bed. While I lied there under the covers, I couldn't think of anything else other than Lisa navigating that snake-like route near her home, where she ultimately surrendered her life. The day that Lisa and I watched the Formula 1 car crash had been a premonition. The roadway near Lisa's house has a series of long stretches and sharp turns, just like the racetrack we witnessed in Sebring. That was where Lisa talked about putting her foot to the floor in a black car, not fearing death. I thought about what must have been going through her mind, as she took the first turn and then the second, before reaching the next straightaway, aiming for the largest tree along the road.

I thought about little Kricket, who must have been scared in the back seat, curled up in her little bed shivering in silence - sensing that something bad was about to happen. I imagined Lisa thinking about all the rapes she endured, her fall from the Cloud Swing, and her accident in Kansas, where she rolled 80 feet down an embankment, and left hanging upside down, bleeding, and unconscious. I imagined her thinking of the days she spent in prison and in Hospice, waiting to die alone. I imagined Lisa thinking about the days her two children were born, and the times that they were ripped from her arms.

Perhaps Lisa was even thinking about the day we first met, the time we were engaged, the moment we split up, and the day in Tampa when we were reunited. Perhaps she was contemplating all the times she reached out to her mother for an apology, which never came. Lisa may have been thinking about how she had to deliver her baby chained to a hospital bed, only to have to give her up, just hours after Joy was born. Perhaps she said goodbye in her mind to her son Geoffrey, who almost never answered her calls. Most of all, I thought about how scared, desperate, and angry Lisa must have been, as she embarked on her journey to the underworld. Lisa was alone, except for her faithful sidekick, as the speedometer continued to climb higher, and the sight of the woods came into view.

I could hear Lisa's final scream and the sound of the impact of the crash, which echoed in my mind. I imagined the Audi lifting off the roadway like an airplane, flying straight into a tree, and then crashing to earth. I thought about Lisa's weary and torn body catapulting forward, as her head slammed into the glass of the front windshield, killing her instantly. I had a vision of her lifeless body slumping back over the steering wheel, where she was found by the police hours later. Lisa wasn't dressed to go out to a club that night. She was dressed only in a white T-shirt, pink sweatpants, and aqua flip-flops, between one and two in the morning. Ironically, it was about the same time of night that Alvin's body had been found in the woods. Lisa's sin had come full circle, and her penance had been paid with her life.

My mind replayed the crash repeatedly in my head, until I became mentally exhausted, and I finally fell asleep. I was drenched in sweat and tears, hoping when I woke up, I would realize that it all had been just a nightmare. When I finally opened my eyes the next morning, I knew that the phone call from Carmen wasn't a dream. Lisa was dead, and I would never see her again in this life. I stayed in bed all day, completely overwhelmed with grief and despair. All I wanted to do was to sleep and escape my inconceivable reality. Lisa's death felt surreal to me. I didn't want to believe she was really gone forever. I wanted to destroy the brain cells which carried this information.

What made matters worse was that I knew I couldn't attend Lisa's funeral because of Dave. I couldn't say goodbye to my lover properly. I couldn't even hold her hand one last time, before her lifeless body was cremated, and her ashes scattered in the wind. I would find no solace from her horrible family or from the memories she and I created together. I felt only bitterness and contempt for everyone who had harmed her, during her miserable life. I stayed in bed day after day, only going downstairs to eat, occasionally. I couldn't work anymore. My depression continued to grow worse as the days went by. At some point, I thought I would lose my mind completely. I cut myself off from my job, my friends, my phone, everything. I buried myself in the sorrow and pain I felt deep inside my soul - I wanted to die!

A couple of weeks later, I finally emerged from my abyss. My fury directed at Carmen and Dave began to grow inside me. I felt like I had reached out of the depths of Hell to resurrect myself from obscurity to seek revenge for my loss. I began to feel rage flowing through my veins. Hatred does in fact make you powerful, and gives you focus and determination to right the wrongs that have been done. I hated Lisa's family for the way they treated her and what they had done to me, by pushing her over the edge. Her parents had destroyed her life and mine, and I was bitterly angry with them about it - I won't deny it.

My feelings of animosity began energizing my motivation, and I used this fuel to light a fire inside of me. It helped me to awaken from my slumber of depression. I was determined to find all the facts pertaining to how Lisa died, and what led to her to suicide. She had posted something on one of her Facebook pages in the past, which read:

"THIS IS NOT THE END OF MY STORY."

Sadly, for Lisa Yvonne French, this time - it was really the end!

26. Searching for Answers

My name was listed as the primary insurance holder on the Audi, which is why the insurance company contacted me, after receiving news of the crash. They told me where the car had been towed and asked me if I could come to Florida to sign release papers. Once I had done that, the insurance company could take possession of the car to evaluate the damage and write a check. When I contacted the man from the towing company, he sent me photographs of the car from his yard. The entire front end of the Audi was demolished, and the windshield had a small round shaped indentation from where Lisa's head hit it during the crash. The airbag deployed but didn't save her life. If she had been wearing her seatbelt, it's likely she would have survived the impact. I believe Lisa deliberately didn't put it on because keeping herself safe was not her intention.

Apparently, the car slammed directly into a large tree at high speed. From the damage to the car in the photographs, it looked like Lisa had been driving over 75 mph in a 30-mph zone. The police initially assumed it was an accident because they discovered that Lisa had been drinking while driving. They concluded prematurely that she lost control of the car while intoxicated. However, there were no skid marks from attempting to brake or any signs of the vehicle swerving along the road. The facts did not support the drunken accident theory; I knew this was not the case.

Gregg speculated that someone might have been chasing her, and that explained why she had been driving so fast. Even though it was an interesting theory, I didn't think this explanation had merit either. However, I knew that Lisa had deliberately killed herself because of the conversation we had just two days prior to her death. Once all the evidence was collected and the autopsy report filed, I was certain Lisa's death would be ruled a suicide.

I believe Lisa really wanted to have a more peaceful life, but she didn't know how to manage it. She had faith in me, but she couldn't trust anyone completely. Lisa never found a way to come to terms with all her painful memories. I did everything I could think of to help her and never tried to take advantage of her, the way other people did. It still wasn't enough to save her. All I wanted was for Lisa to have a better life and to be safe from harm. It wasn't a lot to hope for, but it was still too much to expect.

I asked Lisa once if she could remember a time in her life when she felt the happiest. She told me it was when she had an opportunity to swim with dolphins in Las Vegas. Her face lit up with an exuberant smile when she told me about her experience. I could see the joy in her eyes, as they sparkled with delight, thinking about her childhood memory.

"It was really an amazing experience," Lisa said. "I was able to hold onto their fins while they towed me through the water. They swam around me and jumped over me. It was thrilling. Animals have pure spirits and give unconditional love. If you treat them kindly, they will become your friends for life. They will never harm you - unlike people."

Sadly, there were not many happy memories in Lisa's past. My hope was that she could experience that same level of joy again in the future. Unfortunately, having a happy life stretched far beyond her reach, and it was something Lisa no longer believed in. I think the only thing that kept her going all those years we were apart was the belief that her mother loved her. She finally realized that what I told her was true - that love was more about actions than words, and that her mother's deeds never demonstrated real love toward her. Now that Lisa had become more sober and spoke with me about the facts of her life, she finally faced the sad truth - that her mother never took care of her properly and exposed her to unspeakable harm. I believe understanding this sent Lisa over the edge. Everything she thought she knew about her mother had been an illusion.

Perhaps Lisa always knew the truth but refused to accept it. Lisa may have thought that if her mom didn't really love her, then no one did - so there was nothing left to live for. She may have asked herself – "Why continue suffering if nobody really loves me?" Sadly, Lisa chose Valentine's Day to remind everyone, including me, how much she didn't feel loved or appreciated. The truth was - I loved her tremendously, but for some reason, I couldn't make her believe it.

Now, I had to prepare to make a fourth journey to Florida. This time it wouldn't be to see Lisa. It would be to close the last chapter of her life, without having the opportunity to attend her funeral. I had to sign paperwork to release the car and look to see what might still be inside. I also had to return the license plate to the DMV and consult with an attorney. This was going to be one of the hardest things I ever had to do in my life. I had already been feeling extremely stressed for the past 10 months being involved with Lisa again. I never anticipated what I'd have to go through with her, when her name first came up on my radar again. It would have all been worth it, if Lisa survived and had been living a better life. I wanted to visit the site where Lisa ended her life, but I was already very emotional, so I decided not to go.

Prior to her death, I knew what Lisa had been going through, every step of the way. I also knew that none of the theories related to her death were correct, except for my own. No one else believed her 'accident' had been a suicide. Even Carmen, who knew her best, pretended Lisa's death was an accident. However, there was only one plausible explanation. She decided to end her life and take her little dog Kricket with her, so that she wouldn't die alone. Lisa loved that little dog more than anything else in the world. She had been a loyal and devoted companion. I expected Lisa to make sure I had custody of Kricket if anything happened to her. She didn't trust her parents to take care of her baby, especially since her mom refused to take care of Joy.

Two days before Lisa departed on her final journey from earth, I stopped her from killing herself by causing the police to be sent to her house. By Valentine's Day, Lisa was determined to end her suffering, and she decided not to let me stop her. When I spoke with Carmen on the phone, she told me that Lisa had written me a Valentine's Day card, which she never sent. Lisa did the same thing with a Christmas card, which she finally gave to me in January. I told Lisa's mom that I would send my friend Carrie over to pick it up because I didn't want to have a confrontation with Dave.

By the time Carrie gave me the card, either Carmen or Dave had opened it first, which didn't surprise me. They may have been concerned about what she wrote to me because it might incriminate them in some way. When I read the card, it seemed as if everything was fine when she wrote it. It was lighthearted and funny - nothing profound or ominous. It was just like Lisa to hide her pain with humor and pretend everything was all right - even though her whole world was crumbling around her.

The following day, I started to prepare for the long journey south. This was going to be the worst trip I ever had to make. Along the way, my mind would be free to think about everything that had happened in the past year. I wasn't looking forward to allowing free thoughts to flow through my mind for the next 12 hours. I didn't want to cry anymore, especially while I was driving long distance. After tortuous solitude, I arrived late at night in Orlando. All I wanted to do was go to sleep, so I could stop thinking. I wanted to have energy for what was going to be a miserable day.

The next morning, I drove to the towing company. The man I spoke to previously met me at the gate and led me over to the Audi. Even though I had seen photos of the car already, I still wasn't prepared to see it smashed to pieces up close. There must have been tremendous force from Lisa's body during the impact because the steering wheel had been pushed closer to the dashboard by the weight of her body. Glass and car parts were everywhere, and Lisa's blood had stained the driver's side seat cover and front windshield.

I froze as I looked down on the floor underneath the steering wheel. One of Lisa's blood-stained flip-flops had been left behind, after the police had removed her lifeless body from the demolished pile of junk. I picked it up off the floor and began to cry. I thought to myself that she shouldn't have died this way. It was a horrible end to such a rare and gifted woman. Lisa chose to take her own life, rather than be committed to an institution or maintaining the status-quo. Apparently, all my efforts to help her and show her my love were in vain. Lisa never said goodbye to me because she knew if she did, I would have tried to save her again. This was really the first time her death felt real to me. Her tragic life's story had finally come to fruition.

Lisa often said to me - "If not for you, I'd be dead already."

I guess I should have felt grateful for the time I was able to spend with her before she died, but I didn't feel thankful at all. I only felt pain, sorrow, and emptiness. I was completely lost without her, as I had been every day since we split up. Despite everything, Lisa was still the greatest lover I ever knew. I had lost her once before, but this time it was forever because I failed to save her. No matter how much I did to help Lisa survive, it wasn't enough. It wasn't nearly enough! Lisa's death meant the end of her pain, but for me - it was only the beginning of mine.

After removing some things from the car, including Kricket's collar and leash, I signed the paperwork to release the Audi to the insurance company. Lisa's doctor's office was nearby, so I decided to go there next. When I arrived, I found that her doctor wasn't in on Fridays, so I wasn't able to speak with him that day. The girl at the front desk remembered me because I had been there a few times with Lisa over the past several months. I told her what had happened, but she already heard the news. The office assistant was very sympathetic and had kind words to say to me. We spoke for about 15 minutes before I left to go back to the hotel.

When I arrived, I went to my room, put the 'Do Not Disturb' sign on the door, turned off the lights and closed the curtains. Then, I took off my clothes and slipped under the covers. I cried again until I fell asleep. It had been such a traumatic day, which I wanted to forget. I didn't even wake up to have dinner. Before losing consciousness, I tried to imagine how Lisa must have felt before she died. She had complained to me about how ungrateful her parents acted, after all the housework we did and the attention and care she gave her mom at the nursing home.

Despite all my help and support, Lisa was apparently tired of the daily struggle. She just wanted to leave this world, so that all her pain would finally be gone. At this time, I felt the same way she did. I just wanted this torment and my reality to disappear forever. I closed my eyes, hoping I would wake up and realize my reality was just a bad dream. I tried to sleep, but I felt tortured by the images in my mind and the ache in my heart. On April 11, it would have been Lisa's 52nd birthday. I had hoped that the idea of spending it with me would have given her something to look forward to. Unfortunately, it wasn't enough incentive to keep her from destroying her life.

I'd been depressed before, but the feeling I had now was nothing like what I had ever experienced in the past. I blamed myself for Lisa's death. I had been so focused on helping to put her life back together again, that I didn't realize that she may not have been ready to do that yet. Perhaps what she needed more was time to heal with love, affection, and understanding - free from pressure and criticism. Maybe, I should have fought harder to encourage Lisa to see a specialist, instead of helping her to find a job. It was a total failure on my part, and it all turned out so tragically in the end.

When I woke up the next morning, the cycle of depression started all over again. I kept going over everything in my mind, repeatedly. I thought about what I could have done and said differently. I contemplated why I failed to make sure that Lisa received proper psychiatric care. I also thought about whether I had made a terrible mistake by helping her to have a car to drive. I kept thinking about what I could have done differently to have changed the outcome. These questions will haunt me for the rest of my life.

Suicide obviously ends the life of an individual in distress. However, it also hurts and devastates the people they leave behind. It's a life-long sentence for the people who loved them the most. Some people who suffer from the death of a loved one, don't survive long afterwards because the pain is too intense. People who commit suicide may not understand the impact they cause to others when they choose to kill themselves. Perhaps they want others to suffer. Maybe, they aren't thinking about anything, except the agony they are experiencing. I will never know if Lisa wanted me or her mother to suffer, or if she just wanted to end her own suffering. After someone decides to end his or her life, the people closest to them can become lost in unending despair. This is how I was feeling. I believed that my suffering would never end. I felt as if by dying, Lisa had transferred all her pain to me.

Child abuse is one of the worst crimes against humanity, yet it often goes unpunished. Lisa had been afraid that if she told the police about Alvin, they wouldn't believe her. This is often the case concerning many victims of sexual predators - particularly children. They are victimized twice. Once by their abuser and again by the justice system and society. Unfortunately, sexual predators are protected by their wives, parents, friends, siblings, the government, and society. If these criminals are convicted, their sentences are often far too lenient. The justice Lisa served to Alvin caused her a lifetime of suffering and persecution. Her mother Carmen got away with being an accessory to child abuse, murder, and to her daughter's suicide. It doesn't seem fair that she wasn't held accountable for her crimes against her daughter. However, in 2020, Carmen died under mysterious circumstances - perhaps from guilt and shame. Maybe, it was something more sinister.

The dark clouds of despair had been forming for days, and they were beginning to infect and poison my soul. I was alone and in crisis, and I wondered if there was going to be anyone who would rescue me now. I honestly didn't feel like living anymore without Lisa. I felt torn up inside and responsible for what happened to her during her life. I still had things I needed to do in Florida, but I didn't feel like doing any of them. I wasn't even sure I could leave my hotel room or drive home. I had put most of my time and effort into saving Lisa's life over the past year to no avail. I asked myself what was left for me in this world without Lisa, except to find out if Joy/Megan is really my daughter. I decided to stay in my hotel room for another day in the dark under the covers - continuing to be tortured by my thoughts and emotions.

The next day, I decided I needed to try to feel better, so I thought I would go for a walk around Downtown Disney, which has been renamed 'Disney Springs.' Since I couldn't go to Lisa's house, I couldn't retrieve anything I gave to her that I wanted to keep. I also couldn't sell the bed back to the store because Dave refused to let the movers pick it up. Dave and Carmen were going to keep everything, even though all that belonged to Lisa, by law should have gone to her son Geoffrey - including the car insurance money. I walked around for hours just trying to keep my mind off the image of the car and Lisa's bloody sandal. I couldn't comprehend why she chose to end her life so violently. That question continued to plague my thoughts.

Lisa could have killed herself any number of ways, but she chose to die in the car I gave her on a day which has symbolic meaning about love. She could have overdosed, drowned herself in the Lake by her house or taken poison. She could have even put a gun to her head and shot herself. Why kill herself in this fashion and put Kricket in the car with her? Did she plan it before she left the house or decide to do it after she started driving? These were the questions that tormented me. I didn't want to make Lisa's suicide personal, but that's what it felt like to me. Everything Lisa did was always personal and dramatic. The way she chose to die seemed like she had sent a message to everyone who knew her well. The message may have been:

"I'm done with all of you and everything; you don't deserve me!"

During this whole ordeal, I discovered that Carmen was one of those people who was nice to your face and then talked badly about you behind your back. I was aware that Dave manipulated her, but that was no excuse for how she behaved toward Lisa or me. Carmen was beautiful in her prime, but as she aged, she became increasingly jealous of her daughter. I'm sure there must have been many good men in the circus, but somehow Carmen ended up with the most vile and evil lovers. In her youth, she could have chosen almost anyone she wanted, but unfortunately, Carmen attracted the worst type of men.

As far as I knew, I was one of the few people in Lisa's life who didn't try to exploit or mistreat her. I was probably one of the only ones who tried to help her with no strings attached. Unfortunately, people like Lisa often have no one who wants to help them. As a society, we can't just stand on the sidelines and look the other way when someone needs help - especially if it's someone we know. We all have a responsibility to act when someone is suffering. It's not enough to say you will help, but only if you're asked. People like Lisa are not going to ask for help. We must offer aid to people, even if they say they don't want it. Minds like Lisa's are broken. People like her are incapable of thinking rationally or in their best interests. Lisa was mentally ill and in deep distress and couldn't make good decisions for herself.

Exactly what made Lisa choose this manner of death will remain a mystery that no one will ever solve. However, there was one thing I had no doubt about - Lisa's death was a suicide. Every other explanation that came to a different conclusion was wrong. The only place I might find more answers would be in the police and autopsy reports. Even so, those reports weren't going to tell me what was going through Lisa's mind when she got behind the wheel of my black Audi on February 14th, 2019.

I kept running everything over again in my mind, as I walked among the crowd of people. I couldn't stop thinking about how this tragedy could have been prevented. I wondered if Lisa was upset with me because I didn't call or send her a card and flowers on Valentine's Day. I know I should have - I will regret it forever! "Lose my number" was the last thing she wrote to me, other than the Valentine's card she penned. I had left Lisa alone on Christmas, New Years and Valentine's Day, but if I had the chance to change the past, I would have spent every day with her, if it kept her alive.

Lisa and I lived about 12 hours apart, so I couldn't be with her more than a week or two at a time. She fought with me sometimes because she needed me, but I couldn't be there. I should have realized that causing trouble was her way of demanding attention. I spent almost eight weeks together with Lisa during a 10-month period in 2018 - 2019. However, Lisa needed me to spend more time with her, but it wasn't possible. I had to work and take care of other things, as well as other people. I couldn't be in two places at the same time.

Sifting these thoughts through my mind wasn't going to bring Lisa back again; and it wasn't doing me any good either. So, I continued to walk along the pathway, among the horde of visitors who were eating and drinking and having a good time. I tried to absorb the good feelings surrounding me, but it wasn't working the way I hoped. It seemed like there was a storm cloud following me everywhere; and I knew that it was going to shadow me for the rest of my life. It was going to be there every night before I went to sleep, in my dreams, and each morning when I opened my eyes. I became aware that Lisa's death would always eclipse any sunshine I experienced in the future. She had finally escaped all the pain she endured during her life, but unwittingly she had transferred her burden to me to carry.

I kept thinking about the fact that we were supposed to spend her birthday together in April, but now that wasn't going to happen. I continued to walk among the joyful visitors, who were oblivious to my misery. The same thoughts and questions ran through my head, like a merry-go-round which never stopped turning. I stayed at Disney Springs until after dinner. I finally ate something, despite my mood. I'm not much of a drinker so I didn't get drunk, but I would have liked to. Unlike Lisa, I didn't like to take drugs or drink alcohol to deal with my anguish. I tried hard to recall good memories we shared together to cheer myself up, but it didn't help. All my recollections were overshadowed by Lisa's untimely demise.

Soon, it would be time to go home. I didn't think I could deal with coming back to central Florida again for a long time. I had tried to care for Lisa like no other woman in my life, and it ended in total disaster. I felt completely devastated. I didn't know how I was going to pick up the pieces of what was left of my life and start over. I didn't feel any comfort walking among happy people - nor did I find any pleasure in eating delicious food and drinking good wine. I wondered if I would ever enjoy anything again.

I left for the hotel feeling overwhelmed with grief, wishing that I had not wasted 28 years of my life living without my greatest lover. Tomorrow, I would have to return home with the knowledge that I would never see Lisa's face or hear her voice ever again. Lisa had cried so many tears in her life - enough to fill the Grand Canyon. I took some comfort in knowing that she would cry no more tears in Heaven.

27. Incompetence and Underhandedness

It had been an exhausting trek home from Florida. After heading to bed, I couldn't sleep for hours. Even though I was tired from driving, my mind was restless. I was tormented by everything that had happened in the past couple of weeks. It would be at least a few days before I could leave my bedroom again for more than a few minutes at a time. All I wanted to do was escape my reality and my emotional turmoil.

A few days after returning home, Lisa's doctor called to talk, since he missed me at his office. It was very nice of him to take time out of his day to offer his sympathy. He knew I loved Lisa because I had taken the time to speak with him about her well-being. He tried saying nice things to console me. It gave me the sense that he cared about her too. Lisa told me that her doctor had a son who committed suicide, so I knew he understood the misery of losing a loved one this way.

In my opinion, Lisa's doctor still didn't do enough to help her nor take enough time to understand everything that was wrong with her health. He should have known about her alcoholism, and that she had deep seeded psychiatric issues. He also didn't give her much of a break when it came to his fees, knowing she had no job and no health insurance. Lisa was also a drug addict, who never should have been prescribed opioids. However, I did appreciate that he took the time to call me after her death. He also called to talk to Lisa two days before she died to see how she was doing, after her encounter with the police. As much as I think he cared about Lisa, he fell short of doing enough to save Lisa from killing herself.

Like many doctors in this country, Lisa's PCP was too busy to notice certain things about her condition and didn't take enough time to ask her pertinent questions. I'm sure that Lisa probably lied to him during every visit and withheld valuable personal information. Even so, I think her physician could have helped Lisa more concerning the extra weight she was carrying, stemming from her alcoholism, lack of exercise and depression. I know that doctors can only do so much when their patients are being uncooperative. However, Lisa had been going to see him regularly every month, so he should have been more informed. It's incumbent upon health care professionals to know their patients as well as possible, so they can treat them appropriately.

Many patients are set up for failure based on our current system of healthcare. I think people hoped that the Affordable Care Act (ACA) would provide better coverage for people with limited financial means. Unfortunately, 'Obamacare' has only made things much worse for many people who have extensive medical needs, because it's so expensive and complicated to access. Lisa couldn't sign up for it by herself, so I had to help her to register. Afterwards, I discovered that the premiums would eat up most of her welfare check. It cost about $650 dollars a month and she received only $750 dollars each time in welfare benefits.

By the following week, I finally opened my computer and looked for how I could receive the police and autopsy reports related to Lisa's death. While I was doing this, I wondered why I hadn't heard from the authorities in Florida, inquiring about what I knew. I was sure that Carmen must have given them my number, if they didn't have it already. I was the closest person to Lisa other than her mother, so it felt strange that no one seemed interested to talk to me. She also died in my car, even though it was registered in her name, but my name was still on the insurance. It didn't make any sense to me that I wasn't contacted within a week after her death.

Weeks passed while I checked the internet to see if anything had been written in the newspapers about the fatal incident, but I found nothing. I wondered how they could have missed a story about the death of one of the region's most notorious female killers. It was strange no one in the media seemed to know about Lisa's suicide. The press is constantly in touch with the police to see what's newsworthy. If I hadn't seen the car myself and read the police report, I might doubt that Lisa had died. Certainly, a woman, who had been on every talk show for over a year, and the subject of both 'Hard Copy' and 'Real Detective' exposes, should have made the local news when her life came to an abrupt and violent end.

I decided to write a press release and e-mailed one of the editors at the Lakeland Ledger. I later spoke to a female reporter who had covered Lisa's trial. For some strange reason, she hadn't heard the news about the car crash. When she read my press release, she didn't realize at first that the woman in the story was the notorious Lisa Yvonne French, who had been convicted of second-degree murder in 1991. The reporter and I had a very long conversation over the phone about Lisa's life and my relationship with her. Oddly, she didn't seem to feel that Lisa's suicide was much of a newsworthy event, even though she knew Lisa's famous history.

Lakeland and Winter Haven are small towns in Florida, and not much happens there that makes national news. Cypress Gardens' events occasionally made national headlines, but not much else does, other than maybe the baseball training camp in Lakeland. Not only was Lisa's past relevant in the present, but there were still many unanswered questions surrounding Lisa's death, that a good investigative journalist should have been interested in finding answers to.

For example: Why did Carmen lie about where Lisa was going the night of her death? What led to Lisa's death - was it an accident, suicide, or something else? What happened to Lisa while she was in prison, and after she was released? How about writing a follow-up story on mental illness and the mental health care system in the state of Florida? Why not write about police protocols concerning people suspected of being at risk for suicide, and whether they are sufficient for protecting people's lives?

There was a lot to report on. In my opinion, this editor failed to recognize how significant Lisa's story was to that community. I think she missed an important story about an extremely fascinating woman. There should have been a full-page story written about Lisa, similarly to what had been done in the past. Her murder trial was one of the biggest stories in the region at the time. Lisa was in the news for weeks. The headline should have read - 'Circus Performer Convicted of Murder Commits Suicide.'

How many people from central Florida have made national news, due to a highly publicized crime like the O.J. Simpson Trial? Ironically, his trial followed soon after Lisa's, which took all the oxygen away from her headlines. Lisa's captivating story is still compelling enough to spawn a second documentary, which was produced as late as 2016. That happened only three years prior to her death and about 30 years after the murder in 1985! Lisa's story is still relevant today!

It's hard for me to believe the reporter didn't want to do a feature story to show that Lisa had been a victim and not a villain. She should have tried to correct the record by illuminating Lisa's true character and investigated her history, as well as what brought her over the edge. Instead, she left it up to me to tell her story. Certainly, Lisa's truth about child abuse and neglect is one of great public interest, especially someone as unique and famous as Lisa French. The news of her death shouldn't have been just a three-sentence blurb in an obituary column. Currently, there was no ruling on the cause of her death, and still no autopsy report. The editor should not have dismissed Lisa's story. Instead, she should have dug into the circumstances surrounding the crash to find out what happened. This was no cut and dry case of an unknown citizen having an alcohol related accident.

It wasn't until the first week in April when I finally received a call from one of the detectives, who was assigned to Lisa's case. I was a bit concerned that he might be investigating me, so I was careful about what I told him at first. He said the reason for his call was to ascertain the cause of the accident. Apparently, the police report mentioned the fact that there was alcohol residue in a mug found in the car. The detective and I stayed on the phone for well over an hour. I didn't get the impression that he was interested in charging me with anything, after the first 15 minutes of our conversation, so I opened up about the events surrounding Lisa's fatality.

I was candid about my experiences with Lisa, her behavior and state of mind. I mentioned to him how I thought her parents had contributed to her demise. Before speaking to me, the detective had been leaning toward recommending that Lisa's death was an alcohol related accident. However, I think I convinced him that there was no way that her death wasn't suicide. I told him he will see that I was right, after he reads the coroner's report.

I reminded him that there wasn't any evidence of Lisa breaking or losing control of the car. There were no skid marks at the scene, according to the man who towed the car. I informed the detective about Lisa's history, so that he would have a better understanding of what led to this event. I was surprised to learn that he hadn't heard anything about her. He must have been young or not from the area. Everyone who was old enough to read a newspaper in Polk County in 1991, knew about Lisa's murder trial. Her story made headlines in the Tampa Tribune among other regional newspapers. The detective seemed shocked, as I him her tragic story.

Within just days after speaking to the detective, the autopsy report was finally published. Lisa had apparently taken ten times the prescribed amount of blood pressure medicine, before getting behind the wheel. Even if Lisa had survived the crash, the overdose of pills may have killed her anyway. This fact suggested that Lisa must have had a terrible melee with her parents, just before she left the house. It proved to me that Carmen had lied about Lisa having an accident, while going to Karaoke. If nothing else, Lisa would have dressed better and not worn sweatpants and a t-shirt. She would have also left home closer to eight o'clock and not after ten, because most bars stop doing Karaoke by 11 pm. Also, she would not have taken Kricket along with her either.

In addition to all the problems Lisa's death created, I still had Joy to consider. After hitting a dead end with the Catholic Charities of Lakeland, I had few routes left to pursue. I took a couple of DNA tests to see if she was in any of those companies' databases, but I haven't found a match yet with a woman her age. I thought, perhaps I could hire a lawyer or a detective to help me to find her, but I knew it will probably take a lot of time and money. I had already spent a great deal of money trying to keep Lisa alive. This wasn't the right time to search for Joy.

If only Lisa was still alive today, we could have gone to the adoption agency and the hospital in Bartow where Joy was born to prove paternity. I should have done that during my last visit to Florida, but time was short, and I didn't appreciate the urgency. Lisa had so many immediate needs at the time that I decided to put looking for Joy on the back burner. In hindsight, it turned out to be a mistake. As soon as I discovered the possibility that Joy might be my daughter, I should have investigated the possibility at once.

Once you pass the age of 18, all sealed records from an adoption should become public record, like they are now in New York State. Unfortunately, we seem to care more about protecting parents' images, versus giving children of adoptions pertinent information - important to their health and happiness.

I tried flushing all these thoughts out of my mind for the moment because I was still arguing with the insurance company over the money from the Audi. The policy was under my name, and I had made all the payments. However, they still wanted to write a check to Carmen, which meant I would receive nothing. Under Florida law, Lisa's son Geoffrey should have received any claim from her estate and not Lisa's mother. I spent weeks fighting with the insurance company over this issue with no success. I didn't want to reward Lisa's parents, who were the main cause of her pain and suffering. No matter how long I was able to delay the payment, Carmen was still going to end up with the insurance money because the DMV allowed her to put the title of the car in her name. In my opinion, this was insurance fraud that Carmen and Dave were perpetrating, and the DMV and the insurance company were co-conspirators.

So often, the degenerates of society seem to come out ahead, while innocent victims receive the short end of the stick. There is often no justice for them. In this case, there was no justice for Lisa or me. It was just more salt poured in my wound.

28. Final Curtain Call

It was now April 10, 2019 - the day before Lisa's 52nd birthday. Lisa and I had planned to celebrate it together. It was a hot Spring Day and not a cloud in the sky. I decided to work on making a little patio with stone blocks off my porch in the backyard. It was the middle of the afternoon, so it was becoming hotter and more humid. I probably should have been drinking more water and taken more breaks, but I like to keep going once I start a project.

At first, I felt fine, but a little while later I began to feel fatigued. I was in decent shape physically, but I hadn't been going to the gym as much, since I moved to North Carolina. I was accustomed to working-out with my friend Stuart twice a week in Philadelphia, but now I didn't have my 'mate' from Birmingham with me anymore. After working in the yard, lifting stones, and digging holes for about 45 minutes, I couldn't catch my breath. So, I went inside my house to drink some water and cool down. I had felt a sharp pain in my chest while I was digging which didn't go away. My stress level and heart rate were both very high. I started to feel like I was in a crisis, but I didn't understand what was happening to me.

I drank some more water, but I still felt besieged by internal forces. Instead of calling 911 right away like I should have, I went upstairs to my bedroom to take some aspirin. I struggled to climb the stairs to my bedroom since I felt weak, and the pain in my chest was increasing. I grabbed a bottle of aspirin from my nightstand, while my hands trembled, my heart burned, and my blood pressure rose. I finally called 911 for help, about 45 minutes after I first started feeling badly.

Paramedics arrived about 15 minutes after I called. I dragged myself back down the stairs to let them in the house. The medical team rushed through my front door and flooded the hallway with their bodies and equipment. They asked me all kinds of questions, while one of the first responders lifted my shirt and began sticking electrodes all over my chest. Then, they hooked me up to a heart monitor to record my vital signs and perform an EKG. I was still conscious and standing on my own during the ordeal.

"What's happening to me?" I asked someone.

"You're having a heart attack," the female paramedic replied.

The news took me by surprise, but I wasn't alarmed. However, it seemed to fit with what I had been experiencing. I still couldn't believe it was happening to me. I was only in my mid-fifties, and I had been on cholesterol medicine for over 10 years. I led a relatively healthy lifestyle - I didn't smoke or take illegal drugs. I only drank a glass of wine with dinner usually and didn't eat much fried food. I was still relatively active and had been working-out at least twice a week. However, I had been under tremendous stress during the past year because of Lisa.

In a strange twist of fate, I happened to speak with my half-uncle Alejandro from Panama for the first time, just two weeks prior to being hospitalized. He told me that his father, who is my biological grandfather, had died from heart disease, but later in life. Apparently, I had stress and genes working against me. The heat and heavy lifting that day must have pushed my body over the edge.

"What hospital do you prefer to go to?" a paramedic asked me.

"How about the closest one that performs heart surgery," I replied.

"That would be Wake-Med Raleigh," the paramedic said.

"Ok then, let's get going!" I replied.

Unfortunately, it was going to take at least 30 minutes in good traffic to arrive. I prayed there would be enough time to make it before I went into cardiac arrest. One of the paramedics radioed ahead to the hospital. The other two put me on a stretcher and wheeled me to the ambulance waiting on the street. Once the doors closed, a female paramedic made small talk with me. She was calm but didn't say anything particularly reassuring. It all seemed like routine chit-chat, which was not ideal for my state of mind.

During a crisis, time always seems to move in slow-motion. The ambulance ride felt like the longest journey I had ever taken. I could have died at any minute, and that truly would have been the end of everything. I should have been anxious and afraid, but instead I felt a strange sense of calmness and peace. I thought about Lisa and hoped I would see her again in the Afterlife if I died. I didn't know it, but one of my arteries going to my heart was completely blocked. I was closer to death than I imagined at that moment. However, I didn't feel like I was going to die - at least not yet.

When the ambulance finally arrived at the hospital, the emergency staff rolled me inside on a gurney. When I reached the operating room, the nurses brought the rails down from the cart and pulled me onto the operating table, like a sack of potatoes. They began removing all my clothing, which felt somewhat erotic. Everything happened very fast.

I tried to imagine exactly how the doctors were planning to operate on me. I assumed the surgeons would put me to sleep, cut my chest open, and then go to work. I didn't understand anything about contemporary heart surgery, so I didn't know what to expect. Oddly, the surgeon didn't sedate me, but I still felt tired anyway. I watched as the medical team scurried around the room and hovered over me like drones. It was all very surreal. Then, everything suddenly appeared to be slowing down.

When the surgeon began to operate on me, I couldn't feel anything, except for some pressure around my groin area. Apparently, that was the point of entry for a stent which the doctor planned to place where the obstruction occurred. Surprisingly, the surgery only took about an hour, which is about the same amount of time it takes to have my teeth cleaned. I imagined that I would be on this steely cold table completely naked for a lot longer. I began to feel dizzy from all the commotion around me. I still couldn't believe they were operating on me without anesthesia.

Suddenly, I began to feel strange and lose focus. The clamoring in the room was fading, as the lights appeared to be dimming. I couldn't keep my eyes open any longer, so I closed them and allowed my mind to drift from consciousness. Perhaps, my life was slowly slipping away from me. Suddenly, the thought occurred to me that tomorrow would be Lisa's birthday. We were supposed to be together to celebrate. I began to feel dizzy - then everything went dark.

After what seemed a long while, I woke from a deep sleep and hesitantly opened my eyes. Everything in the space looked hazy at first - silent and empty, with only one bright, blinding light in the corner of the room. I could no longer feel the cold stainless-steel table beneath me, nor could I see anyone moving around the room any longer. I sensed that I was no longer lying naked in a frigid, sterile hospital emergency room. I wasn't sure where I was just yet.

I found myself sitting in the bleachers underneath a grand tent. I was wearing a pair of jean shorts, a white polo shirt and white sneakers. It was nighttime, so I couldn't see much of my surroundings. I thought for a moment that I must be dreaming, while still being operated on, because none of this seemed real to me. I felt unusually energetic and full of life for the first time in years. My body seemed different to me too - I had lost weight and gained muscle tone. I didn't have a mirror, so I caressed my face and gently ran my fingers through my hair. My skin felt smoother, and I had thick locks of hair, like in my youth. Something very bewildering was happening to me. I had no clue how I arrived at this place or why I wasn't in a recovery room. My eyes were finally adjusting to the light, as objects became more in focus.

I heard a creaking sound from above, so I looked up to see what it could be. Surprisingly, it looked like there was someone swinging on a trapeze - high above me. By her silhouette in the dim light, she appeared to be a young woman. She wore a white leotard with silver and gold beading, which sparkled like stars in the night sky. The girl's body pierced the air with great speed. Her hair seemed to ignite into a red ball of fire, when it streamed through the spotlight, like a phoenix rising from the ashes. She glided back and forth with pendulum rhythm, gaining height with each pass, as she stood on the bar. I noticed there was no net below to catch her in case she fell.

"Who is this girl?" I asked myself. "Why is she here with me?"

I stood up clumsily and walked down the steps toward the earth below. I was unable to lower my glance from above. I still couldn't see her face clearly, but I watched intently, as she sat down and wrapped her legs around the swing. Then, she allowed herself to fall back with her hands and hair dangling in the air. Finally, I could see her face for the first time, as she continued to fly over my head. Her expression was joyful. She smiled at me without uttering a word, until I broke the silence.

"Vonnie!" I cried.

"Hi baby!" Lisa yelled back. "What took you so long? I've been waiting here for you."

Her tiny body still floating inverted in the air with her arms outstretched toward me.

"How is this possible?" I asked myself.

Lisa was putting on a private show for me under the big-top. She pulled herself up into a sitting position again and began to swing more furiously. She looked so free dancing in the air, without a care in the world. It brought me so much pleasure watching her, so I stopped trying to solve the riddle of why we were there together. Then, she oscillated over to the platform and hopped off her perch, raising her right arm to wave at me.

A white Cloud Swing hung where Lisa stood, which she wrapped around her arms. The next thing I knew, she leaped from the platform back into the sky, like an eagle circling around me from high above. She descended gradually and gracefully, like the hang gliders at Cypress Gardens. Then she flipped over and dropped into a free fall - headfirst, catching herself by her wrists, only a few feet from the ground. She rolled over and landed on her feet, detaching the Cloud Swing from her wrists. Lisa turned toward an imaginary audience, who were applauding wildly in her mind and took a bow. Then she glared at me, locking her piercing, sapphire eyes on mine, as they sparkled like diamonds in the spotlight. I stood frozen in awe and disbelief, as Lisa smiled with unbridled exuberance, and began running toward me. Her pace slowed to a walk and then she stopped directly in front of me. I could hardly believe my eyes. I felt like I needed to touch her to be sure she was real.

Lisa's eyes were no longer bloodshot, her teeth were her own, and not stained with nicotine. She appeared to be fit and free of pain, exactly as I remembered her when we first met. My heart was pounding because I was so thrilled to see her again. I shivered, as she touched me with her soft hands pressed against my cheek. I wasn't imagining her. I felt overwhelmed by her unexpected reemergence into my life, once again. A teardrop ran down my face, as she wrapped her arms around my neck and kissed me passionately. Then, she whispered to me in a soft tone of voice.

"Don't cry baby, you're here with me now - I knew you'd come," Lisa said. "We'll be together forever now."

I was speechless. Lisa closed her eyes and leaned in to kiss me again. Her lips were always so sensual and sweet. I lifted my hands to her face and caressed her delicate skin with my fingers. Instinctively, we held each other so tightly that we squeezed the breath from each other's lungs, in a warm unending embrace. In that moment, nothing else mattered to me, except being together again, while holding Lisa in my arms. Time stood still. Then she spoke again.

"I've been waiting for you to celebrate my birthday with me," Lisa said.

"What's the date today?" I asked. "I seem to have lost track of time."

"April 11th of course; it's my birthday," Lisa said excitedly.

"Remember, you promised to take me to a nice restaurant for dinner," she continued. You told me I could order lobster and champagne, with yellow cake and white frosting for dessert."

"I would love to celebrate your birthday with you Vonnie," I replied. "It will be my greatest pleasure!"

"Oh wait, I don't have a gift for you," I said.

"Don't worry baby; you already gave me your heart yesterday," Lisa replied.

"Haven't you figured out why you're here with me yet?" Lisa asked.

Only at that moment, I realized what had happened to me.

A WORD FROM THE AUTHOR

Drug addiction is an extremely toxic thing to have to deal with from both sides. My experience with Lisa concerning her mental health issues and drug use was extremely stressful, but she was worth all my efforts.

I think very often people don't want to try to help others in trouble because they think it will negatively affect their lives. I found that some people I asked were willing to do what they could for my sake, and because they are compassionate individuals. Lisa's problems certainly took their toll on my life, but I have no regrets. I would do it all again, but perhaps try even harder for a better outcome.

It's easy to walk by people on the street who are homeless, begging for money, or passed out drunk in an alleyway. Sometimes we give them money and are satisfied that we have done our best to help. However, we haven't accomplished anything, except to pretend we have done our good deed for the day.

People in a crisis need our time, care, and attention. They need to feel loved, like anyone else. They also need us to stick by them and not give up, due to frustration. Sometimes, people who wind up in prison or on the street are there due to their poor choices, but often they feel abandoned, betrayed, and desperate because of neglect, abuse, or exploitation.

My experience with Lisa has taught me to be more compassionate, and not prejudge people who end up in dire circumstances. Many of these people are intelligent, talented, kindhearted, and simply victims.

The worst thing anyone can do is to harm children, especially ones so young, innocent, and fragile. I believe there should be stricter penalties for people who abuse them, and greater care given to those in our society with mental health issues.

How can anyone receive proper medical attention, if they don't have money, a job, or health insurance? The Affordable Health Care Act isn't affordable for many Americans, including those who are on Welfare - at least not in my experience. We must do better for those in need!

If you or someone you know has mental health challenges, please do your best to seek professional assistance and do everything you can to help people, who are desperately in need.

National Alliance on Mental Illness (NAMI)

1-800-950-6264

National Suicide Prevention Lifeline (NSPL)

1-800-273-8255

Made in the USA
Columbia, SC
05 May 2022